Great Exploration Hoaxes

Great
Exploration
Hoaxes

DAVID ROBERTS

SIERRA CLUB BOOKS   SAN FRANCISCO

FOR SHARON

—and the island in Lake Nuyakuk

The Sierra Club, founded in 1892 by John Muir, has devoted itself to the study and protection of the earth's scenic and ecological resources—mountains, wetlands, woodlands, wild shores and rivers, deserts and plains. The publishing program of the Sierra Club offers books to the public as a nonprofit educational service in the hope that they may enlarge the public's understanding of the Club's basic concerns. The point of view expressed in each book, however, does not necessarily represent that of the Club. The Sierra Club has some fifty chapters coast to coast, in Canada, Hawaii, and Alaska. For information about how you may participate in its programs to preserve wilderness and the quality of life, please address inquiries to Sierra Club, 530 Bush Street, San Francisco, CA 94108.

Library of Congress Cataloging in Publication Data
Roberts, David, 1943-
Great exploration hoaxes.
Includes index.
1. Explorers—Biography.   2. Impostors and imposture.
I. Title.
G200.R6   910'.92'2   80-27331
ISBN: 0-87156-325-8   AACR1
Printed in the United States of America
10 9 8 7 6 5 4 3 2 1

CONTENTS

PREFACE

The idea for this book came from writing another one. About three years ago the Sierra Club commissioned me to write a short novel; they gave me no guidelines except that it have to do with mountaineering. An old adage of the climbing world has it that although there are numerous classic expedition narratives and personal memoirs, a decent mountaineering novel has yet to be written. I thought I knew one of the reasons why. Climbing may be intensely dramatic, but it is strangely lacking in interesting moral problems.

The strongest moral aspect of mountaineering—perhaps the only one—is trust. There are few acts in life that bespeak a more total commitment to another person than tying onto the same rope with him. And the antithesis of trust is betrayal.

Musing on these truisms, I was suddenly struck with the idea that it might be interesting to write about a man who fakes an important climb. I knew about Frederick Cook and Mount McKinley (see Chapter 6) and about Cesare Maestri and Cerro Torre (see Chapter 9), but I realized that I didn't know much about Cook and Maestri as people. It was obvious that the most interesting way to write my short novel would be from the point of view of the man who perpetrates the hoax.

Two questions seemed paramount. First, what would lead a man to attempt a hoax? Was it an impulsive or a carefully premeditated act? What kind of man would do it? Was it possibly a matter of self-delusion? Second, what was it like to live with, once the skeptics began pointing their fingers? What was the effect on the rest of a man's life?

I knew I had to do some research. I started with Cook and Maestri, and the trail led me to other explorers, not necessarily climbers, who had tried to pull the wool over the eyes of the world. I was looking for a composite character type, in the way that experts on airplane hijackings have developed a "behavioral profile" to screen potential criminals as they pass through the airport security gates. Almost at once I picked up some remarkable similarities, like the frequency with which hoaxers seem to have lost a parent in childhood. (In the Epiloge of this book I speculate briefly about the "composite type" who attempts an exploring hoax.)

The research was both fascinating and disturbing. I had always thought of myself as a person constitutionally incapable of faking anything, and I had never been aware of the slightest compulsion to misrepresent my climbs in any way. I started and ended my researches with the conviction that the kinds of people I was looking at were unpleasant, vain, and obsessive. But as I began to write my novel from "Victor Koch's" eyes—the name a play on Cook and Maestri—I began actually to see the world with him. I found out why, having told the lie that initiates the hoax, a violent and dogged insistence on one's own story in the face of detractors was preferable to confession. I discovered the dark pleasure of dividing the world into two mutually hostile camps—true allies and villainous betrayers—with the self as fulcrum. I could taste as if it were my own the destruction of Victor's life which his hoax made inevitable.

In the middle of writing the novel, I realized there was a book waiting to be written about the real exploring hoaxes—maybe a more interesting book than I could write about an imaginary person on an imaginary mountain. There had been books about specific hoaxes but not, to my knowledge, a book about the phenomenon or a survey of different frauds over the centuries. There were books about scientific frauds and art forgers, but I wanted to focus on explorers, the field I knew best.

I started talking about the idea at cocktail parties and found that almost everybody, whether interested in exploration or not, had something to say about faked achievements. Many asked, "How do you prove it?"—and, indeed, that is the central question. We can demonstrate the Piltdown Man hoax far more surely than we can prove that Robert Peary never reached the North Pole. I had expected that more people would shrug their shoulders and say, "Does it really matter who climbed a certain mountain first?" Even to those uninterested in geography or voyages, it mattered.

There was a simple reason, I became convinced. Everyone can identify with the hoaxer, because each of us has had the experience of seeing a trivial lie magnify into a nightmare of deception. Late for work, one claims the car ran out of gas. One misses so-and-so's party because of the sudden arrival of a friend from out of town. "That's funny. I thought I saw you alone at the laundromat"—and from such simple seeds the weed of the consistent falsehood proliferates. Most of us, moreover, have had firsthand experience of deception—amatory, financial, professional—more serious than the missed party. The impossibility of confession makes sense to all of us. When I first taught freshman English, I detected one or two plagiarists each term. It astonished me that, confronted with the evidence, they would often indignantly deny any misdeed—it was a matter of sheer coincidence that the words matched exactly, or of unconscious absorption. After living with Victor Koch for several months, I understood.

Once the novel was written, I turned my attention to the nonfiction book. For a year I burrowed through the stacks of Widener Library at Harvard as I ferreted out information. I had no idea how difficult the process would be. Although my book reflects almost no primary research, for the simple reason that there is probably nothing new to be learned about Sebastian Cabot or Samuel Adams, writing it required an exhausting familiarization with historical and navigational arcana, as well as faculties of skepticism and judgment beyond my powers. I owe much of my acquaintance with the individual controversies to deep scholars like James A. Williamson, Jean Delanglez, Wallace Stegner, and Nicholas Tomalin and Ron Hall; but I do not owe my final judgments to them. The soundest scholars, faced with uncertain and patchy evidence, leap to conclusions. For me the most exacting task that writing this book demanded was the sorting out of biases, the toleration of ambiguity. I hope the reader comes away from the book convinced that my verdicts are at least reasonable, not motivated by my own biases, which I cannot pretend not to have.

The book would be more useful to scholars and serious students if it were footnoted. But I did not want *Great Exploration Hoaxes* to scare off the casual reader or to smack of historical pedantry. In each chapter, just as when I was imagining Victor Koch, I was after the man himself. It is the peculiar makeup of Father Louis Hennepin or Admiral Richard E. Byrd that makes their stories interesting, beyond the (in themselves important) questions of who first descended the Mississippi and who first saw the North Pole.

One thing became clear to me about these men: the decision to fake an exploratory achievement determined almost everything about the rest of their lives. The hoax became the central fact of their existence.

The world was reduced to allies and betrayers. Even in the case of relatively successful frauds like Robert Peary and Richard E. Byrd, we cannot envy these men their declining years. They lived out their natural spans in bitterness and proud isolation, even when surrounded by the worship of a credulous public, even when decorated with official honors. Exposure, one suspects, lurked like the wolf at the door.

It is gratifying, in a superficial way, to conclude that perhaps the happiest dotage experienced by any of the ten men I have written about was that of James "Abyssinian" Bruce—the only man in this collection clearly wronged, the only explorer whose real deeds were dismissed as phony. I have included his story for the cautionary lesson it teaches us about skepticism itself. The world needed a Samuel Johnson when Byrd's flight to the North Pole was being celebrated; but Johnson helped to ruin Abyssinian Bruce.

A word about the scope of this book. There is a vast literature, especially in the 17th and 18th centuries, of the *voyage imaginaire*— the outlandish travel tale, often a utopia or an anti-utopia, passed off as nonfiction. *Gulliver's Travels* is the best-known example in English. But this is a different species from the exploration hoax. I verge close to that genre in discussing *Robert Drury's Journal*, which may be a novel by Daniel Defoe. But Robert Drury may also have been a real person shipwrecked on Madagascar, as we are certain Robinson Crusoe was not in the Caribbean. The ten "cases" I discuss involve only controversies about real voyages and discoveries, in which a deliberate hoax is a possible explanation.

The chapters are presented chronologically. For me the earlier ones—about Sebastian Cabot, Father Hennepin, Robert Drury, and Abyssinian Bruce—are every bit as fascinating as those of the 19th and 20th centuries. They were the hardest for me to research, the slowest for me to steep myself in. But they may seem dry and academic to some readers, dependent as they are on textual wrangles, interpretations of phrases, scholars' scribblings in the lacunae. I have written the book so that the chapters are by and large independent of each other, and I invite my reader to pick it up and start anywhere. I have kept my speculations about the phenomenon itself—my "overview"—confined for the most part to the Epilogue. The bibliographies at the end of each chapter tell the reader where he can go to arrive at his own conclusions.

My work in the library was long and solitary, but two men I have yet to meet helped point me in useful directions—Percy Adams, whose excellent *Travellers and Travel Liars: 1660-1800* introduced me to Father Hennepin and Robert Drury; and Dennis Rawlins, whose *Peary at the North Pole: Fact or Fiction* is a monument to careful reasoning.

Three people in particular must be credited for helping me get this book written, though none of them can be blamed for its failings. My agent, Dorothy Parker, stuck with me through enough self-doubts to sink the most seaworthy of projects. Ed Ward, with whom I have taught and climbed for many years, spent more evenings than was good for him hanging out in bars with me while we shared the kinds of whimsies and schemes that drive explorers out of the safe ports of bourgeois domesticity. And my wife, Sharon—my first and best critic—kept me writing, and helped me to understand the men I was writing about.

1

SEBASTIAN CABOT AND THE NORTHWEST PASSAGE

In 1508, Sebastian Cabot set sail from Bristol with three hundred men in two ships. He crossed the Atlantic quickly, visited the great fishing grounds of the Newfoundland Banks, familiar to Bristol men for about a decade, and made a landfall. Cabot had more serious exploratory ambitions, however, and soon pushed on toward the northwest, coasting along the shores of Labrador. He found the ice-clogged passage that would come to be called Hudson Strait, drifted through it, and entered the open water of Hudson Bay, a full century before Henry Hudson would "discover" it. Cabot wanted to push on, but his men were on the verge of mutiny.

He turned back, sailed south past the Newfoundland Banks, and continued along the coast of the present United States, still searching for a westward passage through the American landmass. He may have wintered along this coast. Having explored the Atlantic shore all the way to the tip of Florida, he turned home, arriving in Bristol in April 1509 to find that his monarch, Henry VII, had died and a new Henry, who would turn out to be far less interested in geographical discovery than his father, was on the throne. Though he had not found a route to Cathay, Sebastian Cabot had completed the most significant voyage yet undertaken by English ships.

Or had he?

The leading 20th-century Cabot expert, James A. Williamson, believes that the 1508–9 expedition took place much as described above. But there are strong grounds for concluding—and sound scholars who argue—that Cabot's whole voyage was fictitious, that in fact he never left England.

To a modern observer, it may seem incredible that the true facts about a voyage of such importance remain so conjectural. Surely such a pioneering venture would be bound to leave in its wake dozens of authentic records, even eyewitness accounts. Surely no man, no matter how clever, could fake a voyage that had supposedly involved three hundred men under the patronage of the King of England.

The uncertainty about Cabot's Northwest expedition originates in two sources. One is primarily historical. Although the Spanish, the Portuguese, and the Italians took pains to chronicle their great nautical voyages during the late 15th and early 16th centuries, on the whole the English did not—until Richard Hakluyt began to collect and publish firsthand accounts of his countrymen's discoveries in 1582. Before Hakluyt, English voyages were recorded mainly in the memories of living seamen or in obscure Continental compendia of knowledge. Many great deeds and adventures slipped irrevocably into the dark hiding places of historical ignorance. Of the great mariner John Cabot, Sebastian's father, on whose 1497 voyage England's whole claim to North America rested, no portrait exists today, nor a single scrap of his handwriting. By the middle of the 16th century the facts of John Cabot's life had passed completely out of common memory.

The second cause of confusion surrounding Sebastian's Northwest expedition lies in the very makeup of the man's character. Whether or not the 1508 voyage was a hoax, Sebastian Cabot seems to have been a thoroughgoing confidence artist. He managed to build success-ful careers in both Spain and England as an adviser on northern navigations mainly by fostering the illusion that he was the sole possessor of vast funds of secret geographical lore. He seems to have taken full credit for everything his father accomplished, letting John Cabot's reputation dwindle to that of a mere merchant, while his own burgeoned as the man who had discovered North America. At the peril of his own life, he played the conflicting interests of Spain, England, and Venice off against each other, entering into cabals and intrigues in which he promised worlds but avoided delivering much of real substance. He died on dry land with a comfortable pension, well liked and reputable.

The 16th-century sources for Cabot's expedition—probably all the evidence scholars will ever have upon which to base their judg-ments—consist of some seventeen documents in Latin, Italian, Spanish, Portuguese, French, and English. They tend to be fragments only, some mere offhand allusions a sentence or two long. They contain among them so many mutual contradictions that there is no possible way of reconciling their details in a coherent account of a single voyage. By themselves, however, such discrepancies do not amount to evidence against Cabot. Many of the documenters were sloppy guardians of truth, and nearly all were writing down stories they had heard third- or fourth-hand, sometimes at a remove of seventy years from the events they describe. The closest thing we have to an account by Cabot himself appears in 1556 in a volume of navigations by a Venetian named Ramusio, who claims to have received a letter from the navigator, which he was summarizing.

Cabot's English service ended abruptly in 1512 when, on a visit to Spain, he was invited by King Ferdinand to enter the Spanish marine as a *capitán de mar*. He did not serve an English king again until 1548, when Edward VI appointed him as a maritime adviser to the Admiralty. The long hiatus is no doubt responsible for the absence of any English sources for the 1508 expedition until the last years of Cabot's life, when a man named Richard Eden, who claimed to know the aged pilot, recorded a few skimpy details of that voyage. In 1555 Eden was writing at a distance of forty-seven years from the alleged embarkation from Bristol; and if he did receive the story from Cabot's lips, he may have been listening—so his detractors would insist—to an old man who had never been a reliable source aggrandize a myth of his own deeds that he had spent a lifetime concocting.

Faced with the fragmentary nature of the Renaissance sources and the unlikelihood that new evidence will turn up, the modern student is reduced to choosing among scholars' portraits of Sebastian Cabot. Surprisingly, because of the extreme variation among those portraits, this effort amounts to a fascinating pastime. Thanks to the labors of James A. Williamson, any student can read the original texts of the seventeen sources translated into English. Williamson in fact invites the reader to decide for himself about Sebastian Cabot (see Bibliography).

The full range of judgment can be comprehended by looking at the likenesses that three scholars, each the leading expert of his day, have unveiled for our scrutiny. Richard Biddle, a Pittsburgh lawyer, was the first man to try to assemble all the known documents bearing on Cabot; his 1831 *Memoir* represents the pinnacle of Cabot idolatry. In the last decade of the 19th century, the indefatigable Frenchman Henry Harrisse issued a stream of memoirs and monographs on Cabot, the general import of which was to debunk the explorer as a wholesale fraud. In our own century, James A. Williamson has spent over thirty years studying the controversy, and his works represent the effort, to use his own metaphor, to steady the pendulum of Cabot's reputation. Williamson acknowledges the navigator's shady and dubious sides, but expresses faith in the reality of the bold Northwest expedition.

Biddle's Cabot. It would not be fair to hold Richard Biddle responsible for exaggerations that only subsequent scholarship has corrected. The "rediscovery" of John Cabot was a triumph of late-19th-century research, and crucial documents have been unearthed as recently as 1956. To the Pennsylvania lawyer in 1831, John Cabot was merely a merchant sailor from Venice who had settled in Bristol, and to whom, with his three sons, in 1496 Henry VII had issued a patent for the discovery of lands "unknown to all Christians." Biddle took it for granted that Sebastian Cabot was the man who had discovered the mainland of North America in 1497. Whether or not the father even went on the voyage was a question Biddle briefly entertained, concluding that if John Cabot was on board, it was "merely for the purpose of turning to account his mercantile skill and sagacity."

Thus by 1508, in the American scholar's view, Sebastian Cabot was already an accomplished and experienced mariner, whose "simple, but bold proposition" of 1497 had actually represented his first attempt to find a northwest route to Cathay. When Biddle turns his mind to the 1508 expedition, then, he harbors not the slightest suspicion that the journey may have been a hoax. The only question is just how far Sebastian actually penetrated along the Northwest Passage. His answer is, well into Hudson Bay. To buttress this conclusion, it is an easy matter for him to discover that the 16th-century sources that give Cabot the most northerly latitude at the point where he turned around, notably Ramusio and the Englishman Richard Willes, also happen to have been the work of the soberest chroniclers. The sources that limit Cabot's penetration to more southerly latitudes were the work of historical hacks, or of interested parties such as "Spaniards . . . jealous of the reputation of Cabot."

The most specious piece of Biddle's reasoning springs from a vague similarity between the earliest source for Cabot's voyage, a Latin text by Peter Martyr from 1516, and a very recent traveler's account of the terrain around Hudson Bay. Only six years before Biddle was writing, Captain Edward Parry, as part of the Admiralty's vigorous new attack on the Northwest Passage, had led an expedition that attempted the route by pushing into the northwest corner of Hudson Bay. Biddle turns to Parry and finds:

> Very little snow was now lying upon the ground, and numerous streams of water rushing down the hills and sparkling in the beams of the morning sun, relieved in some measure the

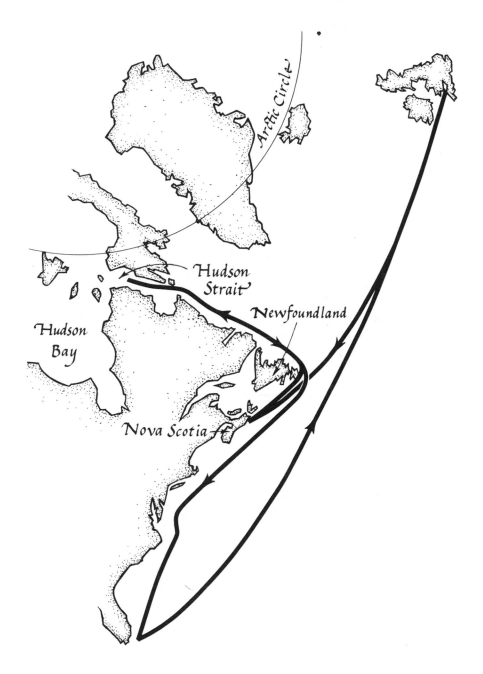

The route of Sebastian Cabot's 1508-9 expedition, as based on a composite reading of those sources that credit him with sailing farthest.

melancholy stillness which otherwise reigned on this desolate shore.

Three hundred and seventeen years earlier, in the same latitude, according to Peter Martyr (as Englished by Hakluyt), Cabot had "found monstrous heaps of ice swimming on the sea, and in manner continual daylight; yet saw he the land in that tract free from ice, which had been molten by the heat of the sun." Such evidence convinces Biddle that the two sailors must have visited the same place. (In other exploration controversies, comparisons like this one are a favorite resort of the credulous.)

Biddle's enthusiasm seduces him into building a model hero. The epithets with which he decorates Cabot again and again are "enterprising and intrepid," "accomplished and enthusiastic." The 1508 decision to turn back south, then, was a simple matter of nerve versus cowardice, of "the dauntless intrepidity that found a new impulse in perils before which his terrified companions gave way."

The full flavor of Biddle's idolatry may be tasted in his handling of Cabot's 1526–30 Spanish expedition to the La Plata River in South America, the only voyage we can be sure Sebastian actually led. The accounts by which we know about this expedition are those of Cabot's underlings and financers, who filed lawsuits against their former commander and tried to have him arrested when he got back to Spain; thus our view of it may be one-sided. But it is hard not to picture the La Plata venture as a four-year disaster. Stimulated by the successful circumnavigation performed by one of Magellan's ships, Charles V put Cabot in command of an expedition "for the discovery of Tharsis, Ophir, and Eastern Cathay." The plan was to explore the coasts of South America in search of a more northerly passage to the Pacific than the one Magellan had found.

Soon after reaching Brazil, Cabot let himself be distracted by Portuguese rumors of great treasures of gold and silver in the interior. He apparently gave up any intention of searching for the passage to Cathay and concentrated much of his next three years on fortune-hunting up the La Plata. As a result of the switch in plans, several of Cabot's officers threatened revolt. Even before he had reached the mouth of the river, he had put the troublemakers under arrest; then he set them on shore, although some were sick with fever, and sailed away, leaving them to die. (The officers managed to befriend the natives and eventually made their way to the Portuguese settlements to the north.) In the harbor near Santa Catalina, Cabot's flagship ran upon a submerged rock. Later allegations reported that the commander was the first man to abandon ship, which so demoralized the crew that the vessel ended up a complete wreck.

Cabot pushed up the La Plata and its tributaries, building forts as he went. Chasing a rumor of gold, he led his men westward up the Paraguay River, despite failing provisions and hostile natives. When a few Indians approached the straggling band of Spaniards and offered to show them where they could find food, Cabot dispatched thirty men to follow the guides, who led them into an ambush in which they were all killed or wounded.

In 1528 Cabot sent one of his ships home to request a relief expedition. Upon its arrival in Seville, the merchant backers of the expedition decided at once they wanted nothing more to do with Cabot. The king, steadfastly loyal, ordered a relief expedition at his own expense; but his instructions apparently were never carried out. Meanwhile Cabot had housed his men in a new fort on the Paraná River. While he was away, Indians attacked and burned the fort, killing most of its defenders. The native victory encouraged further attacks, and even though he had retreated with the remainder of his force to the coast, in the following months Cabot lost another thirty men while they were out fishing or foraging for roots. Late in 1529 the survivors decided to flee for Spain, which they did not reach until the following July.

Cabot returned to face seven years of judicial inquiry. It took the scribes of the Council for the Indies three months simply to draw up the accusations and interrogations brought against the commander by his former subordinates. After two years Cabot was found guilty of maladministration and disobedience. He was sentenced to four years' banishment to Morocco as well as heavily fined. For some reason (perhaps the loyalty of Charles V) the banishment was never put into effect, and, amazingly, Cabot was allowed to continue in his office as pilot-major of Spain.

George Parker Winship, a scholar otherwise sympathetic to the explorer, sums up the La Plata expedition by remarking that Cabot "discovered only one thing—that he was not qualified for the leadership of a maritime adventure." Yet Biddle sees it differently. The La Plata voyage was a four-year conspiracy against a brave man, a "dark treachery" enacted by opportunistic and cowardly subordinates. He finds that some of the incriminating testimony "has that air of vagueness so characteristic of falsehood," yet discovers in the same documents proof of Cabot's "remarkable gentleness of deportment" and the "affectionate attachment" binding his men to him.

Biddle excuses the abandonment on shore of Cabot's officers as "the daring exercise of . . . rightful authority," a bold step necessary to quell a mutiny. "The effect was instant. Discord vanished with this knot of conspirators." Nowhere does Biddle mention the great hurry in which Cabot allegedly fled his own grounded ship. He regards the massacres of Cabot's men by Indians as unfortunate mishaps, denies claims that they were provoked in part by Cabot's barbarous treatment of the natives, and in general assails "the disingenuousness of the Spanish historians." Glossing over the judicial aftermath of the expedition, Biddle resumes his narrative with the bland observation that Cabot took up again his functions as pilot-major. This uninterrupted service goes to demonstrate that "the defence submitted to the Emperor must have been completely successful."

At the end of his biography Biddle sums up his subject's importance by saying, "The English language would probably be spoken in no part of America but for Sebastian Cabot." Lamenting the fact that Cabot's burying place remains unknown, the lawyer concludes, "He gave a Continent to England: yet no one can point to the few feet of earth she has allowed him in return!"

Harrisse's Cabot. In 1897, with Britain at the height of Empire, the four hundredth anniversary of (as it was now known to be) John Cabot's discovery of America was widely celebrated. Buildings were constructed, tablets mounted, a commemorative tower planned, statues commissioned, and orations delivered, not only in Bristol but in Newfoundland, where it was supposed the elder Cabot had made his landfall. The tenor of the celebrations was on the whole honorific to both John and Sebastian Cabot, as evinced by the Bristol statue that portrayed an eager, standing youth being sent out to sea by a bearded, seated patriarch. (In 1937 it was discovered that John Cabot, far from living to be an old man, had vanished on his second expedition in 1498.) Ironically, coinciding with the outburst of commemorative works, the monumental labors of a shrewd French scholar were putting Sebastian Cabot's reputation into the deepest shade it had ever known.

The culmination of Henry Harrisse's work was a large volume that appeared in 1896, entitled *John Cabot the Discoverer of North-America and Sebastian His Son*, in which the scholar declared his purpose to be "to set forth a true history . . . based exclusively on authentic documents" of the explorer "now held by many to have been one of the greatest navigators and cosmographers that ever lived." Winship, an admiring dissenter from Harrisse's conclusions, said of the work, which he thought "magnificent," that it "is not a history; it is rather a laboratory manual." With the painstaking zeal of a born iconoclast, Harrisse examines one by one all of Sebastian Cabot's purported achievements and pokes holes in each of them. Arguing from Sebastian's alleged friendship with chroniclers like Peter Martyr, Harrisse blames the explorer not only for neglecting to mention his father's deeds, but for willfully misrepresenting him as "a sort of itinerant merchant, who had come to England solely to sell his goods," and for deliberately attributing to himself his father's navigations. Harrisse is the first scholar to doubt that Sebastian, who must have been a youth in his teens, was even along on the epochal 1497 voyage.

Underlining a sentence in Peter Martyr which other scholars had tended to overlook, Harrisse begins to build his case: "'Sume of the Spanyards denye that [Sebastian] Cabot was the fyrst fynder of the lande of Baccallaos [the Newfoundland Banks]: and affirme that he went not so far westwarde.'" Detail by detail the revised portrait takes shape, of a man "capable of disguising the truth, whenever it was in his interest to do so." The numerous inaccuracies and inconsistencies in reports from sources supposedly in contact with Cabot, even about basic matters like the country of his birth, derive, the French scholar concludes, not from careless historians but from Cabot's own "usual manner of speaking, vainglorious and erratic." Erratic like a fox, Harrisse means; for the method behind Cabot's unreliability was to gain power by being "constantly engaged in plotting and corresponding in secret with foreign rulers to advance his own interest." Thus the question of whether or not the 1508 Northwest expedition ever took place is inextricably bound up with the possible advantages Cabot might later have gained, first with the Spanish crown, then with the Venetian senate, by pretending he had led such an expedition.

The main source for dating the voyage in 1508–9 is a sentence in a 1536 report to the Venetian senate by the ambassador to Spain, one Marc-Antonio Contarini: "But upon his return he found the King dead, and his son caring little for the enterprise." Harrisse argues, from an allusion by the same author to Columbus, that the voyage he mistakenly records is actually John Cabot's 1497 expedition. All the earliest sources, though they disagree about the latitude reached and other details, repeat the "fact" that Sebastian sailed in two ships with three hundred men. To Harrisse this is proof only that after he had moved to Spain in 1512 Cabot kept telling the same story to different men. Tracing the swift rise in Cabot's fortunes at the Spanish court, Harrisse points to the documents that indicate that the Venetian kept trading on his supposedly unique knowledge of the Baccalaos fishing industry, and possibly of the Northwest Passage, which was widely theorized to exist. "This hyd secreate of nature," as one Italian source puts it, would have been extremely valuable information for the Spanish, who had explored no farther north than 40°.

Harrisse analyzes the remaining sources for the Northwest voyage, and tries to show that they merely borrow from the earlier Italian ones. Though he stops short of declaring that the expedition was entirely imaginary, the French writer's verdict is implicit: there is no evidence other than Cabot's own "vainglorious and erratic" boasts that he ever set sail from Bristol, much less reached Hudson Bay. And there was everything—a lucrative career as maritime adviser to kings—to be gained by misrepresenting himself as a sailor with unmatched experience in the North Atlantic.

The same sharp scrutiny is brought to every phase of Sebastian Cabot's life, and the cumulative effect is devastating. Two details are worth mentioning, as bearing retrospectively on the 1508 expedition. In 1521, though still in Spanish service, Cabot visited England and may have entered into an agreement with Henry VIII to lead a major English expedition of discovery. We know about the plan because the king ordered the twelve great livery companies of London to make a large contribution, and the Drapers objected, in an official protest.

> And we thynk it were to sore aventour to joperd v shipps wt men & goodes unto the said Iland [the Newefound Iland] upon the singuler trust of one man, callyd as we understond, Sebastyan, whiche Sebastyan, as we here say, was never in that land hym self, all if he makes reporte of many thinges as he hath hard his Father and other men speke in tymes past.

As Winship later pointed out, we cannot be certain that the "Sebastyan" of the Drapers' protest is Cabot himself, let alone what the ostensible object of the expedition was. But to Harrisse the resemblances are too close to be coincidental. Whatever posterity had to say, the merchants of London in 1521 knew a fraud when they saw one, and his nine years' absence from the country had not diminished their memory of the man who took credit for his father's expeditions.

A 1544 "planisphere," supposedly executed by Sebastian Cabot, on which the Newfoundland "prima vista" is located and the mouth of the St. Lawrence indicated with great accuracy, was held for centuries to be evidence of Cabot's firsthand knowledge of the New World. Harrisse proves convincingly that the information on the planisphere derives from Jacques Cartier's expeditions, the nomenclature plagiarized from a 1541 French map that incorporated Cartier's discoveries. Thus in Harrisse's view Cabot was a shrewd student of his own hoaxes, and knew how to ransack sources of which the English and the Spanish might be largely ignorant to bolster his claims to knowledge.

In 1522 Cabot entered upon his most dangerous intrigue. At a time when he was privy to all the exploratory plans of the Spanish government, and when the balance of power in the New World was extremely delicate, he sent an agent secretly to Venice to promise to the Council of Ten that he was ready to travel to the Italian city to reveal a confidence on which, he claimed, the future greatness of the Venetian Republic depended. Even to promise this was, of course, high treason. Venice was quite interested, and sent Contarini to Valladolid to feel out Cabot further. Cabot, Contarini reported, grew terrified that the secret might get out. Obviously disconcerted at being approached so openly while he was in Spain, the pilot-major offered vague promises and delays. It may well be that at the very time that he was (probably openly) consulting with Henry VIII about a western expedition, Cabot was secretly offering Venice a slice of the pie. In any event, nothing came of the intrigue.

Harrisse's portrait, while it demolishes Cabot's pretensions as a navigator and cosmographer, establishes a Machiavellian schemer at least as interesting in human terms, however deceitful and self-centered he must have been. Cabot emerges as a kind of three-way double agent, playing Venice against England against Spain, all in the interests of his own power and wealth. To Harrisse, the intrigue and treachery were simply part of the man's "natural disposition." The marvel is that he got away with it all—and escaped banishment to Morocco to boot.

Williamson's Cabot. Despite Harrisse's decimation, the 20th century has been relatively kind to Sebastian Cabot. Winship, the influential bibliographer, writing only a few years after Harrisse, expresses his faith in the 1508 expedition, reasoning that it represented Cabot's attempt to sail *north* to Cathay along the hypothetical "Great Circle" route. Summing up Cabot's achievement in 1973, the historian David Beers Quinn asserts that "modern scholarship—itself a fickle thing—has narrowed down his individual contribution to Bristol voyaging to a single venture, apparently made in the years 1508–9."

Much of the restitution depends on a kind of argument from the absence of evidence—at best a shaky business. Quinn, for example, suggests that Cabot's reason for leaving England in 1512 to serve the Spanish crown may have been the disgrace of having failed to complete the Northwest Passage three years before. Similarly, he argues from the absence of any Bristol records of the financing of the 1508 expedition that it most likely was launched from London instead.

More than any other scholar, James A. Williamson has swayed modern opinion back to a belief in the reality of the Northwest voyage. Williamson is no Biddle. A clear-headed skeptic, he himself casts doubt on details in the sources that even Harrisse left unattacked, as in his lucid demonstration that the ships that would have been available to Cabot could simply not have borne 150 men each. His argument in favor of the 1508 expedition is subtle and logical, well worth an open-minded appraisal.

An outline of the argument follows. In the earliest source, Peter Martyr's *Decades* of 1516, there is no mention of Cabot's purpose in sailing north, nor any northernmost latitude reached—despite the fact that Peter said that Cabot had been a frequent guest in his house. To Williamson the omissions are significant. In 1515 the Spanish were hoping to seize upon a direct passage to the Pacific through the unexplored Gulf of Mexico. The waters farther north they conceded to the Portuguese. It would have been injudicious, then, Williamson argues, for an Englishman in the service of Spain to let on publicly that he knew of a northern route to the Pacific, which would threaten Spain's potential supremacy in the New World. This would have been all the more true after the conquests of Mexico and Peru.

In 1520–1 when Cabot was in England negotiating with Henry VIII for the command of an Atlantic expedition, it would have presented no threat to Charles V if the project were merely a voyage to the Newfoundland fishery, by then a regular milk run for British ships. But the vehemence of the Drapers' protest, with its vague allusion to a "Newefound Iland," must, in Williamson's eyes, indicate a far more ambitious project: the Northwest Passage itself, treason against Spain.

The imprudence of conniving at the same time with Venice was exacerbated by the high ambition of Cabot's project. Contarini's report describing Cabot's reaction to the letter brought him in Valladolid gives a vivid picture of a man mortally frightened by the possible consequences of his own rashness:

> At dinner time I withdrew with him, and delivered the letter, which he read, his colour changing completely during its perusal. Having finished reading it, he remained a short while without saying anything, as if alarmed and doubtful. . . . [At last he said] "I most earnestly beseech you to keep the thing secret, as it would cost me my life."

Williamson argues from the extremity of this reaction that Cabot was not simply bluffing, that he must have believed in the existence of the Northwest Passage because he had already, fourteen years before, discovered it.

In Ramusio's 1556 collection of voyages we hear for the first time that Cabot reached 67°30' N and found open sea, and that "he firmly believed that by that way he could pass toward Eastern Cathay," and would have done so but for his mutinous crew. Ramusio claims to be summarizing a letter from Cabot, and therefore this story ought to be nearly a firsthand account. Williamson believes that by now Cabot could be open and frank about his earlier secrets because in 1548 he had returned to English service, removing himself from the danger of treason. This theory requires that Williamson reinterpret Ramusio's phrase "as was written to me, many years ago, by Signor Sebastian Cabot our Venetian" as actually meaning *not* many years ago.

In this manner the modern scholar examines each of the seventeen sources for reliability, building up the argument that even their contradictions can be squared with a genuine voyage. The proof that Cabot not only embarked, but sailed as far as the entrance to Hudson Bay, hinges on the 1577 testimony of Richard Willes, who wrote that Cabot had reached a strait between 61° and 64° N, sailed west for 10° of longitude, then turned south into a large body of open water which (Williamson suggests) he thought was the Pacific. Willes's account is the most detailed English source, and refers to a map made by one Gemma Frisius in or before 1537, a copy of which is extant today. The crude outlines of a northern water route show on this map, and though most of the place names are attributed to the Portuguese, the south side of the passageway is inscribed, *"Terra per britannos inventa"* (Land found by the Britons). Some scholars have regarded this as a confused record of the Breton Jacques Cartier's discovery of the St. Lawrence. But to Williamson the coincidences are too striking to ignore—including the rough accuracy of Willes's geography when compared to the actual Arctic. In 1508, he concludes, Sebastian Cabot discovered Hudson Bay.

The argument is indeed a possible one; it condenses the mature deliberations of our century's leading Cabot scholar. Yet at half a dozen crucial turns, its logic requires a little tug of rereading here, an extrapolation there. In Williamson's pages one senses the man's lifelong ambivalence toward the Venetian adventurer of four centuries before. Understandably, he would like to see himself as ending a long line of Cabot misrepresentations:

He was no sooner dead than the English made a legend of his name. His reputation grew until it reached exaggeration in the eighteenth century and had scarcely declined a century ago [1829]. John Cabot was forgotten, and Sebastian was revered as the father of English commerce and naval supremacy. Modern research has bred disillusionment and swung the pendulum too far in the other direction. It is time to steady it to rest.

But such is always the scholar's delusion, that he has at last steadied the pendulum of fluctuating error. To shift the metaphor: trying to know the final truth about Cabot's alleged Northwest expedition is like trying to reconstruct a whole tapestry from a few shreds of cloth. We simply know too little. The 1508 expedition will remain eternally an unsolved question.

It is worth pointing out, however, how crucially Quinn and Williamson, in their relatively generous treatment of Cabot, rely on a kind of inverse reasoning. *If* Cabot had indeed been in Hudson Bay, *then* his behavior at such and such a juncture makes sense. For hard evidence they must resort to sources who themselves undoubtedly got entangled in Sebastian Cabot's web of deceitful boasts. As we shall see, it is not often that an explorer with a known record of misrepresentation and secrecy suddenly goes "straight" and pulls off a major achievement. Williamson and Quinn may themselves have fallen prey to the ironic temptations of 20th-century revisionism. It is Harrisse's debunking, in the last analysis, that has the ring of probability. Whether Sebastian Cabot left England at all is one question; but there seems no alternative to the conclusion that the 1508 expedition was in some—probably large—part a hoax.

None of which makes the man himself any less interesting; and we are free to indulge in speculation as to just what kind of fellow Sebastian Cabot was. The only surviving portrait, an engraving copied from a contemporary painting, shows an old man with a doubly forked beard, covetously clasping a globe, his right hand spreading a compass across its northern regions. The face looks shrewd and private, and gives off a sense of great power. Quinn sees Cabot in the Italian Renaissance tradition of businessmen-mystics: "A man of many talents, competent and far-seeing in many respects, he was also vain, and in action arbitrary, while he lived a fantasy life of mysteries and dark secrets alongside his more prosaic everyday activities." Williamson himself emphasizes the "lonely and myste-rious figure, a man without a country, deprived of patriotism yet able to simulate it, of ingratiating manners and secret mind, admired by scholars and respected by the great, successful to the outward view, but a failure by the measure of his own ambitions."

In his last years, with a comfortable pension, Cabot advised the captains of English expeditions attempting to sail by the Northeast Passage, up past Scandinavia and Russia, toward Cathay. The liveliest glimpse we have of him during his whole life comes from these years, when Stephen Borough, one of the captains, setting sail from Gravesend, remarked that Cabot had seen him off.

The good olde Gentleman Master Cabota gave to the poore most liberall almes, wishing them to pray for the good fortune, and prosperous successe of the Serchthrift, our Pinnesse. And then at the signe of the Christopher, hee and his friends banketted, and made me, and them that were in the company great cheere: and for the very joy that he had to see the towardnes of our intended discovery, he entred into the dance himselfe, amongst the rest of the young and lusty company.

In old age, apparently, even the inveterate schemer and loner could raise a glass to hearten a young navigator about to pave his own perilous way north into the frozen unknown.

BIBLIOGRAPHY

Biddle, Richard. *A Memoir of Sebastian Cabot; with a Review of Maritime Discovery.* Philadelphia, 1831.

Harrisse, Henry. *John Cabot the Discoverer of North-America and Sebastian His Son.* London, 1896.

Porter, Rev. Edward G. "The Cabot Quadri-Centenary Celebrations at Bristol, Halifax, and St. John's in June 1897," *New England Magazine*, February 1898.

Quinn, David Beers. *England and the Discovery of America, 1481–1620.* New York, 1974.

———. *Sebastian Cabot and Bristol Exploration.* Bristol, 1968.

Williamson, James A. *The Cabot Voyages and Bristol Discovery Under Henry VII.* Cambridge, England, 1962.

———. *The Voyages of the Cabots and the English Discovery of North America under Henry VII and Henry VIII.* London, 1929.

Winship, George Parker. *Cabot Bibliography with an Introductory Essay on the Careers of the Cabots.* London, 1900.

2

THE SHADOW OF
LA SALLE:
FATHER LOUIS HENNEPIN

O n board the ship sailing for
New France in 1675 was one of the most ambitious visionaries the
American continent had yet embraced. Robert Cavelier, Sieur de La
Salle, who had first arrived in Canada around 1667, had spent the
following eight years trading with the Indians and exploring the new
continent to the westward via the Great Lakes. His travels during
those years remain obscure today, but it seems likely that La Salle
reached the southern tip of Lake Michigan, ventured part of the way
down the Illinois River, a tributary of the Mississippi, and struck off
overland toward the Ohio River. At the vitally strategic eastern end of
Lake Ontario, where the St. Lawrence issues forth, the French had
built a fort in 1672—not without stout opposition from the Iroquois.
La Salle had sailed for France to persuade the court to grant him the
seignory of Fort Frontenac; now he was returning not only with that
title but with a patent of nobility in recognition of his deeds as an
explorer.

A less vigorous man might have used his new post to build up a
trade with the Indians and grow sedentarily rich. But La Salle
cherished three grand ambitions. The first was to fulfill Champlain's
intention of establishing a water passage to China and India across
the mainland of America. The second was to descend the Mississippi
to its mouth and establish a fort there to forestall the Spanish in
Mexico. The third was to develop the vast unknown interior of the
West and thus keep both Spain and England from gaining dominion
over it.

On board the ship an apparently trivial event occurred. Some girls
had been included in the company as potential Canadian settlers.
Their behavior disturbed a Franciscan father, who later recorded:

16

They made a great noise by their dancing and thus prevented the sailors from getting their rest at night; so that I was obliged to reprimand them somewhat severely, in order to oblige them to stop, and to observe due modesty and tranquility.

This afforded the Sieur Robert Cavelier de la Salle an occasion of anger against me, which he never forgot. He made a show of wishing to uphold these girls in their amusement. He could not refrain from telling me one day somewhat angrily, that I acted like a pedant toward him and all the officers, and persons of quality who were on the vessel, and who enjoyed seeing these girls dance, since I criticised them for trifles.

In view of the subsequent career of this frowning Franciscan, there is no good reason to credit his account of the incident. The squabble, however, if it really occurred, may have formed the psychological germ for an act of revenge which the priest would inflict upon La Salle twenty-two years later—a full decade after the great explorer's death.

Father Louis Hennepin, who did not like girls dancing on board ship, was a member of La Salle's expedition to the West four years later. It was this expedition, culminating in the first descent of the Mississippi to its mouth, that won the vast Louisiana for France and made La Salle famous. Hennepin, however, was robbed of a share in the triumph. Sent off on a reconnaissance mission two years before the successful descent, the friar and his two companions were captured by a tribe of Sioux. By the time La Salle led his band of explorers down the great river, Hennepin was back in France writing a book about his experiences. Fifteen years later, in 1697, the friar published a second book, in which he revealed the great secret of his life. In 1680, he claimed, just before their capture by the Sioux, Hennepin and his pair of comrades had canoed down the Mississippi to its mouth and back—a full two years before La Salle.

Of Father Hennepin's early life we know very little, and that mainly from his own lips. He was born around 1640 in Belgium, then Spanish territory. "I was from my infancy very fond of travelling," he would write in middle age. Unsatisfied by youthful peregrinations around Europe, he set his hopes "upon seeing remoter countries and nations that had not yet been heard of." At the same time, by his own testimony, "I always found in myself a strong inclination to retire from the World, and regulate my life according to the rules of pure and severe virtue." While still a boy he became a novice in the Récollet order, the most austere of the Franciscan brotherhoods. Champlain had introduced four Récollet missionaries into Quebec in 1615, so it was not unlikely that Hennepin's twin passions might seek their resolution in the New World. He became a mendicant monk in a convent in Calais, but chafed at the bit. In the most affecting glimpse we have of the young acolyte,

> I used oft-times to skulk behind the doors of victualling-houses, to hear the sea-men give an account of their adventures. The smoke of tobacco was offensive to me, and created pain in my stomach . . . but for all I was very attentive to the accounts they gave of their encounters by sea, the perils they had gone through, and all the accidents which befell them in their long voyages. This occupation was so agreeable and engaging, that I have spent whole days and nights at it without eating.

When a small company of Récollets in Quebec was augmented in 1675 by five members of the order, Father Hennepin managed to get himself assigned to the cloister. He spent his first four years in New France in the nominal post of preacher, but his restlessness drove him out on the trail with the hunters and traders. "I was passionately zealous," he recorded, ". . . for enlarging the limits of Christianity, and converting the barbarous *Americans* to the belief of the Gospel." His zeal led ultimately to his inclusion in La Salle's western expedition of 1679.

At that date the huge interior of the Great Plains and the Mississippi Basin was just beginning to be explored by the French. The Spanish had discovered the mouth of the Mississippi in the previous century, but they had proceeded only a little way up its course from the Gulf of Mexico. Around 1639 a French interpreter on the St. Lawrence named Jean Nicollet heard rumors from the Nipissing Indians of a strange hairless people far to the west, who were heading eastward to trade. Fully expecting to run into Chinese, Nicollet advanced to Green Bay, on the western shore of Lake Michigan, and from there traveled a considerable distance down the Fox and Wisconsin rivers. His native guides made mention of a "great water" only three days away, which the eager Frenchman mistook for the sea. He found no Chinese, of course, but only Winnebago Indians.

The great Iroquois war precluded further exploration for almost two decades. In 1665 a Jesuit named Allouez penetrated into Lake Superior, where he heard rumors about the Sioux Indians and the great river known as the "Messipi." But it was not until 1673 that two Frenchmen, Joliet and Marquette, actually reached the river and floated their canoes upon it—for a full eleven hundred miles, from the mouth of the Wisconsin all the way down to the mouth of the Arkansas. The fear of being killed by Indians or captured by

Spaniards prevented their going all the way to the mouth, along with their virtual certainty that they had proved that the river issued neither into the Pacific nor into the sea of Virginia, but into the Gulf of Mexico. Marquette died of an illness on the return journey, but Joliet survived to carry back the Jesuit's account of the discovery, still a classic of exploration literature.

The middle of the 17th century saw an immense application of Jesuit energy in New France. The goal of the missionary effort went beyond mere conversion; it was to create a colony of pious and obedient retainers in the New World, a virtual empire such as the order had built in Paraguay. The Valley of the Mississippi appealed to the Jesuits as the ideal site for a second Paraguay. In Francis Parkman's memorable evocation,

> It meant a little nation of converted and domesticated savages, docile as children, under the paternal and absolute rule of Jesuit fathers, and trained by them in industrial pursuits, the results of which were to inure, not to the profit of the producers, but to the building of churches, the founding of colleges, the establishment of warehouses and magazines, and the construction of works of defence—all controlled by Jesuits, and forming a part of the vast possessions of the Order.

The Jesuit dream of Canada was doomed to swift collapse; but at the time of La Salle's expedition it dominated French thinking with respect to the little-known Mississippi.

Ironically, La Salle himself, though he had been schooled as a Jesuit, was deeply antagonistic to the order; and the Jesuits in turn distrusted and discredited the explorer. It was no accident that La Salle chose three Récollets, one of them Father Hennepin, for his journey, rather than any of the far more numerous Jesuits. Hennepin himself had the characteristic Récollet chip on his shoulder when it came to Jesuits. Beginning with Champlain, the Franciscan missionaries had gained the first toehold in the New World. But as a mendicant order they had found themselves unable to finance their evangelistic tasks, and in 1624 they had naively invited the Jesuits to help out. When the English made a short-lived conquest of the country in 1629, both orders were sent back to France. Upon retaking possession three years later, the French crown permitted only the Jesuits to return. Récollets were barred for forty years, largely as a result of secret Jesuit machinations in Paris.

In Hennepin's writings the Jesuits get short shrift. He neglects to mention several Jesuit missions in the West at which he surely spent time; he places a wholly fictitious Récollet mission far north of any

Jesuit ones on his map; and in his 1697 book he devotes a pathetic and gratuitous chapter to demonstrating that the Récollets have anticipated the Jesuits in missionary accomplishments throughout the world.

To follow Father Hennepin westward, we must first observe La Salle's Homeric preparations for the Mississippi voyage. His men devoted the winter of 1678–79 to building a boat and a fort. The explorer knew that the Niagara River, which separates Lake Erie from Lake Ontario, was, because of its great falls (of which Hennepin was to publish the first description), the key to all the upper lakes. By erecting a fort just above the falls, at the eastern end of Lake Erie, he might singlehandedly control the trade on the upper lakes, and intercept the Iroquois who regularly brought goods from the West to barter with the Dutch and English at Albany. The boat would serve the dual purpose of monopolizing the trading network on the lakes and of launching La Salle's descent of the Mississippi. As grandiose as the plan was, it was matched by La Salle's persistence in the face of setbacks. The Seneca Indians, who occupied the area, had to be appeased and pacified, and the sabotaging efforts of envious Canadian traders had to be checked. Despite the complete loss of a supporting vessel loaded with supplies, which sank on Lake Ontario, the boat-building proceeded. By spring the *Griffin*, of forty-five tons' burden, was launched on Lake Erie.

In August, La Salle's party, Hennepin among them, set sail for the West. They traveled in four days the length of Lake Erie and entered the Strait of Detroit. On Lake Huron they weathered gale and calm and came at last to the Jesuit mission of Michillimackinac, in the narrow inlet leading to Lake Michigan. Traders, missionaries, and Indians alike greeted the large ship with astonishment; in all of history no sail had ever before been unfurled on any of the upper lakes. In September the expedition crossed Lake Michigan to Green Bay. From there the *Griffin* was sent back to Michillimackinac, laden with furs, under orders to return as soon as possible to the Illinois country, from which La Salle planned to set out for the Mississippi. With great difficulty the remaining men canoed south along the shore of the huge lake until, in early November, they had reached the present site of Chicago. The *Griffin*, however, had not returned. The ship was integral to La Salle's Mississippi plans, for among its cargo were the rigging and anchors for the new vessel he planned to build for the descent of the river.

In the bitter cold of winter the party canoed and portaged to the Illinois River. Constantly faced with starvation, the men lived in a prolonged state of anxiety once they had entered the region of the warlike Illinois tribe. Shortly after New Year, 1680, six of La Salle's men deserted, and an attempt was made to poison the leader. Sorely tried, La Salle nevertheless pushed on down the Illinois and selected a site for a new fort. In January, a little below the present location of Peoria, work was begun on Fort Crèvecoeur: the name reflected the party's mood. The support of the *Griffin* now seemed impossible. The ship, it turned out, had vanished, perhaps during a storm; no trace of it was ever found.

Accepting the worst, La Salle decided to return all the way through the Great Lakes to Fort Frontenac to gather supplies that would be needed for the descent of the Mississippi. He set out on this monumental journey with five companions on March 2. Two days before he had sent three men downstream: strong canoers named Accault and Auguelle, and the Récollet Father Louis Hennepin. Their orders were to descend the Illinois to its junction with the Mississippi, then to push upstream and explore the river's headwaters. La Salle and Hennepin were never to see each other again.

Because he died in 1687 after twenty years of nearly continuous adventure in the New World, La Salle never had the leisure to write a book about his accomplishments. Three long letters that he sent to France form the principal document in his own hand. Yet the memoir of his second-in-command, the Italian Henri de Tonti, can be relied on to trace the movements that brought the party to the Illinois country in January of 1680. Thanks to Tonti, we can follow Hennepin to Fort Crèvecoeur simply because he was a member of La Salle's expedition.

From February 28 on, once the three men pushed off from shore and started paddling down the Illinois, we must turn to the writings of the vainglorious friar. From the beginning, in perhaps minor ways, he dissembled. Hennepin implied that he was the leader of the three-man reconnaissance, that he was virtually La Salle's right-hand man up to that point. But Tonti and La Salle made clear that the experienced Accault was the designated leader of the party. In a 1681 letter from Fort Frontenac, La Salle indicated his candid opinion of the Récollet:

It is necessary to know him somewhat, for he will not fail to exaggerate everything; that is his character. He wrote to me as though he had been all ready to be burned, although he was not even in danger; but he believes that it is honorable for him to act in this way, and he speaks more in keeping with what he wishes than with what he knows.

The incident of the "near-burning" alluded to by La Salle is but one of several hairbreadth escapes Hennepin reported during his three-man jaunt. Yet barring the characteristic exaggeration and the penchant for self-dramatizing, the narrative that he published in 1683 under the title *A Description of Louisiana* probably gives a rough approximation of the friar's adventures during the next few months. In this first work there is no whisper of any dash down the Mississippi to its mouth. Instead, according to Hennepin, the men took seven days to descend the Illinois to its mouth (a little upstream from present-day St. Louis). There they waited for ice floating in the Mississippi to clear, then headed upriver. By April 11, some forty days out, they had reached the Wisconsin River, which enters the Mississippi about fifty miles above what is now Dubuque, Iowa.

At 2:00 P.M. on the 11th the three Frenchmen suddenly saw thirty-three canoes manned by 120 Indians speeding toward them down the river. Hennepin attempted peaceful overtures, but concluded that he was going to die when several old men laid their hands on his head and "wept in a lugubrious tone." The Frenchmen frantically offered presents, but Accault and Auguelle kept hold of their guns, determined to fight to the end. Not so Father Hennepin:

> As for my own part, I determined to allow myself to be killed without any resistance, as I was going to announce to them a God, who had been falsely accused, unjustly condemned, and cruelly crucified, without showing the least aversion to those who put him to death.

The Sioux, however, seemed unwilling to participate in Hennepin's martyrdom. Instead they took the three men prisoner and started north toward their home. Thus began several months (Hennepin is very hazy about dates) of "captivity," during which the Frenchmen enjoyed great freedom: they were allowed to keep their firearms and pretty much to come and go as they pleased. Indeed, one gets the impression that the adventurers chose to associate with their "captors" because they recognized their superior knack of living off the land.

In nineteen days the assemblage paddled up the Mississippi to the falls which the pious father named after St. Anthony (today the site of Minneapolis and St. Paul). From this point the Indians set off overland, walking, Hennepin reports, faster than any European could keep up with, along the banks of the Rum River to their village on Mille Lacs, in east-central Minnesota. All the way, Hennepin complained about the physical ordeal. "If a religious in Europe underwent as many hardships and labors, and practiced abstinences like those we were often obliged to suffer in America, no other proof would be needed for his canonization." Apparently the Indians found their prisoners something of a nuisance. On the forced march to Mille Lacs they set fire to the prairie grass behind the Frenchmen "to oblige us to hasten on."

During the early summer of 1680 the three Frenchmen were kept separate from each other. Hennepin was "adopted" by a chief who he initially thought was going to kill him. On hunting forays the three men occasionally ran into each other. Hennepin complained about the "wretched" fare he was forced to eat, but he seems to have been issued the same rations as the Indians, and his stay in the Sioux village would have made more than one 20th-century anthropologist green with envy. Hennepin learned a few words of the natives' language, and claimed to have started work on a dictionary, but on the whole the Indians were more interested in him than he was in them. He indulged their curiosity by reading them scripture, baptizing a dying child, and warning them about their imminent punishment at the hands of the God who had leveled Sodom and Gomorrah. "But that gross people . . . turned all I said into ridicule," he grumbled.

To avoid being dragged along on a buffalo hunt far to the west, the friar told the Indians that he had promised to meet some other white men at the mouth of the Wisconsin River. (Hennepin asserted, and may well have believed, that La Salle had intended a relief party to meet him at that junction.) The Indians obligingly agreed to hunt to the south instead, and in July a party of 130 families started canoeing downstream. There was a shortage of space in the small vessels, and Hennepin soon found himself standing on shore beseeching one canoe after another to take him in. Accault and Auguelle passed him by, the former muttering that he had already paddled the Récollet far enough to suit him. At last a pair of Indians gave the father a ride.

The hunt ranged across the countryside. Impatient to reach the Wisconsin, Hennepin and Auguelle set off on a two-man expedition of their own; this was fine with the Sioux as long as Accault remained behind. On their own, despite feasting off buffalo, deer, catfish, and turtles, the two adventurers nearly came to grief, once allowing their canoe to drift away from them. With only ten charges of powder left, they were afraid to make a real escape and try to reach Fort Crèvecoeur. The Indians overtook them, and the hunt continued.

In late July two women came into the Indian camp reporting that five "spirits" (as the Sioux called white men) had been encountered near Lake Condé; they, the women related, had heard about the three captives and wished to join them to find out what nationality they were. On July 25, to their mutual joy, Hennepin met the daring explorer Daniel Greysolon, Sieur Du Lhut (or Duluth), and four soldiers. Duluth, who had been two years in the wilds, had just come from the head of Lake Superior down the St. Croix River to the Mississippi. He immediately told the Indians that he was Father Hennepin's brother, and scolded them for treating the friar so badly.

Though Hennepin recounts the meeting in a bland tone, hinting that Duluth was as glad to find him as he was to encounter the explorer, the father must have rejoiced in the knowledge that he was now saved from the savages. With Duluth he traveled for two months, had various adventures, and returned in November to the Jesuit mission of Michillimackinac, where they spent the winter. He just missed La Salle, who had passed through on his dash back to Fort Crèvecoeur a few weeks before. In the following year Hennepin made his way back to Montreal and then sailed for France.

It would be claiming too much to call the experiences which the Récollet had just been through a great feat of exploration. Yet the journey up the Mississippi, the wanderings with Duluth, and above all the time spent on the most intimate terms with the Sioux made up a noteworthy addition to French knowledge of the American West. Parkman, otherwise consistently scornful of the boastful friar, judged that "could he have contented himself with telling the truth, his name would have stood high as a bold and vigorous discoverer." As the first published account of the explorations of La Salle, Hennepin's *Description of Louisiana* could well expect an avid readership. While the father was writing the book, word came to France that La Salle had, in April 1682, fulfilled his dream by descending the Mississippi with Tonti and a large entourage of French and Indians all the way to its mouth. La Salle named the new country Louisiana, after his monarch, and claimed the vast Mississippi Basin for France. Hennepin acknowledged the discovery not only in the title of his book but with a glowing prediction of a great French empire in the New World. The paragraph that credits La Salle with the descent is written ungrudgingly, the magnanimity marred only by the pompous implication that La Salle headed downriver only after "seeing that I had made peace with the nations on the north and northwest."

The feat for which La Salle would be remembered for centuries was, in his mind, a mere prologue to more glorious achievements. He returned to France in 1684, having spent almost the whole of his previous sixteen years in the American wilderness, and immediately presented to Louis XIV a proposal for a new venture that was startling in its audacity. He urged a naval expedition to the Gulf of Mexico, whose personnel would enter the delta of the Mississippi,

Lake Superior

Mille Lacs

St Croix River

Wisconsin River

Michillimackinac

Falls of St. Anthony

capture by Sioux

Illinois River

Fort Crèvecœur

Mississippi River

▬▬▬ Father Louis Hennepin's actual route from February through July 1680, including the approximate route of his travels as a captive of the Sioux.

•••••► The route of La Salle's descent of the Mississippi in the spring of 1682; also the route which, after La Salle's death, Hennepin claimed he and his two companions had followed on a previously unmentioned side trip in 1680.

••••••• The approximate route of Hennepin's return to safety after his rescue by Duluth in later July 1680.

ascend the river some sixty leagues, and build a fortress, from which to control the huge interior. Then with a band of two hundred Frenchmen, supported by an army of fifteen thousand Indian warriors, it should be a simple matter to conquer the "indolent and effeminate" Spaniards who worked the lucrative mines of New Biscay, or northern Mexico.

The crown was sympathetic. Having asked for two ships, La Salle was granted four, their decks peopled with 180 soldiers, mechanics, and colonists, including women and children. The expedition sailed from France in July 1684.

From the outset the enterprise was a disaster. The naval commander of the expedition was at odds with La Salle at every turn, as were several of the chief officers. The ships were delayed by mechanical failures, by unplanned layovers, by La Salle's near-fatal illness, and by separation at sea. Late in 1684 they entered the Gulf of Mexico—waters forbidden to all but Spanish ships ever since the reign of Philip II.

Then occurred the most devastating—as well as the most ironic—of the expedition's setbacks. Only two years before, La Salle had stood triumphant at the mouth of the Mississippi, leader of the first band of Europeans ever to descend the greatest river in the North American continent. No one knew its secrets better than he. At that location, however, though he had been able to calculate the latitude, he had not had the means to make an accurate determination of the longitude. Now, in December 1684, the party of would-be colonists could not even find the mouth of the Mississippi! Believing it to lie much farther west than it actually does, La Salle confidently skirted the coast for mile after mile, until the shore began to trend puzzlingly southward. Beginning to suspect that he was too far west, the explorer called a halt; but he would have been appalled to know by how much he had erred. He lay anchored in what is now Matagorda Bay, between Galveston and Corpus Christi, more than four hundred miles of coastline west of the Mississippi.

The next year and a half bore witness to one of the most demoralizing failures in exploring history. The troubled party managed to build a patchwork fortress in the bay, but already there was dissension. Two men deserted early in 1685, never to be seen again; others tried to flee and were recaptured, one of whom was hanged. A chief officer was bitten by a rattlesnake; his condition worsened, his leg was amputated, but he died. By early summer more than thirty members of the party had perished. To add to their commander's vexation, the supply ship was run aground on a reef—he thought deliberately—and was irreparably damaged. The denizens of "Fort

St. Louis" were further plagued by Indian attacks. Parkman takes a glance at life in the fort during these months:

A lonely sea, a wild and desolate shore, a weary waste of marsh and prairie; a rude redoubt of drift-wood, and the fragments of a wreck; a few tents, and a few wooden hovels; bales, boxes, casks, spars, dismounted cannon, Indian canoes, a pen for fowls and swine, groups of dejected men and desponding, homesick women—this was the forlorn reality to which the air-blown fabric of an audacious enterprise had sunk.

In November 1686 La Salle began a series of desperate overland journeys in search of the Mississippi. He had decided that the only hope for the survival of the colony was to ascend the great river, pass through the Illinois country, traverse the Great Lakes to Fort Frontenac, and send for help from France. During these grim months the more listless of the settlers, deluded by the belief that their country must have sent ships to relieve their sufferings, took to staring out to sea every day, scanning the horizon for a glimpse of the hypothesized sails.

By January 1687, of the original 180 members of the expedition, fewer than 45 were still alive. The mood among the survivors was almost openly mutinous. La Salle's efforts to find the Mississippi failed pathetically; the illnesses that had ravaged the party had left its courageous leader unable to surmount obstacles which five years before would have been trifles in his path.

In March a quarrel broke out among some members of the party searching for the Mississippi. Tempers flared, and La Salle's nephew, with two other men, was murdered in his sleep. The mutineers decided that La Salle had to die, too. They ambushed him, shot him in the head, stripped his body naked, and dragged it into the bushes, deriding his corpse as they did so. In such ignominy died the man who, in Parkman's phrase, was "the heroic pioneer who guided [America] to the possession of her richest heritage."

During the following year a small contingent of survivors, including La Salle's brother, managed to reach the French fort at the mouth of the Illinois River, from which Tonti had been poking southward in search of his former commander, who he had heard was in serious trouble. Eventually the party reached Montreal and sailed in the fall of 1687 for France. To their remarkable survival we owe our knowledge of La Salle's last expedition. The final footnote on the fatal Texas colony was written by a Spanish party who, bent on conquest, finally located and entered Fort St. Louis. They found a scene of utter desolation, with corpses rotting in the sun. The only two Frenchmen still alive, who were taken as prisoners, testified that the colony had been decimated by an Indian massacre three months before. The two men had managed to survive by domesticating themselves as Indian slaves.

We can only speculate what effect the story of La Salle's demise must have had on Father Hennepin, as bits and pieces of it filtered back to France. The tragedy may have loomed, for the ambitious Récollet, mainly as a chance to take over as his own property the glorious deed which now rested as the chief laurel on the brow of the dead La Salle.

At what point did Hennepin decide to steal for himself the descent of the Mississippi? Even to guess at the answer, it behooves us to look at the friar's fortunes during the years La Salle was in Texas pursuing his star-crossed dream of empire. The information is patchy, but we can deduce that these years were not happy ones for Hennepin. His *Description of Louisiana* must have been widely read, for it appeared in two new editions during the decade and was translated into Italian, Dutch, and German. Within the ecclesiastical community, however, there were critics who winced at the pretensions of the book.

During 1683–86 Father Hennepin had a post as guardian of the Récollets at Artois. Here, according to his own account, he fell under the oppressive supervision of a Father Le Fevre, a friend of La Salle's who, in Hennepin's eyes, was to persecute him for years. Le Fevre at first wanted Hennepin to return to America, but the sometime explorer begged off, hiding behind a technicality in the rules of his order. He was instead sent to Rome, then to another convent, and finally banished from France to his native Flanders by royal mandate (Hennepin claimed the orders were forged). He appealed to Louis XIV in vain, and resettled at Gosselies, where he became a confessor for the Penitential nuns.

He spent five years at Gosselies, building, he claimed, a large church and advancing the prosperity of his community. But Father Le Fevre would not leave him alone. His former superior, arguing that Gosselies belonged to France, wanted Hennepin removed to Flanders proper, which was still Spanish terrain. Hennepin objected, but apparently moved once more, back to his childhood home of Ath.

By reading between his own lines (which constitute the main source for the friar's movements during these years), we can picture Father Hennepin as a priest on the down and out, scraping for appointments, followed everywhere by his reputation as a vain and difficult man. After his treatment at the hands of Le Fevre and his monarch's refusal to come to his rescue, he was certainly no longer a partisan of French causes. When he gained the ear of England's secretary of war under William III, he played up his tattered credentials for all they were worth and managed to win an audience with the king at The Hague in 1696. He used William's influence to try to gain a missionary post in America, to which he was willing to travel, we may conjecture, because he now saw the New World as his best remaining hope for advancement. But the Récollet officials parried his request with vague promises. Hennepin, in fact, was never to leave Europe again.

Meanwhile he had been writing a second volume about his adventures on the Mississippi. In 1697 it was published in Utrecht as the *Nouvelle Decouverte d'un tres grand Pays Situé dans l'Amerique.* The *New Discovery* appeared with a fulsome dedication to William III, "the most magnanimous king in the world," who had singlehandedly preserved the Netherlands against a "fatal invasion" by Louis XIV. The friar refers to his own adventure as "the greatest discovery that has been made in this age."

For the most part the *New Discovery* is simply a rehash—even a word-by-word transcription—of the *Description of Louisiana.* But once Hennepin's narrative had coasted down the Illinois again with Accault and Auguelle, the friar suddenly revealed his astonishing secret. During the forty-three days between March 12 and April 24, 1680, the three men, Hennepin claimed, had canoed down the Mississippi to its mouth and back upriver all the way to the Wisconsin. Thus they had made La Salle's great discovery two years before La Salle.

On the surface of it, no boast could have been more preposterous. If Hennepin had gone down the Mississippi, why had he waited seventeen years to inform the world of the fact? Why, indeed, had he made no mention of the sidetrip in his first book?

> I was then obliged [Hennepin explained] to say nothing of the course of the river Meschasipi, from the mouth of the river of the Illinois down to the sea, for fear of disobliging M. *la Salle,* with whom I began my discovery. This gentleman would alone have the glory of having discovered the course of that river: But when he heard that I had done it two years before him, he could never forgive me. . . . This is the true cause of his malice against me, and of all the barbarous usage I have met with in France.

Hennepin went on to claim that La Salle had needlessly risked the lives of several of his men, the friar included.

> God knows, that I am sorry for his unfortunate death; but the judgments of the Almighty are always just; for that gentleman

was killed by one of his own men, who were at last sensible that he exposed them to visible dangers, without any necessity, and for his private designs.

Plunging into his new account of the momentous descent, Hennepin indicates that it was Accault and Auguelle who hatched the scheme of disobeying La Salle's orders and proceeding downstream instead of up. The obedient father, "sure that M. *la Salle* would slander me, and represent me to my superiors as a wilful and obstinate man," nevertheless went along with the scheme for fear that his two colleagues would leave him to starve on the shore if he opposed their resolution. The narrative of the descent continues confidently, sprinkled with adventures and ethnographic observations. At the mouth itself Hennepin wanted to build a cabin and stay awhile "the better to observe where we were," but his more worldly companions, disappointed at finding no natives with whom to trade for furs, were in a fever of impatience to get back upstream. The three men built a cross, knelt and sang the *Vexilla Regis*, and left a letter describing their historic voyage.

The return trip seems to have been accomplished in a few weeks of effortless upstream paddling. Near the mouth of the Illinois, for fear of running into La Salle's men, the adventurers canoed at night and hid on overgrown islands by day. The narrative rejoins Hennepin's 1683 version with the men's capture by the Sioux on April 12 (in the *Description*, the date had been April 11).

The Récollet expected that his new revelation would be met with skepticism. In a paragraph that breathes the essence of Hennepin's peculiar style of grandiose paranoia, the friar dismisses potential detractors:

> I doubt not but that sort of cattle will account of this my discovery as being false and incredible. But what they say shall not trouble me much: They themselves were never masters of the courage and valour which inspires men to undertake the glorious enterprises that gain them reputation in the world, being confined within narrow bounds, and wanting a soul to achieve anything that can procure them a distinguishing and advantageous character among men. It were better therefore for such to admire what they cannot comprehend, and rest satisfied in a wise and profound silence, than thus foolishly to blame what they know nothing of.

Aside from the improbability of Hennepin's alleged reason for keeping quiet so long, the biggest stumbling block he faced in perpetrating the hoax was the matter of dates. His own *Description* had trapped him into asserting that the three men had reached the mouth of the Illinois on March 12 and had been captured by the Sioux near the mouth of the Wisconsin on April 11. Thus Hennepin had barely a month in which to fit his extensive side journey. The dates in the *New Discovery* are themselves internally contradictory. Hennepin tries to give himself an extra thirteen days by averring that he reached the Wisconsin only by April 24; yet a few pages later he gives April 12 as the date of the capture by the Indians. It had taken La Salle two and half months to travel a distance shorter than Hennepin was now claiming in (at the outside) forty-three days.

The narrow time frame required Herculean feats of paddling. The total distance from the Illinois down to the mouth of the Mississippi and back up to the Wisconsin is about 3,000 miles. Had it taken the three men forty-three days for the journey, they would have averaged 70 miles a day; if only thirty days, then 100 miles a day. Least credible of all was the speed upstream: 1,700 miles against a river in flood stage in nine days, or an average of 190 miles per day! As the leading 20th-century student of Hennepin has pointed out, the 1936 Olympic champion canoeing pairs managed to maintain a pace of 7 miles an hour on still water for a few hours only; Hennepin's progress on April 1–2, 1680, would have demanded twice as fast a rate sustained over a continuous twenty-four hours of effort—upstream.

The actual distances on the Mississippi were not well known in 1697, of course. But there were other conspicuous contradictions embedded in the text of the *New Discovery*. The canoes, so light and speedy while going up the Mississippi, were elsewhere the object of Hennepin's complaint that at best they could make only 30 miles a day upstream. The latitudes "observed" by the friar are a jumble of contradictions. One slip, which may have gone unnoticed at the time, would have given the careful 1697 reader a clue as to the sources of Hennepin's imposture. He mentions Easter Sunday as occurring on March 23. But in 1680 Easter was celebrated on April 20. It was in 1682 that Easter fell on March 23.

Discrepancies that glare us in the face today, thanks to modern scholarship, were not so apparent in 1697. Despite its clumsy errors, Hennepin's new narrative became an immensely popular book, running through seven French editions, four Dutch, a German, and a Spanish; the 1699 English edition had much to do with stimulating British interest in colonizing the American West. There were readers from the very first who doubted Hennepin's veracity, among them the author of the preface to the Spanish edition of the book, as well as a Jesuit writing from the mouth of the Mississippi in 1700 who railed against "a thousand falsehoods and ridiculous boasts" to be found in the *New Discovery*. But the tide of opinion was in favor of the Récollet. His two books, after all, were the main sources available in Europe for the complicated but glorious achievements of La Salle's expedition in the West. La Salle's own letters were not published until the 19th century. A Father Le Clerq published in 1691 an account of the Récollet missions in North America, and included the diary of Father Membré, who had been with La Salle and Tonti on their descent of the Mississippi; but this book was quickly suppressed by the pro-Jesuit French government. Thus Hennepin's theft of La Salle went through the whole of the 18th century and much of the 19th largely unchallenged.

Of the rest of Hennepin's life we know little. He followed the *New Discovery* with yet a third reworking of his saga, *Nouveau Voyage d'un Pays plus grand que l'Europe*, which adds nothing of substance to the two previous books. Jean Delanglez, the 20th-century scholar who may be said to have had the last word on Hennepin, speculates that the fervor for colonization in Britain stirred up by the *New Discovery* may have called Hennepin's bluff. An ambitious English scheme to find the mouth of the Mississippi by sea might well have led William III to beseech Hennepin to lead the expedition. Knowing that he had never been to the mouth himself, and that La Salle had died trying to find it by sea, Hennepin may have panicked. We do know that he went to The Hague at this time and begged the French ambassador to return him to France—despite the fact that the remarks in the dedication of the *New Discovery* were virtually treasonous.

The last glimpse we have of Father Hennepin is in Rome in 1701, where he was reported to be in a convent, hoping to return to America. He may have been penning a dedication to the Pope to preface the Italian edition of his famous book. The thought of his switching allegiance from the Protestant William III to the Catholic Clement XI is not at all at odds with his character. We do not know where or when Father Hennepin met his end; "He died," said Parkman, "in a deserved obscurity."

The vague criticism that Hennepin had been a boaster or even a liar went undeveloped for 140 years. In the 1817 edition of the *Biographie Universelle*, for instance, all of Hennepin's claims are accepted as truth, and his rejoinders to his critics are praised as "very plausible." Finally, in 1839, an American reviewer, J. H. Greene, took up the case in the pages of the *North American Review*. Greene noted that Hennepin had never acknowledged Marquette and Joliet's travels on the Mississippi in 1673—while apparently plagiarizing some details from Marquette's map. He went on to point out the impossibly swift canoeing times required by the friar's dash down the Mississippi, and suspected that the account of it was an "inserted journal," borrowed perhaps from Tonti. Greene was answered in another journal, but stuck to his guns.

It remained for Jared Sparks in 1844, in his biography of La Salle, to make the first genuinely devastating attack on the purported side trip. A few copies of Le Clerq's *Établissement de la Foi* had survived the government suppression. Sparks, the president of Harvard, got hold of a copy and found not only that Hennepin had borrowed liberally from it, but that he had "appropriated whole paragraphs, with very slight verbal alterations, contenting himself with changing the dates to suit the occasion." Sparks quoted parallel passages in the original French to clinch the matter. Thus Hennepin had stolen the genuine account of Father Membré, who had accompanied La Salle and Tonti, changing the dates from 1682 to 1680, shifting pronouns and references as need be so that the text referred to Accault, Auguelle, and himself, rather than to La Salle's more numerous party. Among the slips Hennepin had made was leaving unchanged the date on which Easter had fallen. The argument was conclusive. "The records of literary piracy," wrote Parkman twenty-six years later, "may be searched in vain for an act of depredation more recklessly impudent."

Sparks's own view, however, was that the rest of Hennepin's account was by and large reliable. In 1876 a French scholar named Pierre Margry made a startling further claim. Margry had unearthed an unpublished manuscript written by an Abbé Bernou around 1682, called *Relation des descouvertes*. Bernou had been a friend of La Salle's, and it was among the abbé's papers that La Salle's three letters describing his expedition were found. Margry published the *Relation*, adding to the charges against Hennepin the claim that he had plagiarized extensively from Bernou for his own *Description of Louisiana*. As with Le Clerq, the similarities in passages were too exact to be accidental. For example (Bernou first, Hennepin second):

> Enfin, par les essais que le Sieur de la Salle en a fait chez les Miamis au retour de son second voyage, on est persuadé que la terre est capable de produire toutes sortes de fruits, d'herbes, de grains et en beaucoup plus grande abondance que les meilleures terres de l'Europe.

At last, thanks to the efforts which the Sieur de La Salle made in the country of the Miamis upon his return from his second voyage, people are convinced that the land is capable of producing all kinds of fruits, herbs, and grains in much greater abundance than the most fertile lands of Europe can.

Enfin par les essais que nous avons faits chez les Islinois, & les
Issati; on est persuadé que la terre est capable de produire
toutes sorts de fruits, d'herbes & de grains, & en plus grande
d'abondance que les meilleures terres de l'Europe.

At last, thanks to the efforts which we made in the country of the Illinois and the
Issati, people are convinced that the land is capable of producing all kinds of fruits,
herbs, and grains, and in much greater abundance than the most fertile lands of
Europe can.

Hennepin, it would appear, changed only the Indian tribes to ones he
was more familiar with and "le Sieur de la Salle" to "nous."

But why should the Récollet friar have needed to plagiarize from a
secondhand account (Bernou from La Salle) in relating the very
adventures he himself had actually enjoyed? Duluth's rescue of the
three men in the summer of 1680 made it indisputable that they had
indeed been captured by the Sioux after paddling up the Mississippi
to the Wisconsin. In 1880 the American editor of a new edition of the
Description of Louisiana, John Gilmary Shea, argued ingeniously that
the case was really just the opposite: Bernou had plagiarized from a
manuscript copy of Hennepin's book. The relative dates of composi-
tion of the two works became pivotal criteria, as did stylistic and
organizational nuances.

A hearty endorsement of Shea's view came from the civic leaders
of Minneapolis and St. Paul, in Hennepin County, who held in 1880
a lavish bicentenary celebration, complete with a parade, marching
bands, an outdoor banquet, and rousing speeches, to honor "the first
white man in Minnesota." The Shea-Margry debate, at times bitterly
acrimonious, tangled up with scholarly jealousies that derive from
French versus American letters and (still!) from Franciscan versus
Jesuit passions, has waxed strong well into the 20th century. In 1941,
Jean Delanglez reviewed all the evidence, systematically took to
pieces most of Shea's debating points, and concluded that fully two-
thirds of the *Description* was directly plagiarized from Bernou.
Delanglez's argument is dense but precise, and his conclusion seems
unavoidable.

The question lingers—why? Why did Hennepin have to plagiarize
from an account of the very expedition of which he was a member?
Delanglez's suspicion is that the friar kept no journal or even notes
during his long ramble with La Salle. He may have been quite unsure
most of the time just where he was. When he later needed to
remember exactly how and where the expedition had traveled to
reach Fort Crèvecoeur on the Illinois, he turned to Bernou, whose
account was based on La Salle's own letters, to reconstruct the

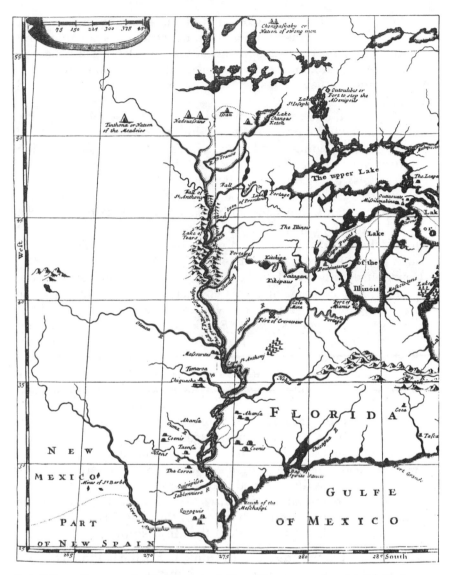

Detail from the map in Hennepin's *A New Discovery*, showing (dotted line) his claimed route in 1680 all the way from Fort Crevecoeur on the Illinois River down the Mississippi to its mouth, then back up to the country of the Sioux, where he was captured by the Indians. (New York Public Library)

expedition. Indeed, in the two-thirds of the *Description* that takes place while Hennepin is with La Salle, the account is coherent. But once the friar is separated from his leader, as Delanglez observes, "his wanderings are hopelessly muddled, and his chronology impossible." Hennepin may have spent most of his time in the New World effectively lost!

As late as the 1920s a handful of French scholars (mostly Franciscans) continued to cling to a faith in the essential honesty of Father Hennepin, going even beyond Shea's last-ditch holding action to reaffirm vaguely the "fact" of the friar's "voyage toward the mouth of the Mississippi." But authentic scholarship leaves us with no alternative to the conclusion that Hennepin was a thoroughgoing plagiarist and fraud. In his adventures among the Sioux he had had a truly extraordinary experience. But he was not a good enough diarist even to offer an accurate account of his own captivity. The need to pose as a great explorer got in the way.

Hennepin's critics and biographers, from the 19th century on, concur in their assessment of his character. "He was one of those restless and aspiring class of men, who are unhappy at the thought of another's fame or success," wrote Sparks. Delanglez, too, singled out Hennepin's "mania for having been first, for having seen more Indian tribes than anybody ever saw before, for having traveled faster and farther than anybody." To the 1903 editor of his *New Discovery*, the friar was a "conceited braggart" whose worldly ambition had "estranged him from all his ecclesiastical colleagues." Parkman could not resist the frequent opportunities to sneer at the Récollet, and even his defender Shea·acknowledged that the man was vain and prone to exaggeration. Delanglez believed that at a certain point Hennepin "had become a pathological case. Subjectively, when he took God to witness, he believed that he was telling the truth."

The definitive appraisal is Tonti's. Hearing in 1700 about the outlandish claim of priority advanced in the *New Discovery*, Tonti wrote his brother from the mouth of the Mississippi:

> I do not·know how Father Louis Hennepin has the boldness to lie so impudently in his relation. He was insupportable to the late M. de la Salle and to all of M. de la Salle's men. He sent the Récollet to the Sioux so as to get rid of him.

BIBLIOGRAPHY

Adams, Percy G. *Travelers and Travel Liars: 1660-1800*. Berkeley, 1962.

Delanglez, Jean. *Hennepin's Description of Louisiana: A Critical Essay.* Chicago, 1941.

———. "Hennepin's Voyage to the Gulf of Mexico 1680." *Mid-America*, vol. 21, no. 1 (January 1939).

[Greene, J. H.]. [Review of *The Life of Father Marquette*, by Jared Sparks], *North American Review*, vol. 48 (January 1839).

———. "Travels of Father Hennepin," *North American Review*, vol. 49 (July 1839).

Hennepin, Father Louis, *A Description of Louisiana*, translated and edited by John Gilmary Shea. New York, 1880.

———. *A New Discovery of a Vast Country in America*, edited by Reuben Gold Thwaites. Chicago, 1903.

Margry, Pierre. *Découvertes et établissements des Français dans l'Ouest et dans le Sud de l'Amerique Septentrionale.* Six volumes. Paris, 1876–88.

Parkman, Francis. *The Discovery of the Great West.* Boston, 1870.

Sparks, Jared. *Life of Robert Cavelier de la Salle.* Boston, 1844.

3

DEFOE IN MADAGASCAR

In May 1729, Londoners were greeted with a new book called *Madagascar: Or, Robert Drury's Journal, During Fifteen Years Captivity on That Island*. The volume told a remarkable story of survival. In 1701 a fourteen-year-old boy named Robert Drury was among the passengers on the ship *Degrave*, which, having traded at Bengal, was headed across the Indian Ocean back toward the Cape of Good Hope. The ship had been dangerously leaky since leaving Bengal, and was now, despite continuous bailing and jettisoning of cargo, threatening to sink. The captain resolved to head for the nearest coast—the island of Madagascar.

The *Degrave* made it almost to shore, where its crew abandoned it as a wreck, fleeing on an improvised raft. Their joy at having escaped death was short-lived, however, for a tribe of natives attacked them in the midst of an overland march and massacred them in the forest. There were only a few survivors, one of whom was Robert Drury. Separated from the others, the fourteen-year-old became a personal slave to one Mevarrow, a deaan, or local chieftain, who spent much of his time gleefully making war.

Drury spent a decade and a half on Madagascar, until he was rescued by a slave trader named William Mackett and brought back to England. His adventures during that time included numerous close brushes with death, marriage to two native women, participation in intertribal warfare, a solo escape from Deaan Mevarrow only to be captured by another master, promotion to captain of his new master's guard, and, of course, a thorough steeping in everything Madagascan.

The title page of this fascinating tome indicated that it could be purchased at booksellers' in Cornhill, Newgate Street, and Fleet Street, or from the author himself, who whiled away his time at Old Tom's Coffee House in Birchin Lane. The narrative itself closed with a warm personal advertisement inviting readers to chat with Drury at the same coffee house, where he spent every day, and was "ready to gratify any gentleman with a further account of anything herein contained, to stand the strictest examination, or to confirm those things which to some may seem doubtful." The book was prefaced by another certificate of authenticity from Captain Mackett himself, who esteemed the young fellow he had rescued as "an honest, industrious Man, of good reputation." As a frontispiece the volume offered a detailed map of Madagascar, and the curious reader could find an extensive Malagasy-English word list in an appendix.

Yet the text was manifestly not that of an unlettered youth who had spent his early adulthood on a remote island peopled with savages. The prose had an easy gracefulness that seduced the reader into Drury's world. A "natural" style, indeed: self-evidently that of an accomplished writer. The book's preface acknowledged an editorial helping hand, that of a "transcriber" who had found it necessary to take Drury's original, "contract it, and put it in a more agreeable Method." This unnamed transcriber also vouched for Robert Drury's character, but admitted that he had altered the text by "putting some Reflections in the Author's Mouth" pertaining to religion. But he swore vehemently that he had tampered with none of the facts, nor had he added any fictions of his own to Drury's tale.

As a story of shipwreck and survival on a remote island peopled with Negroes, *Madagascar* inevitably invited comparison with *Robinson Crusoe*, which had been immensely popular ever since its appearance ten years before. Anticipating the comparison, the transcriber huffed:

> At the first Appearance of this Treatise, I make no Doubt of its being taken for such another Romance as "Robinson Crusoe"; but whoever expects to find here the fine Inventions of a prolific Brain will be deceived; for so far as every Body concerned in the Publication knows, it is nothing else but a plain, honest Narrative of Matter of Fact.

Madagascar was reprinted in 1731, 1743, 1750, 1807, 1826, and 1831. Through the end of the 18th century and most of the 19th, the book seems to have been accepted as a true story. When Madagascar expert Captain Pasfield Oliver decided to publish a popular edition of the book in 1890, he was prompted to do so by the fact that the sailor boy's simple narrative had become one of the most important sources of information on Madagascar—*the* leading source, in fact, in the English language. Oliver, however, was convinced that Drury's tale was completely imaginary, cribbed and patched together by a skillful editor from the tales of pirates and the chronicles of the French governors of the island.

In 1869 William Lee, the biographer of Daniel Defoe, first raised the possibility that the prolific author of *Robinson Crusoe* might also have been Robert Drury's "transcriber." Lee pointed out that Defoe's library was well stocked with travel books, and that two earlier works from his pen, *The Life of Captain Singleton* and *The King of the Pirates*, contained major scenes set on Madagascar. But Lee rejected his own suggestion on the grounds that the style of *Robert Drury's Journal* was unlike Defoe's.

As Drury himself receded into obscurity, the controversy over the book intensified. Oliver was convinced on the very grounds that Lee had cited—linguistic style—that Defoe had written *Madagascar*. Had Robert Drury ever been to the island, then? Oliver was willing to say only that "it seems certain that there was such a person as Robert Drury" and that he had sailed on the *Degrave*. The more rigorous scholarship of the 20th century attacked even that conclusion, and in 1939 the American scholar John Robert Moore, arguing strongly for Defoe's authorship, concluded that "there is no reason to suppose that Robert Drury was more than a convenient name" on which Defoe hung his entirely fictional narrative. Moore, however, was not to have the last word.

There are, therefore, two separate questions. Did Defoe write *Robert Drury's Journal*? And did Robert Drury ever exist, and if he did, did he have anything to do with Madagascar? The questions are logically independent. Even if Drury's adventures were true, Defoe might have been the transcriber who turned the raw material into a marvelous adventure story. Alternatively, Defoe may not have been the author; but that says nothing about whether the book is a "romance" or a "plain, honest narrative of matter of fact."

In order to understand the scholarly snarls in which these two questions lie tangled, it is valuable to take a closer look at Drury's story, and to sample the prose style in which it is told. From the first pages the similarities to *Robinson Crusoe* obtrude. Defoe, posing as an anonymous editor, had given Crusoe a character recommendation and had sent the book into the world vowing, "The editor believes the thing to be a just history of fact; neither is there any appearance of fiction in it." In his first pages Crusoe regretfully calls to mind his father's "serious and excellent counsel" against going to sea, his mother's vexation, and his own perverse obstinacy in disobeying them. Shortly after his shipwreck, Drury laments:

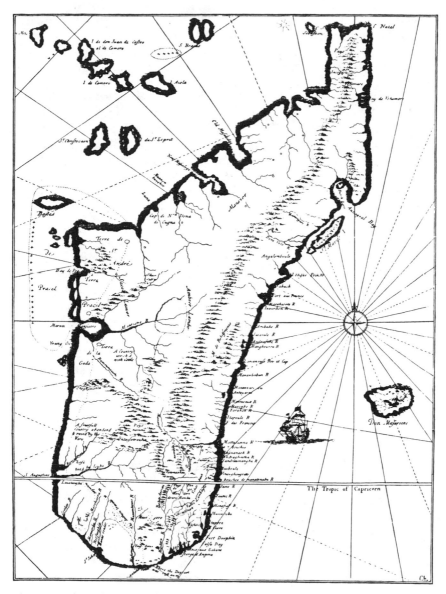

The map of Madagascar (largely plagiarized from Flacourt) that appeared
in Robert Drury's Journal. The dotted line across the southwest corner of
the island, labeled "The Authors Travells to Augustine," gives the
supposed route of the author's escape from Deaan Mevarrow. (New York
Public Library)

Now my wicked obstinacy appeared to my view, and my tender mother begging me on her knees not to go to sea, gave me the most distracting torture. I could see my error now, and repent; but who could I blame but myself?

The similarities, of course, prove little, given the vast influence of *Robinson Crusoe* on adventure books both true and fictional.

Two days after the shipwreck, the survivors from the *Degrave* experienced the sort of coincidence that at first blush seems unmistakably the stuff of fiction: they ran into an Englishman. This man, who was named Sam, had been captured by pirates, from whom he had escaped by feigning illness and asking to be put ashore on Madagascar. Sam told them about two Scottish ship captains, Drummond and Stewart, who could be found in the nearest village. The captains had similarly been seized by pirates, who had spared them, with a few of their crew, by setting them adrift in a longboat. The *Degrave* survivors, Drury relates, united with Drummond and Stewart and their retinue, who briefly bolstered their numbers.

In the native village the Englishmen were for a while the uneasy guests of the local king, Crindo. After an old woman brought them the news that Crindo planned to kill them all, the refugees decided to march 125 miles overland to Fort Dauphin, where a more Europeanized King Samuel held sway. In typical English fashion, they reasoned that an aggressive offensive aided their chances, so they seized the king, his wife, and his son as hostages. As they fled, a force of six or seven hundred natives followed them, menacing them with lances each step of the way. Trying to gain a weapons advantage, the Englishmen bartered away their hostages for guns, but this sealed their doom. On the banks of the Mandrare River the native army, now swelled to two or three thousand, attacked. Drury says that the defenders had only thirty-six firearms among them. The odds were impossible. Before his very eyes the fourteen-year-old saw his captain killed with a lance to the throat and to his sides. The wholesale slaughter swept through the party, and soon the natives had "murdered every man; they then fell to stripping them of their clothes, and even butchering them; for they ripped open several of their bellies."

Drury and three other youths his age alone were spared, to be taken into slavery. The four were immediately separated, and Drury was not to see any of them again during his long stay on the island. The boy was marched at once to a strange town where his master, Mevarrow, Crindo's grandson, took charge of him.

Up to this point in his narrative, Drury has been fairly specific about dates. But from his enslavement onward, the years pass in a seasonless blur of forced labor, warfare, and personal adventures. An odd effect of the book, stemming perhaps from a lack of skill on the author's part, is to make Drury seem not to age: even while he gains in status in the eyes of his captors, he continues to convey a late-adolescent or early-adult sensibility. He remains curious but timid, cooperative but unhappy, principled yet adaptable.

During the years of his enslavement to Mevarrow, Drury's chief occupations, aside from helping his master wage war, seem to have been three: tending cattle, digging for wild yams, and gathering honey from beehives. These labors he performed day in and day out until he became quite the expert at all three, so that, for instance, he was eventually put in charge of a cattle-rustling foray into a neighboring herd. As a soldier in Crindo's army, Drury was a participant in the endless civil war that occupied virtually all the tribes and factions on Madagascar.

He was also a careful observer of native rituals, which he reported in great detail. Shocked and fascinated by the idolatry of it, he vividly described the worship of a household altar called the Owley, a bizarre concoction made out of beads, wood, animal horns, and alligators' teeth, beneath which the natives sacrificed live oxen. At his first ceremony the boy was ordered to worship at the Owley, but he refused, for "I would sooner die than worship false gods." Deaan Mevarrow calmly proceeded to lead Drury out of town to be executed for his impiety, but was at the last minute dissuaded by his brother. Drury had earlier balked, with equally dire potential consequences, at the obligatory obeisance of licking Deaan Mevarrow's feet, which all his underlings, including his wife, performed each time he returned from battle.

At some later point the English youth tried to instruct his hosts in the true religion, but was received with gales of laughter. If no man had ever seen God except some ancient forefathers who beheld him descending in a cloud, the natives asked, how did anybody living know this was true? "I was here at a great loss because they had no knowledge of letters, and therefore I could not make them understand anything of the Scriptures." Drury lost the theological debate when he attempted to explain the biblical account of creation. The idea that God had constructed woman from one of Adam's ribs provoked especially hearty mirth among his auditors, and Drury, to clinch the case, repeated the superstition that living men had one less rib on one side than on the other. A particularly bony specimen was brought forth, his ribs were counted, and Drury was properly chastised for giving credit to "old women's stories."

Drury also served as a local historian, keeping straight the complicated genealogies of the various local deaans and setting down an
extended history of the famed King Samuel, whom he had not yet
met, but who must have been often in his thoughts as a potential
source of rescue and escape.

As an observer Drury also witnessed practices that filled him with
horror. With three fellow slaves, famished from not eating for days,
Drury secretly killed and roasted one of the cows. The masters
apprehended the miscreants and immediately castrated them. Drury
was spared only because he convinced Mevarrow that he had
contrived to spare the cow belonging to him. Later Drury observed
the elaborate circumcision feast of a year-old child, essentially a
drunken debauch.

During these years Drury excited fascination everywhere he went,
for most of the natives had never seen a white man, and had never
heard of one serving as a slave to a black. In a military skirmish into a
remote village, Drury masqueraded as a white prince to instill awe in
the particularly backward inhabitants. Generally speaking, Drury's
importance grew as the years passed and as Mevarrow became fonder
of his slave. After capturing a rival prince's mother and daughter,
Drury was offered his choice of the women to take as a wife. Drury
chose the sixteen-year-old daughter, "being in truth extremely
pleased with her from the very moment I took her." The proud
husband led his bride away by a rope tied around her middle. "She
only laughed and jested with me for it, but I was so fearful of her
getting away that I could not sleep." In a short digression on
Madagascan beauty, Drury attempts to make his reader understand
"how I could so passionately love a black woman." Within weeks, if
our hero can be believed, the passion had become mutual.

Nevertheless Drury had determined to escape from his master.
Deaan Mevarrow, suspecting the young man's intentions, employed a
wizard to cast a charm over Drury so that at the thought of running
away he would be overcome with guilt; if guilt was not efficacious,
the charm would cause him to break his back and legs. The doughty
Englishman persisted in his resolve, however. His only reluctance
stemmed from his failure to persuade his wife to join him in the
escape.

It was some satisfaction that I had no child by her. I was almost
afraid to tell her, but at length, after making her swear solemnly
by the Owley that she would keep the secret I should entrust her
with, I told her I was going, and the only trouble I had was
parting with her. She begged and cried, but there was no staying

any longer for me here. . . . At length she was a little appeased from her first passion, and I broke from her arms by break of day—with what pain those of my readers who are tender lovers can better imagine than I can describe.

Drury fled into the forest, striking out northwest toward the harbor of St. Augustine, where ships were sometimes reported. For twenty-six days he pursued his solitary escape, killing cattle for food, avoiding natives by day, but building fires at night to keep the foxes away. The account of this remarkable journey forms one of the most lively and engaging sections of the book. Drury by now was an expert at living off the land, and seems to have had little trouble coping with the wilderness. Indeed, he was so adjusted to Madagascar, he claims, that he had completely forgotten the English language.

Finally Drury reached St. Augustine Bay, where one Deaan Trongha, an ally of Crindo's, held sway. Trongha greeted him warmly, and recruited him at once for his army. The chieftain also introduced Drury to a Dutchman named Eglasse and a West Indian Negro who spoke English—the first non-Madagascans Drury had met in years. But Drury had scarcely settled into Eglasse's house when he saw the Dutchman murdered before his eyes by some dishonest cattle dealers. Shortly afterward Deaan Trongha himself was killed in battle. Drury spent an indeterminate time as a kind of half-slave, half-lieutenant to a succession of local chieftains. In the middle of the country's interminable civil war he ran into his former master Mevarrow again. Drury licked Mevarrow's feet, made up an excuse about why he had fled, and asked after his wife. "They told me she would not be married to any other man, but continued constantly lamenting for me. This brought unfeigned tears from me."

Drury now determined to put all his efforts into escaping from the island. Hearing of an English ship arrived to trade at a nearby port, he wrote a message on a satter leaf to the captain and begged a native to deliver it. To Drury's anguish, the messenger reported that the captain had glanced at the leaf and thrown it contemptuously away: "' . . . and I am sure it was as good an one as that you gave me; for it's true I dropped yours, but I pulled one of the best I could find from a tree.'" At the news, Drury went off weeping into the woods.

There remained several momentous adventures before the former cabin boy was to be saved. When a new master chided him for living without a woman, Drury consented to taking a new wife, but only on the condition that she agree to the betrothal of her own free will. Drury was now as happy as he had been since the shipwreck, or so he maintains. But almost immediately he underwent his closest brush of all with death. Having innocently struck up a friendship with an East Indian, Drury found himself implicated by association when his new friend uttered an ungrateful remark in the presence of the local king. The king peremptorily ordered Drury executed, and before he could think, he was being led to his death. He arrived, his hands bound, at the place of execution, where the sight of the unburied bodies of other victims caused him to "weep piteously." At the last moment a voice from the distance called out, "Stay, stay! don't kill Robin." (Drury's nickname, among natives and Englishmen alike, was Robin.) The oldest of the king's wives, sure that the death of a white slave would bring ruin to the country, had begged for the reprieve. Drury was told that he was the only man who had ever returned from the place of execution alive.

By now Drury might well have begun to reconcile himself to spending the rest of his life on Madagascar. He was still technically a slave, but his current master, Rer Moume, had not only nudged him into a second marriage, but had conferred upon him a herd of thirty cattle and a black slave of his own. For a castaway who had arrived on the island by shipwreck and had barely survived a massacre, this was uncommon prosperity.

One day the most unforeseen of possible events occurred. Two men delivered a basket of palmetto leaves to Rer Moume, who found enclosed a letter which the bearers indicated was meant for the white man. Drury took the piece of paper and found to his astonishment that it was addressed to him. "I was so surprised, I had not power to open it, thinking I was in a dream." Recovering his senses, Drury read the letter, which was from a Captain William Mackett, who said that he had been sent by Drury's father to procure his liberty.

It would not be until his return to England that Drury fathomed the chain of circumstances that led to his rescue. Two years before he had made the brief acquaintance of an English youth named William Thornbury, who had been nine years on Madagascar, having been the sole survivor of a pirated ship whose crew were murdered or put on shore. Thornbury had been adopted by a much more lenient king than Mevarrow, who had never dreamed of making the lad into a slave and who had agreed to give him his liberty when a ship might arrive. At the time Drury had put great hopes in Thornbury; but two years had passed since he had seen his compatriot, and he had all but forgotten about him.

Thornbury had indeed been rescued and taken to England. In a London pub one day a stranger overheard Thornbury talking about Madagascar and interrupted him. The stranger, it turned out, was Drury's brother. The coincidence led Thornbury to Drury's father, who, rejuvenated at the knowledge that his son might be alive, commissioned Captain Mackett to stop at the island and look for him.

Drury was not free yet: he had to persuade Rer Moume to let him go. The chieftain took an informal caucus of his wives and attendants, who were evenly divided. At last the benevolent despot told Drury that although everyone would be saddened by his departure, he was free to choose it if he really wished. "So I licked his feet, and took my leave of him, and of this custom, too; for this was the last time I licked a black man's feet."

On meeting with Captain Mackett, Drury was given a letter from his father. He was in a fever now to be home. All the members of the ship's crew took the new apparition for a wild man. Drury was "at a great loss for words to speak currently for several days." His hair was cut, his beard shaved, and the wild man was dressed in "a neat seaman's habit." Once aboard, he was seasick for the first three or four days.

On the way home the ship stopped on St. Mary's Island, where Drury was recognized by Nick Dove, who had been one of the other three survivors of the massacre. Dove had escaped the island after only two years by becoming a pirate. From Dove Drury learned that another of the survivors, John Benbow, had long since gotten back to England.

On September 9, 1717, Drury once again stood on his native soil, after an absence of more than sixteen years. He went at once to the neighborhood of the inn his father had once managed, where he found to his great sorrow that his mother had died of grief shortly after learning of the shipwreck of the Degrave, and that his father had died in the past year. He had to content himself with visiting old friends and his sister, who had given him up for dead.

A year later Drury signed up for a second voyage to Madagascar, but on his return in 1720 he gave up the wandering life, settled down to write the account of his adventures, and installed himself in Old Tom's Coffeehouse to entertain the curious. The 1743 edition of Madagascar indicated in an altered concluding paragraph that its author had died, but gave no date. The only other piece of biographical information about Drury published in the 18th century occurs in a letter from William Duncombe, who had known the brother of John Benbow, the other survivor of the shipwreck and massacre. Duncombe, like Mackett, praised Drury as "a downright honest man, without any appearance of fraud or imposture," and indicated that many men knew him in later life, because he had worked as a porter at the East India House.

Thus Drury himself faded into the limbo of historical obscurity, even as "his" narrative gained prominence as the best English book on Madagascar. For a century and a half after its publication, *Robert Drury's Journal* was alluded to as fact by missionaries, travelers, and historians familiar with Madagascar. When William Lee entertained the possibility in 1869 that the book had been written by Defoe, he was not disputing Drury's veracity, but merely puzzling over the identity of the "transcriber." In fact Lee averred, "It is certain that there was a Robert Drury—that he had been a captive as stated—that he wrote a large account of his adventures—that he was seen, questioned, and could give any information required—after the publication of his book."

Apparently the first writer to doubt the authenticity of the *Journal* was a Frenchman named Emile Blanchard, in 1872, and then for somewhat tendentious reasons:

> The truthfulness of the narrator has been affirmed; nevertheless, on several grounds, there is room for doubt. Drury asserts that he was a slave. A European reduced to slavery! that is impossible, say those who know the Malagasy; they might probably kill a European, but would never degrade him to the lowest rank.

Captain Pasfield Oliver, who had lived in Madagascar, at first accepted Drury's book as genuine. But his faith was "considerably shaken," just as Blanchard's had been, when he first read Etienne de Flacourt's monumental *Histoire de la Grande Isle Madagascar*, published in 1661. Flacourt had been the French governor of the island, and his narrative was the leading early source of information about Madagascar. Oliver noted certain details which he thought in their very phrasing resembled passages in Drury's book "almost word for word." Drury could not be expected to know French, and, indeed, discussing the history of King Samuel, he had ingenuously remarked, "Whether any of the French authors of voyages have wrote anything of him I know not, nor have I had the opportunity of seeing their histories of Madagascar to compare with this of mine." But, Oliver concluded, the text gave "patent evidence" that Drury's transcriber not only read French but had borrowed liberally from Flacourt and others.

The map prefixed to the narrative evidently derived from Flacourt. The Frenchman's map, for instance, indicated regions in the interior labeled "Pays tres fertile Abandonée et ruiné par les guerres" and "Pays riche en bestial." The identical regions of the English map noted "A fruitful country, abandoned and ruined by the wars" and "A country inrich'd with cattle." Oliver thought that Drury's editor had borrowed a map adapted from Flacourt by John Ogilby, King

Charles II's cosmographer, in his well-known *Africa*. In 1943, John Robert Moore demonstrated that the map in *Robert Drury's Journal* had actually been taken from a Dutch work, *Blaeu's Grooten Atlas* (1665), which in turn relied on Flacourt. The map, however, does not necessarily bear upon Drury's veracity, for nowhere in the 1729 edition of the *Journal* is there any claim that Drury himself was responsible for it. The dotted line indicating his route of escape from Deaan Mevarrow is so close to a straight line that any editor could have penciled it in.

Similarly, the impressive English-Malagasy word list is nowhere referred to as Drury's work. Oliver persuaded the Reverend J. Richardson, who had compiled the most recent bilingual dictionary, to comment on the word list in an appendix to the 1890 edition of *Drury's Journal*. Richardson concluded that Drury had not written the list himself, but had dictated it to someone else. The republished word list gave "Drury's" versions and modern Malagasy words in parallel columns, testifying to the remarkable accuracy of the vocabulary. Yet there are words in the narrative itself in Malagasy that do not appear in the word list, and the longest single speech in the native tongue that appears in the book, a ritual invocation at the infant's circumcision ceremony, cannot be "translated" with the word list.

Oliver concluded that Drury's "editor" had borrowed liberally from Flacourt, Ogilby, and, for the accurate description of Madagascar ports and coastlines, Thornton's *English Pilot* (1703). He accepted Drury's existence, and believed that he had in fact been shipwrecked on the *Degrave*. He had definitely spent time around Madagascar. It was Oliver's guess, however, that Drury had, like Nick Dove, become a pirate. The Captain White of Drury's second voyage Oliver identified with a pirate of the same name who later died in France.

Finally, Oliver was convinced that Defoe was the author of *Madagascar*. He seconded all of Lee's hints about Defoe's familiarity with the island, his interest in pirates, and his knack for concealing fiction as autobiography. He pointed out in Drury's book the kinds of "cunning artifices" by which Defoe created an air of verisimilitude in his fiction. And he quoted parallel passages to argue, *contra* Lee, that the style of Drury's "transcriber" was remarkably like that of the author of *Robinson Crusoe*.

At the turn of the century the world's leading Madagascar experts were the brothers Alfred and Guillaume Grandidier, authors of or collaborators on nearly fifty books about the island, as well as pioneering explorers of its interior. Despite Oliver's arguments, the

Grandidiers remained convinced that Drury had performed most of the exploits his *Journal* narrated. But when they translated Oliver's 1890 edition for a 1906 French edition, their footnotes indicated dozens of errors and impossibilities—which they assumed were the editor's fault. Their firsthand experience allowed them to debunk the topographical features along the route of Drury's alleged escape from Mevarrow as wholly imaginary. In similar fashion, Defoe had invented a topography in Central Africa across which his fictitious Captain Singleton had rambled. The Grandidiers doubted that a white man would have been kept by the natives as a slave; at the most he might have been detained from escaping. They doubted also the prevalence of feet-licking as a form of obeisance, regarding it as rare or ancient. The French scholars quarreled with Drury's account of the circumcision of a one-year-old; in their experience such a rite was never performed on a child younger than seven or eight.

During his escape, Drury had built fires to keep the foxes away. But, the Grandidiers pointed out, there are no foxes on Madagascar. Could the transcriber have mistaken the fox for the *fossa*, a dangerous feline native to the island? The Grandidiers gave him, or Drury, the benefit of the doubt. Strings of such minor discrepancies did not, in their eyes, damage the basic honesty of the book.

More seriously in error was the attempt to view the Malagasy natives as noble savages, superior to Europeans in qualities like justice, kindness, and chastity, as Drury claimed in a number of expository asides. The Grandidiers blame these sentiments entirely on the book's editor. Certainly they did not come from Flacourt, who abhorred the sexual freedom of the Malagasy, called them "the most vindictive nation in the world," and wrote, "If there is any country in the world given to treachery, dissimulation, flattery, cruelty, lying, and fraud, it is this one."

Such was the state of thinking about Robert Drury shortly after the turn of the century. Despite the vigorous attacks on the authenticity and accuracy of the book, a general belief that it was a true story persisted. The 1910 edition of the *Encyclopaedia Britannica* listed it as a chief source of information on Madagascar.

The 20th-century debate has belonged to two American scholars, Arthur W. Secord and John Robert Moore. Professors at the universities of Illinois and Indiana, respectively, and world-renowned students of Defoe, they struggled for over forty years with the puzzle of Robert Drury in a continuing colloquy, sometimes friendly (Moore tips his hat to Secord in the acknowledgments of one of his books), sometimes acerbic.

Secord began the quest by defining what he called "the Defoe problem" in 1924. One of the most prolific of English writers—the checklist of his productions includes over 550 titles—Defoe was also one of the most careful to keep his name separate from his writings. As Secord puts it, "One has to consider that for thirty or forty years he wrote copiously in both prose and verse on every sort of subject, made use of every medium of publication, and strove for anonymity by every possible subterfuge." The reasons for his invisibility were largely political: he was a radical mercantilist and Whig and, as modern scholarship has discovered, a spy and a double agent as well. Knowledge of his life remains sketchy: it is only in the present century that such basic things as the name of his wife and the fact that he was married only once (tradition held twice) were learned.

Secord's seminal contribution to Defoe scholarship was to concentrate on the question of the sources in his reading and experience on which the exquisitely detailed and realistic structures of his novels were based. Moore used the approach developed by Secord to analyze *Robert Drury's Journal* in terms of both authorship and authenticity. In 1939 he published his first analysis of the problem, which reduced Drury himself to the most ephemeral status he had yet held.

Moore argued simply from internal improbabilities that the work had to be almost wholly fiction. Drury, for instance, claimed that for years on Madagascar he had completely forgotten English; yet nine years after his return he was able (according to Richardson's conjecture) to dictate an extensive English-Malagasy word list. If the cabin boy had spent most of his fifteen years in the interior of the island, it was perplexing that there were so few details of the interior, and so many of the coastal regions, which could of course be learned from sources other than Drury.

Moore pinpointed as the germ of the idea for the book a brief item in the diary of Narcissus Luttrell, recording a news item on April 21, 1705:

A boy lately arrived in a gally from the Indies gives account that the Degrave, an East India ship of 800 tun, valued at 100,000 l., sprung a leak some time since on the coast of Madagascar, where the men landed, with their effects, and also carryed their guns on shore, but could get no provisions of the inhabitants, who said 'twas not customary to supply strangers till they delivered up their arms; which they had no sooner done, but these barbarous people killed them all but the boy now come over.

From this news item, Moore argued, the author of the book had fleshed out a full and realistic narrative. To do so he needed two things: a name on which to hang his tale, and a wealth of Madagascan detail to inform the adventures of his hero. For the former he chose Robert Drury—perhaps the East India porter mentioned in William Duncombe's letter; perhaps a pirate associated with the slaver William Mackett, who needed to keep his doings for the last fifteen years quiet. In any event, the nameless boy of the news item, who had returned to England within three years of the shipwreck, became "Robert Drury," who had not returned until fifteen years after the *Degrave* had sunk. For details of Madagascar, the author had ransacked Flacourt, Ogilby, and others, and also oral traditions from returning seafarers and the gossip, both oral and written, of notorious pirates.

That the author was Defoe, Moore maintained, had not been seriously doubted since 1890. Nevertheless he spent some effort clinching the case. The argument for Defoe hinges on numerous cases of similar turns of style in *Robert Drury's Journal* and books known to be by Defoe; on the prevalence in both of idiomatic phrases, like "made a tolerable shift to make candles;" on Defoe's recurring interest in Madagascar; on the commonality of political and religious views between Drury and other Defoe protagonists; and on the kinds of human activity which catch the author's eye in the *Journal* as well as in Defoe's other novels.

In a second work, published in 1943, Moore listed what he felt were the six principal sources for *Robert Drury's Journal*, besides the Luttrell diary entry. These included the name only of John Benbow, the other survivor of the *Degrave*. A tradition held that Benbow had written a manuscript journal of his experiences, but that it had been burned in 1714. Moore doubts that Defoe got any real information from the lost journal. Another source was Robert Knox's *Ceylon*, since Knox also had extensive experience in Madagascar. And Defoe, having just written his *History of the Pirates*, had in his head rich troves of Madagascan lore from talking to brigands who had sailed the seas near that prime slaving and pirating island.

If Defoe wrote *Robert Drury's Journal*, and if he spun it essentially out of his own fancy, it represented his last extended fictional narrative. Two years later, in 1731, the prolific author died at the approximate age of seventy.

Moore's analysis was soon countered by a pair of papers from Secord. The Illinois scholar accepted Defoe's authorship, but argued from documentary evidence that the account in *Madagascar* of the homeward journey of the *Degrave*, as well as of Mackett's return in 1717, was surprisingly accurate on a number of minor details. Secord saw his research as making "some slight progress . . . in reconnecting

Drury with the book which bears his name." Moore was not convinced, and the two engaged in a "discussion" about the issue in *Notes and Queries*.

By 1945, however, there was no real proof that Robert Drury had ever existed. In the last years of his life Secord traveled to London to search through parish records and the manuscripts of the East India Company. His hunch was that the debate over Drury had been altogether too conjectural and literary. And indeed, he found in London what he called "an embarrassing quantity of documentary evidence" that scholars had never bothered to seek before. Secord died suddenly in 1957, before he could publish his results; but his colleagues found two papers in all but finished form among his manuscripts and brought them out in a posthumous collection called *Robert Drury's Journal and Other Studies* (1961). The "years of patient research in many libraries," to cite his editors, serve to throw the Drury question back into the arena of debate, and to leave students more perplexed than ever.

Secord's findings were remarkable. After an exhaustive search of parish records, he came across the birth notice of one Robert Drury on July 20, 1687 (this date is only four days off the date in Drury's own account). For the first time Drury's existence was conclusively proved. Next Secord searched the East India Company records for evidence as to the fate of the *Degrave*. Many details of its outward voyage to Bengal and its return as far as Mauritius could be traced, and these agreed remarkably with Drury's brief account. Secord pushed the search as far as a terse note in the log of a ship that had picked up five deserters from the *Degrave* on Mauritius: "Capt. Young from Bengall very leaky."

The indefatigable scholar managed to prove also that Luttrell's diary entry was truthful: another survivor of the shipwreck had indeed arrived in England in 1705 on board the *Raper*; the boy's name, however, could not be ascertained. At this point Secord had his great breakthrough. He found a source that no one else had suspected existed: a series of abstracts published by a Dutchman named Leibbrandt just before the Boer War. Leibbrandt was Keeper of the Archives at the Cape of Good Hope, where every ship bound home from the Indian Ocean stopped. Even though the abstracts were published in English, scholars seemed unaware of them. We can imagine Secord's excitement as he pored over these obscure documents and found, amid masses of relevant material, a summary of John Benbow's journal—reported to have been burned in 1714, and by now suspected of being purely apocryphal. The summary of Benbow for the first time gave hard documentary evidence of the

Degrave's shipwreck on Madagascar. Not only that, it included an account remarkably close to Drury's of the survivors' arrival in the village of a chief named Decrindo (Drury's Deaan Crindo), the taking of royal hostages, the flight, and the massacre.

Furthermore, the Cape records gave independent corroboration of the existence of the Scottish captains Drummond and Stewart, whom Drury said the survivors had run into in Crindo's village. After the massacre Benbow and Drummond evidently were separated from Drury and made their way to Fort Dauphin. Drummond died there, but after several years Benbow was rescued by a Dutch ship that took him to the Cape.

Secord could hardly "prove" the details of Drury's long stay on Madagascar, since for most of the purported fifteen years Drury would have been alone among nonliterate natives. But two aspects of the *Journal's* account of those years led him to believe the narrative could not have been written except by an eyewitness: the history of King Samuel, much of which was verified by Dutch records; and Drury's handling of the intricate genealogy of five different family groups of Malagasy. "This complicated genealogical pattern could not," Secord argued, "have been invented by Defoe or even by Drury; it must deal with real people in the areas assigned to them, and it is almost incontrovertible proof that Drury lived long in the regions in which the *Journal* says he lived." Almost, but not quite.

Sifting through once more the records of St. Katherine Cree parish, Secord found a burial notice for Drury's mother in 1703 and one for his father in 1716—the very years the *Journal* gave for the deaths. A secondhand account of Drury's father's will implied that despite the long absence of his son without news, the father expected his return and in fact feared grandchildren by native women. To Secord this was indirect proof of the remarkable Thornbury connection by which Drury says he was rescued. (The scholar was unable to find independent traces of Thornbury.) A last East India record in 1730 reflected a petition from Drury asking leave to be employed by the Swedes on a Madagascar expedition. Secord, however, found no trace of the man's having ever served as a porter for the company. But he did find Drury's burial record, on March 15, 1734.

It is a pity Secord did not live long enough to push his investigations a little further, or to counter the still-dubious skeptics. The clinching corroboration—any record that Drury himself sailed on the *Degrave* or returned on Captain Mackett's ship—still eludes scholarship. We can imagine, even in the light of Secord's findings, that Defoe took Benbow's story of the shipwreck and massacre and grafted it onto the genuine Robert Drury, possibly because Drury had fifteen years he would rather not account for; patched the tale together with Madagascan history and pirate lore; and produced a charming romance.

Moore, Secord's longtime rival, responded grumpily in his 1971 *Checklist* of Defoe's writings: "Drury seems to have been a real personage; but he was not possibly the author of the major part of the original narrative." A disinterested Defoe expert, James Sutherland, summed up the state of the Drury question as follows: "The answer is still to be found; but *Robert Drury's Journal* may contain less of Defoe than Moore believes it does, and more of him than Secord was prepared to admit."

Whatever the true disposition of this fascinating scholarly wrangle—and the true disposition may never be made—can we by any stretch of the imagination accuse Daniel Defoe of perpetrating a hoax? If so, was *Robinson Crusoe*, also an allegedly true story, an attempt at a hoax? One answer, albeit a hostile one, comes from the mouth of the great belletrist Leslie Stephen, who said of Defoe: "In other words, he had the most marvelous power ever known of giving verisimilitude to his fictions; or, in other words again, he had the most amazing talent on record for telling lies." The distinction between the art of fiction and the art of lying, Stephen believed, was not always clear in Defoe's mind. "He was merely aiming at true stories, which happened not to be true."

BIBLIOGRAPHY

Flacourt, Etienne de. *Histoire de la Grande Isle Madagascar.* Paris, 1661.

Grandidier, Alfred and Guillaume. *Collection des ouvrages anciens concernant Madagascar,* vol. IV. Paris, 1906.

Lee, William. *Daniel Defoe: His Life and Recently Discovered Writings.* London, 1869.

Moore, John Robert. *A Checklist of the Writings of Daniel Defoe.* Hamden, Connecticut, 1971.

———. *Defoe in the Pillory and Other Studies.* Bloomington, Ind., 1939.

———. *Defoe's Sources for Robert Drury's Journal.* Bloomington, Ind., 1943.

Oliver, Captain Pasfield, ed. *Madagascar; Or, Robert Drury's Journal During Fifteen Years' Captivity on That Island.* London, 1890.

Secord, Arthur W. "Defoe and Robert Drury's Journal," *Journal of English and Germanic Philology,* vol. 44 (1945).

————. "Robert Drury and Robert Drury's Journal," Notes and Queries, vol. 189 (1945).

————. Robert Drury's Journal and Other Studies. Urbana, Ill., 1961.

————. Studies in the Narrative Method of Defoe. Urbana, Ill., 1924.

Stephen, Leslie. Hours in a Library, vol. I. London, 1907.

Sutherland, James. Daniel Defoe: A Critical Study. Cambridge, Mass., 1971.

4

THE TRAGEDY OF
ABYSSINIAN BRUCE

As we shall see, the personal consequences of having an exploring hoax exposed can be genuinely tragic for its perpetrator. But far more tragic—and far rarer—is the plight of the authentic explorer who is universally discredited as a phony. Such a man was the Scot James Bruce, Laird of Kinnaird, the greatest African explorer of the 18th century—but a man who died in 1794 with the laughter and ridicule of England ringing in his ears. In 1769, Bruce disappeared somewhere in Northeast Africa. Four years later he emerged at Marseilles to claim that he had penetrated Abyssinia as far as the source of the Blue Nile. The tales he had to tell of that unknown country were so exotic that they were to make Bruce first widely celebrated, then, as skepticism hardened around his report, just as widely lampooned and derided. The publication, shortly before his death, of a five-volume account of his travels only served to intensify the mockery. It was not until the 19th century that his reputation was restored.

Had the discrediting been the work of philistines alone—acidulous journalists and salon dilettantes—the tragedy of James Bruce would be less interesting. Instead, some of the most sober and sagacious men of the day, including Samuel Johnson, Horace Walpole, and James Boswell, held Bruce at arm's length, perused the man, and then discarded him with a shrug or a sneer. They did so on much the sorts of grounds by which true frauds have been debunked: the wild and improbable character of Bruce's tales, their internal inconsistencies—and the difficult personality of the explorer himself.

What sort of man was the Laird of Kinnaird? Physically he was awesome—six feet four inches tall, with dark-red hair, a loud voice, and an energetic disposition. His first biographer, Alexander Murray, noted that "his person was large and well-proportioned; and his strength correspondent to his size and his stature." In later years he grew prodigiously fat, but in Abyssinia he must have struck everyone he met as an athletic giant.

At the age of two, James Bruce had lost his mother. His own health remained poor through adolescence. Another early biographer, Francis Head, described Bruce at sixteen:

> He was much too tall for his age; his breast was weak; his general appearance indicated that he had grown faster than his strength; and his relations were alarmed lest he should become consumptive.

(It is fascinating to come upon, in Bruce's early years, two of the childhood circumstances that characterize a surprisingly high proportion of the men who later perpetrated exploring hoaxes—a sickly constitution or physical defect that must be overcome, and the loss of a parent while young.)

After a conventional schooling at Harrow, Bruce contemplated first a career as a clergyman, then one as a lawyer. At seventeen he went to the University of Edinburgh to study law, but did poorly, for he found himself seduced instead by Italian poetry—the first step on his curious journey to Abyssinia. Within the initial year his health worsened, and he dropped out of Edinburgh and returned to the family estate.

In 1753, at age twenty-two, Bruce went to London nursing the vague idea of signing up with the East India Company. Instead he hung out with former university acquaintances, living, as Murray put it, "in the gay manner of a stranger who was soon to leave them, and probably to be long absent." He fell violently in love with a beautiful young woman to whom his friends introduced him, and gave up all thoughts of India to claim the hand of Adriana Allen, the daughter of a prosperous wine merchant. With the marriage came a share of the family business.

James Bruce would surely have ended up a London businessman, of no importance to history, had his young wife not, like his mother, possessed a delicate constitution. Within months after the wedding Adriana came down with unmistakable signs of tuberculosis. Bruce, accompanied by Adriana's mother, tried for a cure first at Bristol, then in the south of France. In Paris in October 1754, after less than a year of marriage, three months pregnant, Adriana died.

At this point, for the first time, the intensity and passion that were later to stamp Bruce's Abyssinian travels came to the fore. In Paris some Catholic priests had crowded around Bruce's door trying to "persecute" Adriana, as a heretic, in her dying moments, and after she was dead they refused her public burial. Bruce stole out at midnight with her body, seized a plot of earth in the burying ground assigned to the English embassy, interred his wife, and then rode on horseback all night, wild with grief and fury, through "the most tempestuous night I ever saw" to Boulogne. He arrived sick and exhausted, and soon set sail for England.

During the next four years, perhaps to purge his grief, Bruce plunged himself into the study of languages, adding to his Latin, Greek, French, and Italian an acquaintance with Spanish and Portuguese. He also studied drawing. On the business pretext of sampling Portuguese and Spanish vintages, he spent a year traveling from Portugal to Holland, steeping himself in culture and language. In the latter country he collected the best Dutch and Italian texts on Oriental languages, his newest interest. Soon he had learned Arabic, and came across the works of the great 17th-century German scholar of Ethiopian languages, Job Ludolf. The discovery of Ludolf was the spark that led Bruce, a decade later, to travel to Abyssinia.

Once back in England, however, Bruce again seemed ready to settle down to a quiet domestic life. There had been rumors of war against Spain, and the Scotsman, seizing a chance at advancement, had proposed an attack on the port of Ferrol, which his recent travels through Spain had led him to believe would be entirely vulnerable. The Pitt government listened carefully, but decided at last not to make an attack. Disappointed, Bruce returned to Scotland, bent on an early retirement to manage his estate.

Lord Halifax, however, sent Bruce an exhortatory message which was to determine the whole remainder of his career. Chiding him for the thought of retiring so early in life, Halifax pointed out that "the way to rise in the present reign, was by enterprize and discovery"— and that no field lay riper for such efforts than Africa. With a sly knowledge of his sovereign's private tastes, Halifax suggested that Bruce be assigned to Tunis and Algiers to make drawings of the ancient Roman ruins there to add to King George III's collection. There happened, Halifax continued, to be a vacancy in the consul-generalship at Algiers.

Bruce readily accepted the post, and set out from England in June 1762. He was not to return for twelve full years. In Italy he practiced his trade by drawing ruins and cataloguing antiquities, and the following March he arrived at Algiers. There he found himself in the midst of a political nightmare. At times during the next two years the Dey of Algiers was on the verge of declaring war against England.

During Bruce's tenure an English ship that came into port was seized and destroyed, its captain and crew converted into slaves. At the nadir of his relations with the dey, Bruce was threatened with death if he did not leave the country within three days.

Bruce's reaction was stubborn hauteur, which won him the grudging admiration of the dey. Nevertheless, he was relieved of his consulship after two years' service. A younger Bruce might well have returned to Scotland, humiliated by his unsuccessful diplomatic career. By now, though, Africa had got under his skin. He proceeded on his own to Tunis, where he began enthusiastically to make the drawings of Roman ruins that had been his original mission. In the service of that task he acquired his most important accomplice, a young Italian painter named Luigi Balugani, who was to accompany him to the very source of the Blue Nile, but who would die, still young, in the remote city of Gondar. (It is characteristic of Bruce's reluctance to share his laurels that he scarcely mentioned Balugani, his companion of six years, in his *Travels*; that he would claim Balugani's death had occurred a year earlier than it did—leaving Bruce as the sole European at the source of the Nile; and that he would pass off many of Balugani's exquisite drawings as his own.)

During the next four years Bruce wandered eastward among the half-known kingdoms of North Africa. In essence, he was perfecting the exploratory style that would make possible the bold penetration of Abyssinia. He endured shipwreck, disease, and hostile Arabs. Adding medicine and astronomy to his talents, he pursued his travels and inquiries with an obsessive voracity that he had never before exhibited. The feature of his adventures during these years (1765–69) that impresses the modern student most is Bruce's indomitable—indeed, almost tyrannical—will.

There were private clues in the European years to the existence of such a will. At the end of his journey from Portugal to Holland, in Brussels in 1758, Bruce had fought a duel, seriously wounding his antagonist, and had fled the city. The circumstances of the conflict are obscure today: Murray recorded that "he was involved in a quarrel with a person who had behaved rudely in his presence to a young gentleman, a stranger, but whose appearance had inclined him to interfere in his defence." A man who would fight a duel over an insult to a stranger had to be a man of passion and principle, and probably of stubborn willfulness.

Even more telling is the relationship with Margaret Murray, the sister of a neighboring laird, whom Bruce had fallen in love with in 1761. Only sixteen at the time, she fell just as deeply in love with him, declaring she could not live without him. Despite that avowal,

Bruce convinced himself that Margaret was encouraging him to go to Algiers. She (we imagine) envisioned a separation of a year or two; little could she foresee an absence of eleven years, during the last five of which Bruce was given up for dead. Yet when the explorer returned to Italy in 1773 to find that Margaret had married a Roman nobleman, his outrage prompted an immediate challenge to a duel. "Without any provocation or injury from me," he wrote the husband, "you have deprived me of my honour—me, an innocent man engaged in the service of my own country—by violating all the rights that are most sacred before God and man." The poor marchese wrote back that he could hardly have intended to betray the Scotsman, since he did not even realize that he existed. The duel was averted. (According to an old tradition, Margaret never got over the shock of seeing Bruce again; she died shortly thereafter.)

To follow the wanderings of Bruce in Abyssinia, some historical background is useful. Ethiopia (as even in the 18th century the country was more comprehensively called) had been from very early times under the sway of Judaism introduced from Arabia. (Moses is mentioned in Numbers as having married an Ethiopian woman.) About the middle of the 4th century A.D., Abyssinia proper—the central and northern highlands of Ethiopia—was converted to Monophysite Christianity. (The Monophysite heresy was that Christ had only a divine, not a human, nature.) Throughout the Middle Ages, however, European contact with Ethiopia was negligible. The country thus took on in the Western mind the quality of a fabulous, unknown land; its mystique was enhanced by the popular notion of Prester John, the legendary "Eastern" Christian emperor, whom many placed in Ethiopia.

In the Renaissance the first explorers and missionaries to penetrate Ethiopia were Portuguese, beginning in 1487. In terms of Bruce's subsequent travels, the two most important were the Jesuit priests Pedro Paez and Jerome Lobo. Father Paez performed the considerable feat of converting the Emperor Susenyos to Roman Catholicism, and was almost indisputably the first European to reach the source of the Blue Nile, in 1618. Bruce's lifelong hatred of Catholics was to join with his vanity in an almost hysterical attack on Paez. The delusion that he was the first to reach the source of the great river was one of several crucial instances of willfully ignoring the facts on which we can legitimately indict Bruce. (Another was pretending that the Blue Nile, rather than the much larger White Nile, was the true main course of the river.) Father Lobo's *Voyage to Abyssinia*, the translation of which was Samuel Johnson's first major work, became the primary source for Johnson's *Rasselas*, whose philosophically romanticized picture of Abyssinia shaped the Englishman's conception of that mysterious country in the late 18th century.

After the Jesuits were expelled in 1633, exploration of the country by outsiders reached a near standstill. The last European to make a deep penetration of the interior before Bruce was a Frenchman named Poncet, who in 1699 spent a year in the interior capital of Gondar, leaving a sketchy account of his experiences. Fully seventy years without an exploratory effort intervened before the Scotsman arrived at Massawa, on the coast of the Red Sea, in 1769.

Bruce's adventures during the next four years were so elaborate, the events he witnessed so outlandish to Western eyes, the landscapes he traversed so wild, and the dangers he braved so extreme, that to summarize his peregrinations is to bleed them of their exotic life. His five-volume *Travels to Discover the Source of the Nile*, a bestseller in 1790, has not been reprinted in full since 1813, and is unread today. A quirky, rambling, lavishly detailed account, it nevertheless remains an eccentric masterpiece of exploration literature. The work is still our primary source for knowledge of pre-20th-century Ethiopia.

Bruce was, of course, fascinated by Abyssinia in its own right; but the abiding motive for his visiting that country was to get to the very headwaters of the Nile. He seems first to have been fired with the idea during conversations with Lord Halifax and the explorer Robert Wood, although the discovery of the river's source, he wrote later, "was always mentioned to me with a kind of diffidence, as if to be expected only from a more experienced traveller." The great naturalist the Comte de Buffon, having heard of Bruce's ambition, wrote to encourage him, and went so far as to persuade the French king to ship Bruce a quadrant.

Despite the incredible richness of the explorer's four years of adventure, intrigue, and danger, he never lost sight of his primary goal, even though his Abyssinian friends would laugh at the absurdity of traveling so far merely "to see a river and a bog, no part of which you can carry away were it ever so valuable."

Two circumstances in particular made Bruce's mission almost suicidal. Ever since the expulsion of the Jesuits in 1633, hatred of Catholics (called "Franks") was so extreme in Abyssinia that the prescribed treatment was stoning to death on sight. To most natives, the distinction between a Scotch Presbyterian and a Catholic was mere sophistry. Bruce took every opportunity to declare his own revulsion against Catholics; but more than once he was accused of being a Frank, and at Sennar he saw the graves of the last three Catholic missionaries to enter the country (all three had indeed been

Alexandria

Aswan

Nile

Red Sea

Berber

Massawa

Adowa

Sennar

*F*U*NG*

Gondar

Lake Tana

White Nile

Blue Nile

source

ABYSSINIA

Much simplified, the course of James Bruce's travels in Abyssinia between 1769 and 1773, including his visit to the source of the Blue Nile. In his lifetime the whole of Bruce's four-year expedition was dismissed as a fake.

stoned to death). To make matters worse, Bruce happened to blunder into the midst of an extremely bitter civil war. It was a mark of his extraordinary diplomatic skills that he managed, at different times, to ingratiate himself with the leaders of both the main warring camps. In general, part of Bruce's success in Ethiopia—simply to survive for four years was brilliant success—derived from his insouciance in the face of probable death.

A simplified three-part schema helps to render Bruce's intricate travels intelligible. The effort of his first five months was to traverse deserts and mountains, river cataracts and high plateaus to the palatial fortress of Gondar, then the country's only true city. The Scot spent the next year and a half in and around Gondar, reaching the source of the Blue Nile at last, but also serving as a general in the war. During most of that time he was not allowed to leave Gondar at all, and more than once he pondered gloomily the old Ethiopian custom of retaining foreign visitors for life. The last third of Bruce's long pilgrimage was indeed an escape from Abyssinia north into Egypt, capped with a nearly fatal five-hundred-mile desert "short cut" between two great bends of the Nile.

Any *Rasselas*-based illusions Bruce might have cherished as to the mildness of the Abyssinian disposition were dispelled early. In Digsa he encountered traders selling Christian children into slavery, and at Adowa he found three hundred prisoners chained in cages, in order to extort money from them; some had been confined for twenty years.

It was on the way to Gondar that Bruce witnessed the event, in itself rather trivial, that would come to be the most famous incident in his four years of wanderings, and that would, in the British imagination, epitomize the explorer's wild fictions. A short distance beyond Adowa, Bruce reported,

> I overtook on the way three travellers, who seemed to be soldiers, driving a cow before them. They halted at a brook, threw down the beast, and one of them cut a pretty large collop of flesh from its buttocks, after which they drove the cow gently on as before.

As much as the notion of cutting steaks from a living cow, it was the idea of eating raw meat that struck Englishmen as unbelievable.

In February 1770 Bruce reached Gondar. The whole region was under the control of the violent, seventy-year-old rebel leader Ras Michael. Clearly Bruce's plans—in fact, his very life—depended on getting himself into Michael's good graces. He could hardly have done so more quickly or dramatically than he did. Upon meeting Michael's beautiful young wife, Ozoro Esther, he learned that her sons were near death from smallpox. Bruce's medical treatment resulted in their immediate cure. Esther was won over, and even the stern Ras Michael professed his deep gratitude.

Throughout the years in Abyssinia, Bruce was to use his extensive "first-aid kit" and his smattering of medical training to the cagiest of ends. In Sennar, where the missionaries had been stoned to death, Bruce pleased the ailing local king mightily by giving him ipeca-cuanha to make him vomit. The sovereign immediately required the traveler to perform the same cure on his three obese queens, who stripped to the waist for the operation; in gratitude, they demanded that he take off all his clothes to show them his strangely pallid skin. By the end of his tour of the country, Bruce's reputation was that "he could bring a dead man to life."

In the same fashion the canny Scot turned his astronomical observations to his advantage. When he found that the natives thought his hours spent with quadrant and telescope were a kind of sorcery, he played up the impression. The climactic event came when, frustrated by a treacherous despot in the kingdom of the Fung, Bruce grandly warned that unless his will prevailed an ominous sign would appear in the skies in four days' time. (He knew from his tables that a lunar eclipse was due then.) The despot relented, but Bruce demonstrated the heavens' responsiveness to his will just to underline the point.

One can analyze Bruce's brilliance as an explorer largely in terms of his capitalizing on his personal skills. In addition to his astronomy and medicine, his horsemanship and his shooting ability won him astonished awe wherever he went. While familiar with guns, Ethio-pians had never seen small shot, and so thought it a miracle that Bruce could shoot birds out of the air. The man's grounding in Ethiopian languages, of course, stood him in good stead everywhere.

But beyond his talents, there were two personal traits that won the day for Bruce again and again. The obvious one was bravery. Linked with it was a poker player's kind of obstinacy—half bluff, half arrogant manliness. Time and again Bruce seemed to imply to equally obstinate nobles that any interference with his plans was unthinkable. It was a stance perilously close to megalomania, and back in Britain the effects of it would contribute to the public joke the Abyssinian adventure became.

Having already gained the good favor of Ras Michael, Bruce spent much of the next year and a half as a semiofficial general in the rebel's army. During that time he weathered the rise and fall of Michael's fortunes, from a peak in which the chieftain was on the verge of conquering the country to the depths of his eventual banishment from it. Bruce rode into more than one battle, involving as many as seventy thousand native warriors, at the head of an Abyssinian black horse guard. In these campaigns he was, for all his valor, an unwilling officer, bent mainly on personal survival while he bided his time before he could go to the source of the Nile. Every week he was reminded of the ferocity of his colleagues. Soon after meeting Ras Michael, for instance, Bruce witnessed the punishment of twelve captured enemy leaders: they were blinded with iron pincers and sent to starve in the valleys below Gondar.

The explorer also bore witness to another form of Abyssinian excess—the banquet. His description of a typical dinner party was one of the passages which most shocked English readers in 1790. Bruce described the cow being led into the banquet room, and the pieces of meat cut from its side; "the prodigious noise the animal makes is a signal for the company to sit down at table." The men cut strips of meat until the cow bled to death; the women rolled the raw strips into cartridges of teff bread and stuffed them into the men's mouths. As the drinking progressed, the company grew more mirthful, until

> love lights all its fires, and every thing is permitted with absolute freedom. There is no coyness, no delays, no need of appointments or retirement to gratify their wishes; there are no rooms but one, in which they sacrifice both to Bacchus and to Venus. The two men nearest the vacuum a pair have made on the bench by leaving their seats, hold their upper garment like a screen before the two that have left the bench; and, if we may judge by sound, they seem to think it as great a shame to make love in silence as to eat.—Replaced in their seats again, the company drink the happy couple's health; and their example is followed at different ends of the table, as each couple is disposed. All this passes without remark or scandal, not a licentious word is uttered, nor the most distant joke upon the transaction.

Bruce avoided comment on the extent of his own involvement in such debauches.

Finally, in October 1770, the explorer got permission to set off for the headwaters of the Nile. Since these springs lay in Gish, then enemy territory, Ras Michael appointed Bruce governor of the whole province to facilitate his progress. In the course of his journey Bruce met Fasil, the enemy chieftain. As a deputy of Michael's, the Scot could well have been put to death at once. Instead he charmed Fasil out of his hostile intentions, and defended his own courage by offering to fight any two of the warlord's men on horseback.

In early November Bruce at last reached the goal that had been the obsession of most of his last ten years. He pulled off his shoes and ran barefoot down the final hill to the fountain that his guide had told him was the true source of the Nile. As he reported later, he "stood in rapture" on the spot, pondering the efforts of "near three thousand years" to reach the place he now occupied. He drank a toast of the fountain's waters to the woman he evidently still assumed was waiting for him in Scotland (in the book her name is camouflaged as "Maria").

Then all at once, like so many explorers when they at last attain a cherished goal, Bruce was seized with despondency, "blasting the crown of laurels I had too rashly woven myself." From this point on in his Abyssinian travels, Bruce was prey to an emotion he had scarcely felt before: homesickness. One night soon after his triumph, as he lay in bed trying to sleep, he suddenly saw before his eyes the Scottish hill where the Tweed, the Clyde, and the Annan all had their sources. "Grief, or despondency now roll[ed] upon me like a torrent . . . I started from my bed in the utmost agony."

Bruce's 1790 account of the Nile was seriously distorted by two blind spots. Throughout the book he ridiculed every aspect of the memoirs of the Jesuit priests Lobo and Paez. If he found a town prosperous that Father Lobo had described as poor, this served as further proof of the spuriousness of the Portuguese explorer's record. He quibbled fiercely. Lobo had described Tissisat Falls, near the source, as 50 feet high; Bruce, measuring them at 40 feet, made that discrepancy another pretext to discount the Jesuit. (The falls are actually about 150 feet high.) All the derision Bruce could muster only points, for the modern reader, back to the man's refusal to accept the priority of anyone else.

The same need dictated the "absent" treatment of Balugani, who was with him at the source. The *Travels* goes for hundreds of pages without mentioning the Italian's name, even though it is evident that Bruce had a European companion. Besides fudging the date of Balugani's death by a full year, Bruce managed, even in the heat of the controversy surrounding him after his return to Britain, not to appeal to the Italian's separate manuscript account of the journey, which was among the papers Bruce had brought back with him. The powerful corroborative effect the manuscript could have had was overbalanced by the potential shame of acknowledging that he had shared his triumph with an Italian.

Once back from the Nile source, Bruce wanted only to return to Europe. The civil war, however, was reaching its climax, and the leader of the black horse guard could hardly be spared from battle, let alone permitted to escape the country. For a year and two months

Bruce fought valiantly, and his medical wonders were in such demand that Fasil actually persuaded him to cross battle lines to tend to his own wounded and sick (Michael allowed the transfer in hopes of using Bruce as a spy). He witnessed numerous examples of Ethiopian cruelty and vengeance. Traveling through a thicket on horseback with Fasil and the youthful Emperor of Abyssinia, Bruce saw the emperor's headdress get tangled in thorns and pulled loose from his head, baring his face, which was considered disgraceful to royalty. With utter calm, the emperor called for the governor of the district, a man of sixty, who came with his son. At a sign from the ruler, the two unfortunates were seized and hung on the spot.

As the war grew more bitter, Bruce became appalled by the constant slaughter and regular executions.

> The bodies of those killed by the sword were hewn to pieces and scattered about the streets, being denied burial. I was miserable, and almost driven to despair, at seeing my hunting dogs . . . bringing into the court-yard the heads and arms of slaughtered men; . . . the quantity of carrion, and the stench of it, brought down the hyaenas in hundreds from the neighboring mountains.

Dejected and increasingly homesick, Bruce resolved to leave the country by whatever means he could; and at last, the day after Christmas 1771, he started north into the kingdom of the Fung, having been freed, as much as by anything, by the capture of Ras Michael.

His adventures were far from over. In fact, he would later judge the eleven months it took him to reach Aswan to be the most perilous part of his long journey. Particularly in the kingdom of Sennar (now part of Sudan) Bruce found himself in a region where it was terribly dangerous simply to be a white man. There were bizarre natural hazards as well, including three on which, because they had not been seen by any other living Englishman, much of the subsequent ridicule directed against the explorer was heaped.

In this unknown kingdom Bruce came across herds of cattle and camels fleeing wildly from swarms of buzzing insects. Bruce was the first Westerner to describe the *tsaltsalya* fly, and to view the fatal bloating and putrefaction it brought to its victims. (The *tsaltsalya* is entirely different from the tsetse fly, then equally unknown to Europe.)

When he crossed the desert, Bruce's party was threatened by gigantic cyclones, or sand pillars, as he called them. These were less devastating than the simoom, a violent hot wind that swept over the party, blistering every square inch of exposed skin. The only defense against it was to fall to the ground and cover one's face. Bruce claimed that two years later in Italy he was still afflicted by an "asthmatic sensation" from "imbibing" the simoom.

The most nearly fatal was the last of Bruce's trials, the five-hundred-mile traverse of the desert between Berber and Aswan. The trek took only twenty days, but was so severe that several of his party died, and all his camels expired or were killed for the water in their stomachs. The travelers' shoes wore out in the first few days. Afflicted not only with thirst but with sandstorms and the simoom, the party struggled across the wasteland, apprehensive at every moment of encountering the nomadic bandits who ruled the desert. The trail they followed was a virtual gauntlet of human bodies and bones—the victims both of thirst and of murder.

Finally, with all the camels dead, Bruce made a decision that was the most agonizing for him of any in the last four years: to abandon all his belongings—papers, collections, drawings that he had carried with him throughout his tribulations. Thus unburdened, the survivors managed to limp into Aswan. Bruce rested several days while his swollen feet started to recover, then borrowed some fast camels, returned to the place where he had left his records, and, astonishingly, and to his "unspeakable satisfaction," found them piled there, untouched.

In March 1773, Bruce's ship arrived at Marseilles, and the "civilized" world began to learn about the astounding expedition he had returned from. He was met by Buffon, among others, and traveled with the naturalist to Paris, where he was lionized. Bruce spent the next year and a quarter in France and Italy, recovering slowly from a guinea worm that had so diseased his leg the doctor in Marseilles had recommended amputation. Everywhere he went, the explorer was treated as a hero, and in neither country did he breathe even a whiff of the suspicion he would provoke in England. The baths at Bologna seemed to work a cure on his leg. Indeed, except for the shock of learning that his beloved Margaret had married the Marchese Accoromboni, his year, one imagines, was a thoroughly happy one.

In June 1774 he arrived in London. He had been absent from Britain for twelve years. At first his reception seemed to match the fashionable furor of Paris. The king received him, thanked him for his "labours in the cause of discovery," and accepted the drawings of ruins that had been the original justification for his mission to Africa. No man, during those first months in London, was more sought after for dinner engagements than was James Bruce.

Among the first to encounter the traveler was James Boswell, himself recently returned from his walking tour of Scotland with Dr.

Johnson. An inveterate collector of great men, Boswell planned to milk a pair of articles for *London Magazine* out of the Abyssinian adventurer. The articles appeared in August and September, scooping any journalistic competition. In them Boswell betrayed no hint of skepticism as he gave highlights from Bruce's travels, including the story of the steaks cut from the living cow. Boswell even accepted Bruce's assertion that the Portuguese had not found the source of the Nile. Yet already there was an indication of public grumbling.

> Some people have complained of Mr. Bruce, as being close and reserved since his return to Britain, and have represented him as *Nec visu facilis nec dictu affabiliş ulli* [Neither easy to look at nor amiable to speak with]. But it should be considered, that a gentleman of fortune, and who has the *blood of Bruce* in his veins, is entitled to maintain a dignity of character. He has travelled for his own instruction and amusement, and he is not bound to communicate his knowledge, but when and how he himself pleases. Besides, Mr. Bruce is above being made a show, or talked to, and stared at, as a strange man. When teased with idle or ignorant questions, no wonder that he should repulse troublesome people, but when he meets with men of knowledge, and of classical enquiry, he is very ready to take the trouble of giving them the satisfaction of which they are worthy.

Privately Boswell offered a less generous portrait of the explorer. Already, Boswell indicated in his diary, Bruce's expectations of universal acclaim were being disappointed, and "this had soured his temper, not sweet originally." The journalist found his subject "impatient, harsh, and uncommunicative."

> As he grew more rough I grew more forward; so that I forced in a manner a good deal from him, while he looked big and stamped and took me short and held his head high and talked with a forcible loudness as if he had been trying whether the room had an echo.

Boswell recorded a sample of the interchange:

> I asked what kind of architecture they had in Abyssinia. BRUCE. "Architecture, Sir, in a barbarous, mountainous country!" BOSWELL. "What kind of houses have they?" BRUCE. "Huts."
> In this manner was information dug from him, as from a flinty rock with pickaxes. . . .
> I afterwards found that Mr. Bruce was communicative enough if you let him alone, but could not bear to be questioned. . . . He

was like a ghost, which, it is said, will tell you a great deal of itself, but nothing if you question it.

In December Boswell learned that Bruce had been displeased by the Latin tag the journalist had used to describe him, which was from Vergil's description of the Cyclops Polyphemus. Boswell wrote peevishly in his diary:

I could see plainly that he did not like me; probably because I had given the public a good dish of his travels, better dressed than he could give himself. . . . Bruce is a rough-minded man, and has not such principles as that one would court him. I had seen him as a curiosity and extracted from him a good essay for *The London Magazine*; and there was enough.

A curiosity, indeed, was what Bruce was fast becoming. The irrepressible Fanny Burney, then only twenty-two, met the explorer at tea. She was struck by his "handsome and expressive face," but wished that he smiled more; she found him generally imperious. She had been warned that he hated company, having found "abominably provoking" the fact that other men had gathered anecdotes about his travels from him and had rushed them into print. Yet Fanny's account of the tea indicated that Bruce could be light and flirtatious.

Bell Strange then carried him his tea. She is about twelve years old, a very good-looking girl. Mr. Bruce, turning to me, said, "Do you know, Miss Burney, that I intend to run away with Bell? We are to go to Scotland together. She won't let me rest till I take her."

"How can you say so, Sir?" cried Bell; "pray, ma'am, don't believe it," colouring, and much fidgetted.

"Why, how now, Bell," returned he, "what! won't you go?"

"No, Sir."

"This is the first lady," said Mr. Bruce, rising, "who ever refused me!"

Fanny's assessment of the Scot, in the end, was a negative one.

He seemed determined not to enter into conversation with the company in general, nor to speak upon any but trifling topics. It is a pity, that a man who seems to have generous feelings, that break out by starts, and who certainly is a man of both learning and humour, should be thus run away with by pride and self-conceit.

At a later tea attended by Fanny, Bruce made an offhand remark that was strikingly revealing in terms of his own psychology. The company had been talking about Captain Cook's second expedition, which had just returned from the South Seas. Cook had brought home with him a Tahitian named Omai, who was to be returned to the island on a subsequent voyage. "But this poor fellow, Omai," Fanny reports Bruce as saying,

> "has lost all his time; they have taught him nothing; he will only pass for a consummate liar when he returns; for how can he make them believe half the things he will tell them? He can give them no idea of our houses, carriages, or any thing that will appear probable."

By March 1775 there were signs that Bruce was about to undergo a fate more ominous than being treated as a curiosity. Boswell recorded in his diary that the distinguished physician and professor Sir John Pringle "told me Bruce was thought a brute here, and was not fully believed." On April 1 Samuel Johnson met Bruce for the first time, and questioned the explorer closely. That very day Boswell reported the meeting in his diary.

> BOSWELL. "Is not Bruce a sensible man, Sir?" JOHNSON. "Why, Sir, he is not a distinct relater. I should say that he is neither abounding nor deficient in sense. I did not perceive any superior sense." BOSWELL. "But has he not a nobleness of resolution?" JOHNSON. "That is not to the present purpose. We are talking of his sense. A fighting cock has nobleness of resolution." He said that Jackson, the Member of Parliament, was a man who knew a great deal; that he was sometimes called "sensible Jackson" and sometimes "all-knowing Jackson," and that he did not believe Bruce.

A clue as to why Dr. Johnson might not have swallowed Bruce's tales can be found in the preface to his own translation of Father Lobo. Forty years before, Johnson had written:

> The Portuguese traveller, contrary to the general vein of his countrymen, has amused his reader with no romantic absurdities or incredible fictions: whatever he relates, whether true or not, is at least probable. . . .
>
> He appears, by his modest and unaffected narration, to have described things as he saw them; to have copied nature from life; and to have consulted his senses not his imagination. He meets with no basilisks that destroy with their eyes; his crocodiles devour their prey without tears; and his cataracts fall from the rock without deafening the neighboring inhabitants.

Horace Walpole was another of the influential Londoners who dismissed Bruce as a fraud. His grounds for not believing the man were the same as Johnson's—the improbability of his tales. Walpole ridiculed Bruce's "story of the bramble," and in a letter to a friend repeated a pun that was making the rounds:

> [Bruce] was asked before George Selwyn if the Abyssinians have any music? he replied, they have one *Lyre*. Selwyn whispered his neighbor, "They have one less since he left their country."

Walpole cautioned his correspondent, however: "Remember this letter is only for your own private eye; I do not desire to be engaged in a controversy or a duel."

Bitterly stung by his public reception, Bruce retired to his estate in Scotland and withdrew from society. In 1776 he married the daughter of one of his neighbors, a woman who apparently brought him considerable happiness before her death in 1785. The world awaited the publication of his memoirs, but year after year Bruce put off writing them. He filled his time with an interminable lawsuit against a nearby coal-mining company and with a fruitless campaign to gain a pension from the king. He hunted deer on his estate, entertained company, and escorted visitors through a small museum room stocked with relics from his travels. And he grew fat.

Finally he applied himself to the mammoth task of penning the narrative of his journey, hoping thereby to gain in his lifetime the recognition that was his due. In 1790 the five-volume quarto edition was published—seventeen years after Bruce had left Abyssinia.

The work was a runaway best seller; most of the edition sold out within thirty-two hours. But Bruce's hopes of vindication were cruelly dashed. The controversy of 1775 revived overnight. A few reviews were favorable, but the wittiest and most widely credited laughed the explorer into caricature. The tone of the raillery can be judged by a sample from a popular broadsheet, "A Complimentary Epistle to James Bruce, Esq., the Abyssinian Traveller," by "Peter Pindar" (the satiric poet John Wolcot). The author complained that, although he himself had been as far as Madeira, he had seen no wonders of the kind Bruce claimed to have beheld.

> Alas, I never met with royal scenes!
> No vomits gave to Abyssinian queens!
> Drew not from royal arms the purple tide,
> Nor scotch'd with fleams, a sceptred lady's hide;
> Nor, in anatomy so very stout,
> Ventur'd to turn a princess inside out;

> Nor, blushing, stripp'd me to the very skin,
> To give a royal blackamoor a grin . . .
> Nor have I been where men (what loss, alas!)
> Kill half a cow, and turn the rest to grass.

In closing the poem by urging Bruce to undertake a second voyage, Wolcot nudged him:

> And mind, ('tis HIST'RY'S province to surprise)
> That tales are sweetest, that sound most like lies.

The crowning insult, perhaps, came when a new supplement to the adventures of Baron Munchausen, the immensely popular comic liar, appeared, dedicated to Bruce and based directly on his Abyssinian travels.

In his last years Bruce was given to wearing a turban on his head and carrying a long staff in his hand as he ambled about the grounds of Kinnaird, and he had a small observatory built to house his telescopes. In April 1794, after entertaining company, he was helping an elderly lady down his staircase. He slipped, fell down the flight of steps, and was knocked unconscious by his own weight. By the next morning he was dead.

It was not until thirty years after Bruce's expedition that another European would enter Abyssinia. The first subsequent voyagers seem to have been motivated in large part by the intention to disprove Bruce's fictions once and for all. But as they revisited the scenes of the Scot's adventures, they not only found natives who remembered Bruce well, but were reluctantly forced to acknowledge that virtually all the details of the man's account were accurate, even down to the incident of cutting steaks from a live cow. Gradually during the 19th century Bruce's reputation grew, until at last he was regarded as one of the greatest explorers of Africa, as well as the single most important source of information on Ethiopia.

Why, in retrospect, was James Bruce so thoroughly discredited? The reasons are complicated. Some have to do with the climate of the age. One of the most popular literary forms in the 18th century was the *voyage imaginaire*, which was always presented, as it were, with a straight face. (On the title pages of their best-known works, Defoe's and Swift's names did not appear; the pretense was that the books were nonfiction travel narratives, written by Robinson Crusoe and Lemuel Gulliver, respectively.) At the same time, there was a huge demand for authentic accounts of journeys to the remote parts of the world.

It was important to be able to tell the one from the other. The credulous bishop who voiced his doubts about *Gulliver's Travels* only because he could not find its countries on his map of the world became the laughingstock of London. Thus the chief complaint against Bruce was that his descriptions and incidents were too wild to be believed.

This explanation, however, is not sufficient by itself. Captain Cook had brought back equally extraordinary stories of life in the South Seas, and no one doubted his word for a minute. Cook, to be sure, was an officer in the Royal Navy, under an official command, while Bruce acted pretty much on his own. And Cook had the corroboration, if he needed it, of the full crews of two Admiralty ships, whereas Bruce's only European companion had died at Gondar.

But a stronger reason for the differing receptions Bruce and Cook received had to do with what the English public wanted to hear. Rousseau's essay *On the Origin of the Inequality of Men* had made a vogue of the myth of the Noble Savage, and when the French explorer Bougainville had come back from a 1769 visit to Tahiti depicting the place as an earthly Eden, the Savage was placed on the map. In the 1770s it was fashionable to give the South Sea Islanders, because their native names seemed unpronounceable, Greek and Roman sobriquets like Lycurgus or Hercules. Joshua Reynolds painted a portrait of the Tahitian Omai posed as the Apollo Belvedere. The account of Cook's first expedition had been rewritten by a Dr. Hawkesworth, ostensibly because Cook was not a well-educated man. Among Hawkesworth's silent emendations were changes in the text to suppress the "defects" of Tahitian life in keeping with the preconception of the Noble Savage.

Bruce had returned from Abyssinia with a far different image of the savage: barbarous, treacherous, despotic, given to the most open kinds of debauchery, all set in a landscape dominated by mysterious diseases and desert heat. His was a view of primitive life which England did not want to see. Moreover, the current notion of Abyssinian life was based on the philosophic rationalism of *Rasselas*, which Bruce's "fictions" violated as thoroughly as they did the idea of the Noble Savage.

Finally, it is undeniable that Bruce's character itself contributed to his misfortune. The vignettes from Boswell and Fanny Burney confirm what Alan Moorehead called "the cold impression of an intensely self-reliant man, one of the kind who repels sympathy by his own conceit." Bruce's abrupt and condescending treatment of the very men who could have sealed him with their approval grievously damaged his public image. The seventeen-year delay in publishing must have seemed to many a furtive dodge against his own guilt. And

Bruce did lie, or at least willfully obscure the facts, in three crucial instances: the prior claim of Paez, the relative sizes of the White Nile and Blue Nile, and the presence of Balugani at the source.

The very strengths that made him a great explorer—above all, the indomitable self-reliance—ill adapted him for the London world of patronage and preferment that he also yearned to conquer. He died, it is reported, firm in the conviction that his daughter would live to "see the truth of all I have written completely and decisively confirmed." James Bruce's personal tragedy was that he did not live long enough to savor that confirmation himself.

BIBLIOGRAPHY

Boswell, James. *Boswell: The Ominous Years, 1774–1776*, edited by Charles Riskamp and Frederick A. Pottle. New York, 1963.

———. *Boswell for the Defence, 1769–1774*, edited by William K. Wimsatt, Jr. and Frederick A. Pottle. New York, 1959.

———. "Some Account of the very extraordinary TRAVELS of the celebrated Mr. Bruce, which at present engages the attention of the Public," *London Magazine*, no. 43 (August and September, 1774).

Bruce, James. *Travels to Discover the Source of the Nile, in the Years 1768, 1769, 1770, 1771, 1772, & 1773*. 5 vols. Edinburgh, 1790.

Burney, Frances. *The Early Diary of Frances Burney, 1768–1778*, edited by Annie Raine Ellis, vol. II. London, 1889.

Head, Sir Francis Bond. *The Life and Adventures of Bruce, the African Traveller*. London, 1838.

Lloyd, Christopher. *Captain Cook*. London, 1952.

Lobo, Father Jerome. *A Voyage to Abyssinia*, translated from the French by Samuel Johnson, LL.D. London, 1735.

Moorehead, Alan. *The Blue Nile*. New York, 1962.

Murray, Alexander. *Account of the Life and Writings of James Bruce, of Kinnaird*. Edinburgh, 1808.

Reid, J. M. *Traveller Extraordinary: The Life of James Bruce of Kinnaird*. London, 1968.

Ullendorff, Edward. *The Ethiopians: An Introduction to Country and People*. London, 1960.

Walpole, Horace. *The Letters of Horace Walpole*, edited by Peter Cunningham, vol. IX. London, 1866.

[Wolcot, John]. "A Complimentary Epistle to James Bruce, Esq. The Abyssinian Traveller." London, 1792.

5

CAPTAIN ADAMS
RUNS THE COLORADO

Sebastian Cabot and Abyssinian Bruce continue to figure prominently in the history of exploration. Father Hennepin, though a mere ghost of the late-17th-century celebrity he once was, manages still to stir the waters of Jesuit historiography, and his name squats proudly on the county that includes the thriving cities of Minneapolis and St. Paul. But Captain Samuel Adams, who briefly challenged the great Western explorer John Wesley Powell for the honor of having led the first expedition down the Colorado River, has come very close to slipping for good through the cracks of history. One of the most outrageous mountebanks in a Wild West that was full of liars and braggarts, Sam Adams died an embittered and deluded old man only sixty-six years ago in his hometown of Beaver, Pennsylvania.

We owe the survival of the Adams story to that most diligent and lively of Western archivists, Wallace Stegner. In the course of writing his *Beyond the Hundredth Meridian*, a splendid account of the importance of John Wesley Powell in "the second opening of the West"—a book by turns acerbic and lyrical, in the long run devastatingly sound, as well as strikingly original—Stegner came upon the nearly obliterated footsteps of Captain Adams. Hunting down sources from Washington to California, poking through stale Congressional documents, musty newspaper clippings, and overlooked letters and journals, Stegner pieced together the fascinating tale of a man who, though self-evidently a crank, came surprisingly close to convincing men in high places that he, not Powell, was the true discoverer of the course of the Colorado River. In Stegner's book the Adams saga weaves in and out, like a comic subplot, a series of Shakespeare's buffoonish throwaway interludes. But the intensity with which the scruffy mountain man prosecuted his farce and the bitterness with which he aged into sedentary madness still have something to tell us about envy and disappointment.

To understand Captain Samuel Adams, it is important to look at some of the actual conventions by which real mountain men lived. The man's background was emphatically different from John Wesley Powell's, and when he left the mining town of Breckenridge, Colorado, and tried to play at the politics of Washington, D.C., he was decidedly out of his depth. In the whole of the Adams saga, more than with most exploratory fakers, the question of just how much the man believed what he said keeps thrusting itself disquietingly forward. It would be easier to dismiss him at every step, as Stegner is sometimes tempted to do, as a conscious fraud and nothing more.

The myth of the mountain man is not wholly, or even primarily, a recent invention. As the increasingly scholarly biographical studies of the last two decades make clear, later "adapters" of the mountain men's tales about themselves created sentimental utopias in the American wilderness, in which their heroes could act out half-imaginary dramas of survival and combat. As early as 1837 Washington Irving was making a frontier legend of the explorer Captain B.L.E. Bonneville, who he claimed had discovered the Great Salt Lake. Irving's careless historiography helped obscure the facts, and today, though we can be certain Bonneville did not discover the salty inland sea, we may never be able to ascertain just what white man first saw it.

Much later, to cite another example, the popular accounts of Grace Raymond Hebard managed so thoroughly to obfuscate the true facts about the important mountain man Jean Baptiste Charbonneau, Sacajawea's son, that we remain in the dark about many of the basic circumstances of his career. Hebard managed, among other things, to have both Sacajawea and her son dying in old age on the Wind River Reservation in Wyoming in the 1880s, even though an authentic record had placed the death of the courageous scout for Lewis and Clark in the year 1812 on the upper Missouri.

As his biographer J. Cecil Alter points out, Jim Bridger deliberately adapted the earlier Paul Bunyanesque Arkansas travelers' tales to fit his own doings; his motives seem in part to have been consciously parodic. But the tall tales made such good telling that (as with later Western gunslingers like Billy the Kid) they soon became canonic anecdotes. Well into the 1950s and 1960s biographers like Stanley Vestal were uncritically passing on as sober fact the wildest tales that had caught like burrs on the leggings of the early trappers and scouts.

The effect of the kind of whimsical self-promotion indulged in by the likes of Bridger and swallowed by an eager public was to create a climate of opinion that, by the 1860s when Samuel Adams flourished, unmistakably linked entrepreneurial ambition with taletelling, no matter how wildly exaggerated. Government explorers like Lewis and Clark or Zebulon Pike went to considerable pains to measure the West, to make accurate maps, and to report reliably what they had discovered. But for trappers and hunters and guides who lived off their unique knowledge of parts of the West barely or not at all penetrated by other whites, the important pose to strike was one of authority—no matter what the actual experience on which the pose was based.

Overlying the essentially oral tradition of the mountain men's deep acquaintance with the wilderness backwaters of the West was the Arkansas vein of braggart humor—a code of conduct as much as it was a literary taste. To a venal upstart like Sam Adams, trying to make his fortune thirty years after Jim Bridger, the legacy of the mountain man, we may imagine, meant several practical lessons. Lie all you want, as long as no one (especially no one in power back East) can contradict you. Pose as the authority. Promise great things in a tone of apparent modesty or willingness to serve. Imply that you are a leader of men and an intimate of little-known Indian tribes. Get yourself outfitted or grubstaked in advance.

Of Captain Adams's early life we know almost nothing. He first surfaces in March 1867 with a letter to Secretary of War Edwin M. Stanton. At that time, two years before Powell was to embark on the Colorado, the vast plateaus of what are now Utah and Arizona and the deep canyons through which the great river bisected them were the least-known part of the continental United States. The river had been forded here and there, in places like Gunnison's Crossing (near what is now Greenriver, Utah) or Lee's Ferry, at the mouth of the Paria. But nearly a thousand miles of canyon-guarded river remained unknown, and the rumors of huge waterfalls and impassable cataracts were known throughout the West.

Thus it may have been of more than passing interest to Secretary Stanton in 1867 to receive a letter from a "Captain" who proclaimed that he was an expert on the river. Adams wrote that he and Captain Thomas Trueworthy had ascended the river from its mouth in the Gulf of California for over 620 miles in a small stern-wheeler. Adams represented his motive as the altruistic one of determining whether or not the river was navigable by steamers. Apparently he counted on the likelihood that Stanton's knowledge of the lower Colorado was fuzzy; for two steamer pilots had already ascended the Colorado to

The full extent of Sam Adams's two forays on the Colorado River. The
journey upstream from Yuma to Callville, which Adams bragged about in
1867, was by then a paddlewheeler milk run. On the aborted descent
from Breckenridge in 1869, Adams's party narrowly avoided several fatal
disasters. Meanwhile John Wesley Powell was completing the true first
descent of the Colorado—which Adams was soon to claim as his own—
from Green River to Callville.

Callville—just as far as Adams claimed—nine years before, in 1858. The original stimulus for paddlewheeler exploration of the great Western rivers had been the Gold Rush of 1849. Steamers were probing up from the mouth of the Colorado as early as 1852. By 1867 the trip up to Callville was a milk run, and there were dozens of landings and miners' tent cities and small adobe-shack villages along its banks. There was, in fact, even a regular steamer service operated by the California Navigation Company.

Adams went on to inform Stanton that from Callville he had gone eleven miles farther upriver, built a raft, and successfully floated through Boulder Canyon. He had climbed the canyon wall above his highest point on the river and gazed northeast across the unknown country, where, he claimed, he saw an open valley some sixty miles in length. This was probably the valley of the Virgin River, a tributary of the Colorado that empties into what is now Lake Mead. Adams was convinced that there were in that vast unknown area no serious obstructions to river travel: "the imaginary canyons and rapids" were the products of fearful and timid souls, or (he hinted) the deliberate fictions of "corporations" entrenched on the river who were afraid of competitors moving in.

Adams then outlined a grand scheme of travel and commerce on the Colorado. He envisioned the river playing the same role in the development of the West that the Mississippi had done in the Midwest. He told Stanton that Boulder Canyon, which he had run, was the most dangerous rapid on the whole Colorado.

Here we must pause. It is easy to see Captain Adams's letter as a grandiose con game, an attempt to bilk Washington out of at least a steady pension for Adams to pursue his Western schemes. But is it not possible that the man had fooled himself? Having climbed out of the canyon to see an open valley stretching away to the northeast, he might have made the leap of extrapolation and simplification that would convince him the going was relatively easy the rest of the way. Wanting to see something can powerfully precondition an explorer to see it. (In 1576 Martin Frobisher, sailing into Frobisher Bay—he thought it a strait—on the southeast side of Baffin Island, was serene in the conviction that on one hand lay America, on the other Asia.)

How much of Adams's misrepresentation, at this point, was fraud? Stegner compares the man to William Gilpin, who after decades of personal hardship in the West could still portray it in books and on the lecture platform as an Arcadia of effortless agriculture and pastoral abundance. "His spiritual relative," as Stegner calls Adams, might indeed have lulled himself into a comparable dream of commercial ease.

Adams's letter gained him a resolution of thanks from the House of Representatives, but nothing more. He appears next two years later, arriving uninvited in May 1869 at Powell's camp on the Green River in what is now southwestern Wyoming, where the Union Pacific crossed the main northern tributary of the Colorado.

Adams knew that Powell was about to embark on his well-conceived descent of the Colorado. Undaunted by the high government connections of his host, he made himself at home in the camp and let the party know that he had been appointed to the expedition as a scientist. When Adams arrived, Powell was at first briefly absent. Unwilling to deal with underlings, Adams indicated that he would present his letters and orders when the major returned.

Adams's bravado was skillful enough to persuade some of the less well educated of Powell's entourage, like Billy Hawkins, that the newcomer must be another Washington expert authorized by their leader. They let Adams camp with them, although they teased him, as a supposed intellectual, with pranks and jests.

When Powell returned, Adams presented him with Secretary Stanton's letter from two years before, representing it as an authorization to join the expedition. Powell asked to see Adams's papers, and the self-styled "Captain" brought forth more letters from men in Washington, wishing him success in his upcoming exploration of the great river. Powell perused the letters, sniffed out the fraud immediately, and banished Adams from his camp.

Miffed but unrepentant, Adams boarded the train and headed for Colorado Territory. If Powell would not take advantage of the extraordinary services he had to offer, he would find other backers who would.

Two months later Adams resurfaced in the Colorado mining camp of Breckenridge. Powell's approach to the great river had been a logical one: to descend the Green through Flaming Gorge, past the famed trappers' rendezvous at Brown's Hole, and join the Colorado at its hitherto unknown junction a little below what is now Moab, Utah. Thus he was not, in the strictest sense, running the whole of the Colorado (or Grand River, as it was called in 1869), whose headwaters lie in the mountains of northeastern Colorado, just west of Longs Peak. Powell knew this well, since only the year before he had joined with *Rocky Mountain News* founder William N. Byers to make the first non-Indian ascent of Longs Peak, from which he had looked down upon the headwaters of the Grand.

By attempting the descent of the river from central Colorado rather than from southwestern Wyoming, Adams was actually tackling the longer, more difficult, and, to purists, more complete passage of the

Grand. But in choosing an out-of-the-way mining boom town for his launching point, Adams was also banking on the ignorance of parochial Westerners as to just how mammoth an enterprise he was promoting, and how unlikely the race with Powell—who by now had almost reached the junction of the Green and the Grand—was to yield success.

In Breckenridge the putative captain seems to have won a certain following. His speeches recruited a party of ten, and the town outfitted him with four boats. In mid-July, amid speeches and cheers, Adams's flotilla set forth upon the waters of the Blue River, a mountain stream only inches deep where it flowed past the two-mile-high mining camp, one of the minor southern tributaries of the upper Colorado River.

Once again we must speculate what Adams's intentions were. No one in the country in the year 1869 had a comprehensive knowledge of the canyons of the Colorado, or anything like a thorough acquaintance with the river. The rudimentary maps of the territories could have supplied a careful geographer with an accurate notion of the distance to be traveled from Breckenridge to Callville, where Adams had been two years before. But the man was a swashbuckler, not a geographer, a schemer, not a true expeditioneer. Yet history clouds the question of whether he believed his party capable of the smooth descent of America's most remarkable river that he was later to claim, or whether in July 1869 he was already planning a hoax. It remains entirely possible that he thought the trip he was embarking on was a feasible one, that the dream of a commercial highway through the West which he had tried to fob off on Secretary Stanton was a sincere vision.

The boat trip itself was an unqualified disaster. Decked out with a flag woven by the Breckenridge ladies that proclaimed "Western Colorado to California, Greeting," and laden with hundreds of pounds of supplies, guns, and ammunition, the four boats floated down the Blue on July 12. Two days later, less than twenty miles downstream, the party came to the first of several griefs in "Rocky Canyon." Three boats overturned; their occupants found themselves hanging onto rocks in the middle of the river; and what Adams's journal is pleased to call the expedition's "instruments" and "papers" were swept away for good.

In all fairness to Captain Adams, it must be noted that the canyons of the lower Blue are regarded even today as difficult white water. It took undeniable nerve even to try to float them in 1869. Nevertheless, the swamping began to take its toll upon the volunteers. On July 18 one man was sent back to Breckenridge for more matches and instruments; the next day another, on the verge of mutineering, was sent packing as "a common nuisance." Three days later four more party members deserted, leaving Adams with a crew of only five, including the man who had returned from the Breckenridge errand.

Undaunted, he launched out once again. Eight miles of what the captain's journal reveals as easy boating led the group to the broad valley where the Blue joins the Grand. With three boats remaining, they had traveled a grand total of fifty-five miles from Breckenridge in twelve days.

A week, unrecorded in the journal, passed before Adams's band pushed on. The boats made a paltry five miles and camped again, at the head of what Stegner surmises must have been Cedar Canyon— the spot where Powell himself, two years earlier, had first dreamed of descending the great river. With the bravado of a conquistador, Adams sent off newspaper dispatches congratulating himself on the progress his party had already made. The three days' rest at this spot undoubtedly had another motive as well: fear. For here Adams was first confronting white water of a truly awesome power.

On August 2, only a few hundred yards into the canyon, one of the boats lost most of its cargo and was severely damaged. The next day the intrepid river rats managed to line their boats (lower them with ropes held by men on shore) all of three hundred further yards. Two days later, while lining it, the party first swamped, then lost completely another of their craft. Reduced to a single boat, the undeniably courageous men threw away all their excess clothing and equipment and made ready to proceed, all six in their only boat. By now even lining and portaging were hazardous enterprises; and sure enough, on August 8, the fourth boat went the way of the third, swamping, breaking its line, and hurtling downstream never to be seen again.

Having lost all four of the boats supplied in Breckenridge, Adams was, if his diary can be trusted, still not ready to give up. He had only 120 pounds of dampened flour and 20 pounds of bacon left, but he urged his men to build a makeshift raft to get these precious provisions around a "perpendicular corner" in the stream. The next day three more men gave up the expedition, leaving Adams with only two accomplices. They built yet another raft and blundered three miles downstream before wrecking it. On August 13 even the indomitable captain had to admit the project was a failure. The three men turned their backs on the river and headed overland back to "civilization."

At this point in his career Adams was guilty of nothing more serious than vague self-misrepresentation to Powell and Stanton and a harebrained assault on the most awesome river in the West. None of his men had died, although a dog taken aboard as mascot had apparently drowned. But the passion to be first, to supersede Powell, seems at this point to have taken over Adams's senses. Once again we are left wondering what part of the extravagant boasts of his next few months to attribute to conscious fraud, what part to self-delusion.

The latter is suggested by the fact that, before contacting outsiders, Captain Adams wrote in a second, polished version of his diary:

> I am fully satisfied that we had come over the worst part of our rout in 95 miles we had descended about 4500 feet. The vallies were open up river, the mountains bec smooth the pine and cedar larger everything indic a prosperous passage was ahead of us had we been in a position to have gone on. Three years before as I stated in my Report to the Sec of War, I looked up the Colorado River from a point 650 miles from its mouth and could then see a vally exten 75 miles to the NE. I could now look to the SW & almost see the narrow gap which divided us.

The phrases breathe self-delusion, with their grandiose posturings ("my Report to the Sec of War") and their wishful rationalizations. But the enormity of that "narrow gap" that Adams may have imagined he could almost see across—a full eight hundred miles containing all the most formidable rapids the Colorado had to offer, including Glenwood, Cataract, and Grand canyons—gave Stegner more than enough cause to reject Adams as a preposterous and deliberate fraud.

As in the case of that kindred river-runner Father Louis Hennepin nearly two centuries before, the goad that seems to have driven Samuel Adams over the brink of mere braggadocio into the seething currents of hoax was the intolerable news that his rival had succeeded. Major Powell emerged from the lower end of the Grand Canyon on August 30, 1869, and almost immediately the electrifying news of his epic river trip began to spread eastward by telegraph. The celebrity instantly conferred on Powell was well earned; as Stegner puts it, "He had unlocked the last great unknown region in the country and made it his own."

But on September 19 the *Omaha Republican* printed a letter of protest against "a recent explorer, who has expended nothing individually and incurred none of the hardships inseparably connected with the development of the west." The correspondent, who was of course Captain Samuel Adams, went on to deny that Powell had made the first ascent of Longs Peak because, it was well known, men and even women had regularly climbed the mountain for at least ten years before Powell. Similarly, Adams claimed, he himself had preceded Powell on the Colorado. "Through all the cañons I have ascended and descended several times within the past three years."

Had the "narrow gap" shrunk, in Adams's bitterness, to no gap at all? Or was this nasty letter a calculated attempt to steal Powell's laurels just as they were being bestowed? Whichever the case, Adams's arrogation of priority, unlike Father Hennepin's, fell mainly on deaf ears. But not for want of energy on his part. Within months Adams, unasked, had submitted a long report of his purported exploration of the Colorado to Secretary of War Belknap. Belknap passed the document on to the chief of the Corps of Engineers, who puzzled over it briefly before deciding that it did not need to be answered with a monetary reward.

Adams did not give up. A few months later he managed to persuade Representative George W. Julian to introduce a House resolution calling for a grant of $20,000 to the doughty captain in recognition of his services. The resolution stayed alive for two years before it was lost in committee. Throughout the 1870s, with inexhaustible pertinacity, Adams nursed his claim through various Congressional bodies. With what may well have become authentic paranoia, he based his case on the claim that "the true facts of the [Colorado] country" were being kept from the public. In 1876 he won an apparent minor victory in the form of a House recommendation of compensation in the amount of $3,750; but finally even this stipend fell through.

Bitterly convinced of personal persecution, Adams went back to his hometown of Beaver, Pennsylvania, and settled down to practice law as, in Stegner's phrase, "the oldest member of the Pennsylvania bar, and probably the craziest." Whether or not the decades of mountain-man-like boasting about his exploratory blunders and failures had permanently distorted his sense of the past, as Stegner suggests, the cranky old man evidently convinced some of his fellow townspeople that he was the genuine article. Upon his death in 1915 the local newspaper noted, generously if inaccurately, that

> he spent a number of years exploring the Colorado River, being sent unofficially by Secretary Stanton, who died before Mr. Adams returned, and his claim from the government was never adjusted.

BIBLIOGRAPHY

Alter, J. Cecil. *Jim Bridger*. Norman, Okla., 1950.

Anderson, William Marshall. *The Rocky Mountain Journals of William Marshall Anderson*, edited by Dale L. Morgan and Eleanor Towles Harris. San Marino, Calif., 1967.

Lingenfelter, Richard E. *Steamboats on the Colorado River 1852–1916*. Tucson, Ariz., 1978.

Powell, John Wesley. *The Exploration of the Colorado River and Its Canyons*. New York, 1961.

Stegner, Wallace. *Beyond the Hundredth Meridian: John Wesley Powell and the Second Opening of the West*. Boston, 1953.

6

DR. COOK
AND MOUNT McKINLEY

By its very nature, an exploration hoax is difficult to expose. A plaque, a flagstaff, or a name carved in a rock may serve to prove an explorer's claim; but the absence of such calling cards cannot by itself disprove it. Because the North Pole is a featureless expanse of drifting ice pack, no visitor can plant a lasting mark there. Because the summits of high mountains sleep under the snows of each successive winter, signs of human passage vanish there as surely as do footprints in the shifting sands of the desert.

Thus when an exploration hoax is exposed, the evidence amassed against its perpetrator tends to be circumstantial: inconsistencies in the explorer's tale; absent or conflicting observational data; the lack of corroboration by subsequent travelers; contradictory testimony by the man's companions; or the inherent unlikelihood of the feat's having been performed in the way alleged. At best, years or centuries after a hoax, its students can say only that the overwhelming preponderance of the evidence weighs against the explorer's claim. There remains a germ of doubt, the long-shot possibility that after all the man really did do what he said he did.

In the history of exploration no hoax was ever more conclusively exposed than the claim by Dr. Frederick Cook to have reached the summit of Mount McKinley in September 1906. Cook was a double fake, for three years later he emerged from the Arctic to announce that with two Eskimo companions he had reached the North Pole— an assertion almost as conclusively debunked as the McKinley claim. The doctor lived the last thirty years of his life in public ignominy, and even spent five years in a federal penitentiary for oil-land fraud.

Yet he never cracked, never confessed, and went to his deathbed in 1940 protesting that he was innocent, with lawsuits pending against his detractors.

Such a man seems an unlikely candidate for a book of martyrs. Perhaps the most extraordinary facet of the phenomenon of Frederick Cook has been his ability to inspire true believers, revisionists who insist that the doctor performed every exploit he ever claimed, and that he was, in the words of his most recent biographer, "not simply one of the greater victims in America's history, but the all-time champion."

McKinley, at 20,320 feet the highest mountain in North America, had been seen by prospectors in the 1890s, but its existence was not widely known until one of them, W. A. Dickey, named it after the then President and, upon his return to the States, wrote a newspaper article about it. In 1903 two expeditions—one of them under the leadership of Dr. Cook—attempted to climb the mountain from the north. Not the least of the problems McKinley posed was its extreme inaccessibility, and it required a formidable overland traverse of unmapped tundra, river, and glacier simply to reach the base of the mountain. The 1903 expeditions found themselves staring up what would later come to be known as the Wickersham Wall—the largest precipice in North America. It was not surprising that they made only a small dent in the mountain's defenses.

In 1906 the first expedition to approach McKinley from the south reached the lower moraines of two gigantic glaciers that spilled from a complex jumble of granite cliffs and icy buttresses. On this attempt Dr. Cook was joined by two of the most redoubtable of the McKinley pioneers, Professor Herschel Parker and the artist Belmore Browne, men who would later be instrumental in exposing Cook's hoax. Having penetrated to the outer edge of the mountain's ramparts by July, the party of seven retreated via the Susitna River all the way to the Pacific Coast. It was late in the season for mountain exploration, but Cook declared that he wanted to return to make a further reconnaissance, and with one other man, the Montana blacksmith and horse-packer Edward Barrill, he set out in mid-August for the interior once again. They were back in civilization in a little over a month. And Cook announced to the world that the pair of them had stood on the summit on September 16.

Browne and Parker disbelieved the doctor the minute they heard his tale. Browne took Barrill aside as soon as he met him, and later reported that the horse-packer said, "I can tell you all about the big peaks just south of the mountain, but if you want to know about Mount McKinley go and ask Cook." Even so, the ensuing controversy might have amounted merely to one man's word against another man's doubts. But in 1910 Browne and Parker, in the course of a second attempt on McKinley from the south, managed to tear a huge hole in the fragile fabric of Cook's claim, although it would not be until 1957 that this fabric would be reduced to tatters. For Cook had made a fatal mistake. He had returned from Mount McKinley with a summit photo.

The story of Frederick Cook is a parable of ambition and deceit, pathetic in its details, tragic in its personal consequences. The man was no mere bungler or incompetent. The abiding irony of his career is that had he taken credit only for the geographic feats he actually accomplished, he would be esteemed today as an explorer of no mean significance.

By 1906, at the age of forty-one, Cook was the veteran of six major expeditions. In 1891–92 he had served as "surgeon and ethnologist" on an expedition under the command of Robert E. Peary—who was later to become his bitter opponent in the 1909 polar controversy. Peary's expedition, the first of four Arctic expeditions Cook would participate in, attempted to reach Greenland's northernmost point and thereby prove the landmass an island. Cook had also served as the doctor on the Belgian Antarctic expedition in 1898–99, the first ever to be forced to winter over in the seas surrounding that continent. Two years later he became one of the founding members of the American Alpine Club.

The reports of most of Cook's comrades during these six voyages testify to a skillful and enthusiastic explorer. On the boat trip to Greenland, Peary had broken his leg; Cook set the bone expertly. Peary later gave high praise to the doctor's services, both medical and ethnographic. Roald Amundsen, his companion on the Belgian Antarctic expedition, called Cook "the finest traveler I ever saw." The 1903 journey, though it failed in its goal of climbing McKinley, made a complete circumnavigation of the mountain, a feat not duplicated until 1978.

Yet there were hints before 1906 that Frederick Cook was a difficult, perhaps even an untrustworthy, man. The strongest criticism appeared in the pages of Robert Dunn's *The Shameless Diary of an Explorer*, a book unique in expedition literature. Dunn, a journalist and protégé of Lincoln Steffens, set down an iconoclastic, no-holds-barred account of the 1903 expedition, of which he was an essential member. The portraits of several of his colleagues were so candid that Dunn felt it necessary to change their names. "The Professor," pompous, lazy, dogmatic but confused, makes a fascinating character study, especially for the reader looking for clues in

Cook's personality that might help account for the later hoaxes.

Indeed, what sort of man was Frederick Cook? Not very much is known about his early life, but two facts leap from the pages of his biographers' otherwise unexciting accounts of Cook's formative years. The first was the loss of his father to pneumonia when the boy was only five. The second was a lisp which afflicted him throughout his life (Dunn mentions it, sometimes disparagingly).

The primary experience of his childhood, he would write years later in *Return from the Pole*, was poverty, which seemed only to fuel his natural ambition. "With abject want as my best driving force," Cook succeeded in putting himself through medical school at New York University. At the age of twenty-four he married, and soon after settled down to private practice in Manhattan. But during his first six months he saw only three patients. Then, as if to echo the childhood blow of losing his father, the doctor's wife died of peritonitis in childbirth; and the baby also died. In his grief Cook turned to long books about travel and exploration. When he read a newspaper story about Peary's needing a surgeon for his upcoming Arctic expedition, he sat down and wrote a letter of application—and thus became an explorer.

Aside from Dunn's snide but penetrating vignettes, the main sources for a study of Dr. Cook's character are his own books. He was a smooth writer, capable of both clarity and evocative power; his "ideas" tended to be conventional ones, however, and he had a weakness for the purple passage. If there is a single salient characteristic of his view of things, it lies in Cook's penchant for seeing all of creation in terms of an elemental struggle between life and death. In the North he would come to regard the very landscape in such terms: "These Arctic rock lichens represent a form of living death. It would require the use of a microscope to determine in the substance of the plant where life ends and where death begins." At a critical point in the half-fictitious journey that Cook passed off as his "return from the Pole," the doctor and his Eskimo friends, he relates, had to abandon their dogs. Rejecting the idea of shooting them to save them from starvation, he decided, "No. Where there is life there is a chance. Death is too permanent for thought to grasp it—it is the end."

Like many an outdoorsman of today, Cook romanticized the wilderness and in *Return from the Pole* placed it in dramatic opposition to "the life-sapping conditions of modern city life," in which

physical exercise is prohibited by the limits of space and the ease of mechanical locomotion; mental energy is strained to cope with the maddening pace of this material age. The stomach is abused by unnatural foods, the liver and kidneys are hardened by poisonous drink, the lungs breathe a hothouse, germ-cultivated air, the muscles wither from disease.

The corollary attitude, a strong belief of Cook's, was the attribution of a renewed "mystery and promise" in the world to those who undergo extreme deprivation and hardship.

One cannot escape the impression that Cook was a lifelong loner. His official accounts of his expeditions give almost no sense of who his companions were. In *To the Top of the Continent* the 1903 party is never introduced, and the only sentence that reveals their full names is the caption of a group photo—which of course omits the name of the photographer, the fifth of the expedition's stalwarts.

Yet many explorers were loners, and many good ones were intensely driven men, of the sort given to simplistic dichotomies between life and death, action and contemplation. In Dunn's *Shameless Diary* the portrait of Cook begins to take on particularity. In the muckraking tradition of Steffens, the *Diary* sets out to tell exactly what happened on the 1903 expedition—not omitting interpersonal squabbles and private embarrassments. In this sense Dunn's very aims ran counter to the gentlemanly tradition in exploration writing of keeping a party's "dirty laundry" out of the public eye, and more than one contemporary who was otherwise unsympathetic to Cook would echo the opinion of Hudson Stuck, the man who in 1913 finally did make the first true ascent of McKinley:

> The book has a curious, undeniable power, despite its brutal frankness, and its striving after "the poor renown of being smart," and it may live. One is thankful, however, that it is unique in the literature of travel.

Yet the modern reader cannot resist the book, nor can he doubt that Dunn's "Professor" is Dr. Cook himself. From an early point in the expedition on, Dunn lost all faith in Cook's abilities as a leader.

> I think he would face death and disaster without a word, but through the insensitiveness of age and too much experience, rather than by true courage. I cannot believe he has imagination; of a leader's qualities he has not shown one. He seems our sympathetic servant.

Among Dunn's most serious criticisms of Cook, especially in view of the later claim to have reached the North Pole, was that he had "no sense of locality," was always losing the trail, and tended to choose the worst routes through the alders. More than once the expedition was somewhat lost in the (admittedly uncharted) Alaskan wilderness.

The arguments of Cook's modern detractors vis-à-vis the later polar controversy—most notably the scholar Dennis Rawlins—include the suspicion that Cook did not even know how to use a theodolite, without which skill he would have been hopelessly lost in the Arctic once he left the shores of Ellesmere Island. The 1903 expedition had a theodolite. Writing before Cook was suspected of any hoaxes, Dunn unconsciously foreshadowed this pivotal critique:

The Professor has just "worked out our position," with a map, a pencil, and a straw. . . . "There's a good chance to use your theodolite now," said Miller today, pointing to an angle of Muldrow [Glacier], whose direction of flow we had been arguing about. The Professor only smiled, and never touched an instrument—as often before when we've wanted an observation.

Years later, in the pages of his autobiography, *World Alive*, Dunn crystallized his impressions of his first encounter with the doctor.

Now at forty, old to my twenty-five years, he still had a spark for exploring. But otherwise he was dumb, with a bovine face, straight pale hair and walrus mustache, milk-blue eyes, a set smile, and a slight lisp. . . . Cook was optimistic, although a puzzling lassitude often beset him. He made desultory decisions, seemed indifferent; yet his confident, pompous solemnity killed criticism.

Many of the details of Dunn's portrait are strikingly corroborated by a journalist named W. T. Stead, who was among the first to greet Cook in Copenhagen in 1909 when he returned from his "polar" journey. Stead fully believed that Cook was telling the truth, even though the controversy was already raging around the heads of the doctor and of his archrival Peary. And yet, in Stead's eyes,

He does not strike us as a man, but rather as a child—a naive, inexperienced child, who sorely needed someone to look after him, and tell him what he ought to do in his own interest. . . . A rather annoying thing about this infantile side to his character was his inability to make up his mind and stick to it about almost anything. . . . If he had been as indecisive and as changeable in the Arctic regions he would never have got anywhere, and certainly could never have got home. . . . He is not, I should say, an imaginative man.

An unimaginative child who could not settle on a coherent story? How, then, did Cook, as hoaxer, fool anybody? Stead gives an unwittingly paradoxical clue: "He is both too honest and too limited to have conceived so colossal a fraud."

Through August of 1906, it must be remembered, Cook stood unaccused of any dishonesty, with a record most explorers might envy. The just-completed attempt on McKinley from the south with Belmore Browne, Herschel Parker, and others had made an important reconnaissance, and as the party traveled down the Susitna River toward Cook Inlet (named after the great English sailor, not the doctor) they were not plunged in the gloom of failure. September, which in the Alaska Range heralds the beginning of winter, was fast approaching. Suddenly Cook decided to return north. His motivation was unclear. According to Browne, when Cook suggested heading back to the foothills of McKinley for a further reconnaissance, Browne wanted to go with him. "He answered that he would do no exploring outside of seeing whether or not the water route [up the Susitna and Chulitna rivers] was practicable and he again urged me to aid him with his game collection." The implication is obvious— that Cook had already in the back of his mind the notion of a hoax, and did not want the scrupulous Browne along to contradict his story.

Cook's own account in *To the Top of the Continent* is opaque and evasive:

> In the middle of August there were various changes made in the personnel of the expedition and in the working programme. . . . Owing to repeated failures and the advancing winter we decided that our energies for the short period of the remaining season would be better spent in exploration than climbing, and to this end our plans were now made.

Yet, says Browne, just before parting from him Cook wired a well-known businessman in New York City, "Am preparing for a last, desperate attack on Mount McKinley."

With Edward Barrill and a prospector named Dokkin, Cook quickly reascended the glacial rivers, itself no mean feat. Near the snout of the Ruth Glacier (which Cook named after his daughter by his second marriage) Dokkin was dropped off to hunt for gold, and the remaining two pushed on up the majestic highway of the glacier. From Cook's photographs we know that he reached an altitude of about five thousand feet on the Ruth. In doing so, he and Barrill became the first men ever to enter what would come to be known as the Great Gorge, a glacial corridor walled on both sides by stupendous granite cliffs, a climbing challenge so formidable that it would not be until the middle 1970s that these cliffs would begin to be attacked by alpinists.

The two men were about fifteen miles south of the summit of McKinley, and a full fifteen thousand feet below. The head of the Ruth Glacier abuts against two massive, high, intricately corniced ridges, later called the South Buttress and East Buttress; they were not to be ascended until 1954 and 1963, respectively. At this point, according to Cook's puzzling admission in *To the Top of the Continent*, he and Barrill still had no intention of going for the summit, for

> the winter, with its heavy snowfall, its death-dealing avalanches, its storms and awful cold, was far too advanced in the upper world. We hoped only for an opportunity to discover a route that would permit a future ascent.

Nevertheless, Cook maintained, the pair pushed on, going extremely light, with packs of only forty-five pounds in which they carried food for ten days and the minimal clothing and gear, including sleeping "robes" made by the doctor's wife out of cravenette, camel's hair, and eider-duck skin, which doubled as overcoats. At this point in his narrative, Cook's prose becomes more and more melodramatic as the descriptions grow vague and general. Bradford Washburn, the McKinley expert responsible for exposing Cook's hoax beyond a shadow of a doubt in 1956–7, believes that he can pinpoint the very sentence in *To the Top of the Continent* where truth leaves off and the lies begin. Indeed, Hudson Stuck reported that upon the appearance of the book in 1908,

> the writer well remembers the eagerness with which his copy (the only one in Fairbanks) was perused by man after man from the Kantishna [gold] diggings, and the acute way in which they detected the place where vague "fine writing" began to be substituted for definite description.

According to Cook's text, the two men advanced toward the "north-east ridge." (The true northeast ridge, by which Stuck was to climb McKinley, is inaccessible from the south. Cook's believers have usually taken him to mean the east ridge of the East Buttress—a route still unclimbed today.) Three days of dodging avalanches supposedly brought them to its crest. The sentence that completes this monumental struggle is typical of Cook's vagueness: "Rising from ridge to ridge and from cornice to cornice we finally burst through the gloomy mist on to a bright snowfield."

During the next four days, according to Cook, the pair slept in snowhouses and, on a particularly difficult night at fourteen thousand feet, in seats they had carved out of a 60° ice slope, their gear and their bodies tied to their planted ice axes. Even now they had only "a half notion to climb to the summit," feeling that they were still reconnoitering a route for future parties. Despite such a modest goal, they struggled against the cold and altitude until, on September 16, they stood on the summit. Cook described the "heaven-scraped granite" near the top and mentioned leaving "a record of our conquest" and a small flag, wrapped in a metallic tube, which they deposited "in a protected nook a short distance below the summit." The climb back down Cook dealt with in a single sentence: "The descent was less difficult, but it took us four days to tumble down to our base camp."

What did Cook and Barrill really do during the twelve or thirteen days on the Ruth Glacier? We can deduce their movements with surprising certainty. Having penetrated the Great Gorge to the foot of a striking mountain now known as the Mooses Tooth, they turned around and walked back down the glacier. Before leaving the mountains, however, they headed up a tributary arm of the Ruth, toward the northeast—actually farther from McKinley than they had been in the Great Gorge. They picked out an insignificant dwarf of a mountain, its summit less than six thousand feet high, and climbed it. On the top Cook took a photo of Barrill holding an American flag. In February 1908 the photo was published in Cook's "official" account with the caption, "The Top of Our Continent."

Belmore Browne, as noted, suspected a hoax from the moment he heard about Cook's claim. Besides Barrill's ambiguous admission ("If you want to know about Mount McKinley go and ask Cook"), Browne had as evidence the impossibly short time Cook had been gone. As he wrote later, "I knew it in the same way that any New Yorker would know that no man could walk from the Brooklyn Bridge to Grant's Tomb in ten minutes." Upon returning to New York, Browne and Parker presented their evidence to the Explorers Club and the American Geographical Society. As good sportsmen, the pair felt that no formal accusations should be made before Cook committed the hoax to print. By the time To the Top of the Continent was published, however, the doctor had sailed secretly for the North.

The matter might well have blown over at this point. The ascent of McKinley, as Browne and Parker viewed it, was a "sporting proposition," and therefore "our claims against [Cook] were really more or less private and personal." But the North Pole seemed, in Browne's words, "a question of international importance," and so when Cook arrived in Annoatok, Greenland, in April 1909 claiming that he had reached the northernmost point on earth a year previously, he thrust himself instantly into the public eye.

It was the bitter polar controversy that attracted the attention of the world—as opposed to merely Alaskans and mountaineers—to the prior McKinley claim. Cook's return "scooped" Robert Peary by about four months, to the latter's chagrin and anger. In the first blush of news Cook seemed to win the day. Copenhagen received the doctor as a hero; President Taft wired congratulations; and the journalist W. T. Stead wrote, "Some believed in Dr. Cook at first; all believe in him now." Peary hurt his own image by becoming Cook's chief detractor, claiming that the two Eskimos who had traveled with Cook had told him, Peary, that the doctor had gone no distance north and never out of sight of land. Cook, on the other hand, treated Peary with magnanimity, accepting his polar claim as genuine—although posterior to his own by a year. In the fall of 1909 a poll conducted by the *Pittsburgh Press* found 73,238 voters who believed in Cook, only 2,814 in Peary.

It was the Peary Arctic Club, a group of rich backers of the older explorer, who, as much as anyone, revived the McKinley dispute. In October, amid conflicting rumors that he was coming to exonerate Cook or to sell out to Peary's cronies, Edward Barrill arrived in New York. On the 15th the front page of the *New York Times* announced the shocking story that Barrill had signed a sworn affidavit denying that he and Cook had ever been near the summit of McKinley. The Montana blacksmith's testimony indicated that the two men never got closer than fourteen miles away from McKinley and never climbed above eight thousand feet (in actuality, they never climbed above six thousand). Nor did they build any snowhouses. Barrill kept a diary, he said, whose entries were dictated by Cook. On September 12 the doctor ordered him to stop making entries and to leave the appropriate pages blank. That same day they made the easy stroll up "Fake Peak," and on the summit, according to Barrill, Cook said, "We will go back down and get a picture of this. . . . That point would make a good top for Mount McKinley." On September 16, a few days before rejoining the prospector Dokkin, Cook asked Barrill for the diary and proceeded to "doctor" the entries.

Why, then, had Barrill gone along with Cook's lies for three years? At first it was simply "a brag," Barrill confessed, and he figured that if he stuck to Cook's story he might get more money out of him. The implication was clear that Barrill never dreamed the truth of the matter would be of such universal interest.

The same issue of the *Times* carried corroborating testimony from Walter Miller, the 1906 expedition's photographer, and from Captain

Armstrong, another of its members. Armstrong revealed that during the expedition Browne had emerged as the real leader of the party because his talents were so superior to those of Cook, the nominal leader. "Browne was the sunshine of our party," Armstrong wrote, "and it was a positive joy to travel with him."

Doggedly Cook maintained his innocence. "I never even knew Barrill kept a diary," he reported. But the affidavit deeply undermined Cook's credibility, not only in the McKinley case but in the polar battle: it might well be regarded as the turning point in the gradual elevation of Peary to public acceptance as the true discoverer of the northernmost point on earth.

Cook did not go down meekly. His many friends in the Explorers Club and the American Geographical Society rallied to his support. Contempt was heaped on Barrill, and Browne later wrote:

> In looking back on that remarkable controversy I am still filled with astonishment at the incredible amount of vindictive and personal spite that was shown by the partisans of Doctor Cook. Men who had never seen an ice-axe or a sled-dog wrote us reams of warped exploring details and accused us of untold crimes because we had dared to question Cook's honesty.

A confrontation before a committee of the Explorers Club was arranged. Browne and Parker were called as witnesses. Cook was told that he was not to regard himself as a guilty man trying to prove his innocence, but rather, in Browne's words, "as an honest man who was being given a chance by his friends to clear himself from suspicion." Nevertheless, Cook refused to testify. "He said that his hardships in the long polar night had affected his memory and that he could not answer any questions without consulting his diary." He asked for two weeks' time—then disappeared.

Browne and Parker were planning another attempt on McKinley from the south for the summer of 1910. The thought inevitably occurred to them that if they could find the peak on which Cook had shot his fake summit photo, and shoot their own duplicate of it, they could settle the McKinley issue for good. This might have seemed a hopeless needle-in-a-haystack proposition. But Cook had made a bad slip: in the corner background of the "summit photo," behind Barrill standing with the flag, the crest of a distant mountain could be seen— a mountain which the two men thought they recognized as one of the sharp peaks on the western margin of the Great Gorge. The angle was all wrong for a photo shot from anywhere near McKinley (from which summit, in fact, the peak shown silhouetted against the sky in

Cook's photo would be dwarfed almost into invisibility). So confident of success were Browne and Parker that they felt they could actually locate "Fake Peak" before leaving New York.

On the 1910 expedition, the pair of sleuths carried copies of Cook's photos—not only the summit shot but photos from the Great Gorge which had been misleadingly captioned with titles like "Clouds and Cliffs, 13,000 feet." The party climbed up the Ruth Glacier, through the head of the Great Gorge into what is now called the Don Sheldon Amphitheater (after one of Alaska's greatest bush pilots). They made a strong push into the western edge of the basin, but were stopped cold by the precipitous slopes sweeping down from the South Buttress. McKinley would not be climbed by this approach for another forty-four years. But the expedition had succeeded brilliantly in its secondary aim—to copy exactly the photo Cook had passed off as showing the "top of the continent."

When Browne and Parker found Fake Peak they were surprised at how diminutive the mountain was—little more than a bump on a ridge protruding out of the glacier. They had thought that at least Cook had ascended a moderately high peak; but apparently "climbing with printer's ink was far easier." As they neared the top of the tiny mountain, Parker shouted out, "We've got it!" They could stand at approximately the place where Cook had photographed Barrill and compare the outlines, even individual rocks, with the details in the photo they held in their hands. The peak on the western edge of the Great Gorge stood on the right skyline, exactly as it did in Cook's photo. Every detail clicked, for, as Browne knew, "no man can lie topographically. In all the mountain ranges of the world there are not two hillocks exactly alike." The only significant difference was that in September 1906 Fake Peak had been covered with much less snow than was there in July 1910. But this seemed of scant importance to the men as Browne carefully photographed Herman Tucker, complete with flag, in the very spot where Barrill had stood.

During the following year Cook's star fell dramatically, in inverse proportion to the rise of Peary's. The "loss" of Cook's observational data from the Arctic hurt his case, as did the reported disclaimer of his Eskimo companions and, of course, Barrill's affidavit. The controversy grew nasty enough to prompt a Congressional investigation. There were good reasons to doubt Peary's claim as well as Cook's, particularly some suspiciously long distances covered during the last days of the dash to the Pole. But Peary had the powerful backing of his Arctic Club, which reportedly poured as much as $350,000 into a defense of their hero. Finally, on March 4, 1911, President Taft signed a bill crediting Peary with reaching the North

Pole; with the honor came a pension from the U.S. Navy for life. Cook, on the other hand, was kicked out of both the Explorers Club and the American Alpine Club.

Browne and Parker rightly thought that duplicating Cook's summit photo ought to settle the McKinley question for good, no matter what the resolution of the polar furor. But such was not to be the case. Cook began to attract a new kind of support, born mainly out of sympathy for the underdog. In 1913 a geographer accused Browne of *painting* the duplicate summit photo. Two "experts" published analyses of the McKinley controversy, each arguing that there were at least six significant differences between Cook's photo and Browne's. One of them, Edwin Balch, used a very strange kind of indirect reasoning to maintain that because a British mountaineer had published an unskeptical review of *To the Top of the Continent* in the *Alpine Journal,* therefore the ascent was "accepted unquestioningly" by experts in the field.

Partisans claimed that the Peary Arctic Club had paid Barrill to write a phony affidavit. In Hamilton, Montana—Barrill's stomping grounds—Cook actually debated his former companion in public. Eyewitness accounts called attention to the beads of sweat on Cook's brow, and recorded his lame efforts to defuse the air of confrontation. Barrill stuck doggedly to the facts of his affidavit, and added that Cook had sent him a letter from Labrador that said, "For God's sakes, keep still and when I come home I will bring you a chunk of the Pole." The evening ended, predictably enough, with a public resolution crediting Barrill's side of the debate.

The rest of Cook's life was a stoic exercise in enduring humiliation. He went on one further expedition, an anthropological trip to Borneo. He became first a Wyoming geologist, then an oil promoter near Fort Worth, Texas. In the latter state he created a Petroleum Producers' Association and sold its stock by mail. A government investigation declared that the lands his company owned were worthless, and in 1923 Cook was convicted of using the mails to defraud. He served five years in Leavenworth, on top of nearly two years in jail while he pursued a futile appeal. Characteristically, he was a model prisoner, reputed to be the most popular inmate in the penitentiary. He steadfastly maintained his innocence, and in fact during his confinement some of the "worthless" lands he had sold stock in were developed by their subsequent owners with immense profit. (John L. J. Hart, an expert mountaineer and a lawyer who was involved in some of the litigation surrounding Cook's land speculation, believes that the doctor acted essentially in good faith in these dealings.)

When he was paroled in 1930 Cook was sixty-four years old, a broken man. He spent the last ten years of his life in poverty, supported by his fanatically loyal daughter Helene. During the first five of those years he slowly penned *Return from the Pole,* his account of the twelve-month voyage during which, with his two Eskimo companions, he traveled, according to his reckoning, 4,000 miles, living off the land, wintering over, and circling Ellesmere Island after a comparatively easy initial jaunt to the Pole. (How Cook actually spent the year remains a matter of conjecture.) Published posthumously, *Return* has a gloomy serenity absent from his earlier books; even if the whole work is fantasy, it gives a greater insight into this "unimaginative" man than does anything else he wrote.

Cook died in 1940. On his deathbed he was pardoned by President Roosevelt. With his passing, one might have thought, the scandals of thirty years before would recede into history. Cook would be remembered as an explorer who pathetically tried to hoodwink the entire world. But the perseverance of the doctor's few staunch believers, spearheaded by his daughter, Helene Cook Vetter, kept the controversies about both the Pole and McKinley smoldering. Partisans seized on Balch's "significant differences" between Cook's and Browne's photos. Browne himself was subjected to an endless barrage over the years. His grandson Brock remembers today, "Aunt Evelyn (Browne's daughter) used to say, 'What we should have done was simply offer *anybody* $50,000 to climb McKinley by the route Cook claimed, with the gear he carried, in the time he said it took. That would have settled the whole thing.'"

Indeed, one expedition tried to do something like that. In 1956 a party headed by Walter Gonnason, financed in large part by Helene Vetter, attacked the east ridge of McKinley's East Buttress, identified as the one Cook "must" have climbed. The Gonnason party made a plane landing on the Ruth Glacier, obviating the exhausting approach march; they had modern lightweight gear and forty-five years of advances in climbing technique. Even so, in fourteen days they managed to reach only 11,400 feet, a good 9,000 feet below the summit, having been stopped cold by a knife-edged, doubly corniced ridge, the first highly technical obstacle on their very long and potentially difficult route. As Bradford Washburn points out, Gonnason was the single believer in Cook's McKinley claim over all the years who knew the first thing about mountain climbing.

In the mid-1950s Washburn decided to settle the McKinley dispute beyond a shadow of a doubt. The first man to climb the mountain three times, Washburn knew that Cook's description of the summit bore no resemblance to the real place: there was no "heaven-scraped granite" within a hundred vertical feet of the summit, no "protected nook" where Cook's metal canister might have been hidden. He knew that Cook could have described the general configuration of the upper ridges of McKinley (which had served as a major debating point for his partisans over the years) simply from two views he had had from the lowlands—one from the north in 1903, the other from the south, in the Great Gorge, in 1906. Above all, Washburn wanted to destroy the "significant differences" argument by making a perfect copy of what he called "probably the most controversial picture in the entire history of exploration." For the latter task he was admirably equipped. Over two decades Washburn had become not only the leading expert on McKinley, but the world's outstanding aerial mountain photographer.

In the summer of 1956 Don Sheldon flew Washburn's party onto the Ruth Glacier. Carrying copies of Cook's photos as Browne had forty-six years before, the party managed to locate the exact spots from which all but two of Cook's incriminating photos were taken (the remaining two "unidentified" photos are of close-up detail, the general quality of which is strongly suggestive of the Great Gorge). After duplicating these photos, none of which indicated penetration beyond the upper neck of the gorge, Washburn turned his attention to Fake Peak.

At the base of the tiny bump of the mountain, the party made some fascinating discoveries. Nile Albright came across the note Belmore Browne had left documenting his visit in 1910; it was still perfectly readable. Other members of the party found three one-pint fuel cans, apparently Cook's, a tent peg and a cotton sack, and an obsolete film carton later identified by Kodak as the kind Browne must have carried. It was little trouble to scramble up Fake Peak. On the summit Washburn once again duplicated Cook's photo of Barrill. With camera gear vastly superior to Browne's, Washburn could isolate features in the mountain's configuration as small as a man's fist. Although the rock surface of the peak had crumbled badly over the fifty years since Cook's visit, almost every detail still corresponded—this crack snaking from upper left to lower right, that boulder with the knob protruding in the middle. The evidence was unmistakable. Yet somehow the angle of Cook's photo was slightly different from what the men were now seeing. Washburn gradually realized that the snowbank on which both Cook and Browne had stood had simply disappeared—melted away or sloughed off the ridge. The point where Cook had stood in 1906 was now about forty feet up, in midair!

Washburn's photos were conclusive; but an old climbing friend of his, Adams Carter, decided to return in 1957 to cement the case absolutely. Carter's party arrived with a number of pieces of aluminum pipe which could be assembled into a long pole. Guying the pole firmly to the rocks, the team made it stable enough for a man to climb. On top of the pole Carter took photos from a spot that was within ten feet of the point where Cook had stood in 1906.

The photo evidence, together with a detailed critique by Washburn, were featured in the 1958 *American Alpine Journal*, the annual publication of the club of which Cook had been a charter member. Mountaineers the world over perused the exhaustive research and documentation Washburn and Carter had assembled. And they told themselves that here, for once, a hoax had been completely and irrefutably exposed.

Astonishingly, the believers in Cook did not give up. Helene Vetter plugged away undaunted with her campaign of vindication. Two biographies of Cook appeared, in 1961 and 1973, exonerating the doctor of deceit. Hugh Eames, the author of the most recent (called *Winner Lose All*), is not so mad as to argue that there are still significant differences between Washburn's photos and Cook's. He concedes that Cook faked the summit picture. By thus "cutting a corner" Cook hoped to make up for the absence of summit photos that was, Eames would have us believe, owing only to the difficulty of getting cameras to work at high altitude in extreme cold. The "proof" that Cook made the summit is based on ridiculously vague similarities between Cook's prose and that of later McKinley climbers. Cook had written, for instance, that on the summit "We felt like shouting, but had not the breath to spare." Grant Pearson, of his 1932 visit to the top: "It was much too cold to yell." And so forth. One need not be a mountaineer to see through the specious logic of Eames's claims. Yet it is perhaps a sign of American credulity that *Winner Lose All* was reviewed in popular periodicals and newspapers with considerable acceptance.

To Washburn, the continuing will to believe in Cook's martyrdom is a source of indignation and disgust. As he wrote in the *American Alpine Journal*, "Americans seem to rally nobly around an underdog at bay, and nobody ever likes to face the facts of a gigantic lie or hoax." Yet, as Watergate proved, the American people can seize gleefully upon an exposed faker, and can indulge in his public humiliation—as they did in 1911, when Cook fell from the status of conqueror of the Pole to that of a sideshow charlatan. There is something about the man's consistency over all the years, the fact that he never broke down and confessed, that may begin to account for the lingering belief in him as a victimized hero. He was a brave man; there is no denying that. In the preface to *Return from the Pole*,

Frederick Pohl, one of Cook's champions, compares his fate to that of an Italian sailor four centuries before:

> His tragedy paralleled that of Columbus. He was rejected, despised, imprisoned, and neglected. Columbus turned to divine support; Dr. Cook relied upon the innate sense of justice in men.

Eames concludes that "he stands, in the history of the American democracy, as its most uniquely grand and somehow royal person, its Prince of Losers."

As baffling as the persistence of faith in Dr. Cook's honesty is the enigma of the man himself. Why, at forty-one, with an enviable exploring record behind him, did he decide to fake the climb, and having decided to do so, why did he so inadequately guard himself against the inevitable suspicions of his former colleagues? Robert Dunn, years later, imagined Cook lying impulsively.

> "Did you make it?" a sourdough might have asked him at timberline, and Doc would have said, "Sure." After that, the lie about the Pole would be easy. He might not know how far north he did get. No man could spot the Pole except with instruments, and taking right observations always seemed beyond the Doc.

But there are strong hints in Cook's personality of deliberate premeditation about things. There is the telegram Browne insists Cook sent to the New York businessman. Was he planning the hoax even then, on board a ship in Cook Inlet? By 1906 the doctor was already obsessed with the North Pole. More than one observer has suggested that he faked McKinley because he thought it would bring him the fame and money necessary to support an Arctic expedition.

The fame he got. And in a single stroke—or rather two—he ruined his life, turning it into an obsessive struggle against his detractors. As noted, Cook had a predilection for seeing the world in terms of an elemental struggle between life and death. There is something in the life of more than one exploration hoaxer that yearns for the simplistic and the dramatic. The choice to fake a glorious achievement, especially when one cannot help foreseeing the controversy that will ensue, may spring from a reductionist hunger to align the world in two warring camps—enemies and loyal friends—with the Self as focus. In Cook, as in other hoaxers, there were touches, discernible in 1903, if Dunn can be believed, of both megalomania and paranoia. So the man's dogged persistence in trying to clear his name makes perfect sense: it was the enactment of a desperate need to cling to the Self, surrounded as it was by smirking mockers who (one always knew) were there from the beginning.

Let the last word be Dunn's.

One night I walked into the Waldorf's old square bar, deserted but for one man alone at a table, sipping champagne. I went over; Doc beamed placidly.

"Hey, Doc. Put it all over on the world, didn't you?" I greeted him.

An hour we must have talked, his stream of words repeating his published story. Whether or not he believed what he said, I couldn't tell, but his justification of his claims grew pathetic. I never saw him again.

BIBLIOGRAPHY

Balch, Edwin Swift. *Mount McKinley and Climbers' Proofs*. Philadelphia, 1914.

"Barrill Says Cook Never on M'Kinley's Top," *New York Times*, October 15, 1909.

Browne, Belmore. *The Conquest of Mount McKinley*. New York, 1913.

Cook, Frederick A. *Return from the Pole*. New York, 1952.

———. *My Attainment of the Pole*. New York, 1911.

———. *To the Top of the Continent*. New York, 1908.

Dunn, Robert. *The Shameless Diary of an Explorer*. New York, 1907.

———. *World Alive: A Personal Story*. New York, 1956.

Eames, Hugh. *Winner Lose All: Dr. Cook and the Theft of the North Pole*. Boston, 1973.

Freeman, Andrew A. *The Case for Doctor Cook*. New York, 1961.

"McKinley Guide Comes to See Cook," *New York Times*, October 14, 1909.

Rawlins, Dennis. *Peary at the North Pole: Fact or Fiction?* Washington, 1973.

Rost, Ernest C. *Mount McKinley, Its Bearing on the Polar Controversy*. Washington, 1914.

Rusk, Claude E. "On the Trail of Dr. Cook," in Howard Palmer, *Pamphlets on Mountaineering*, vol. 3, no. 39, American Alpine Club, New York.

Stead, W. T. "Dr. Cook: The Man and the Deed," *Review of Reviews*, vol. 40 (October 1909).

Stuck, Hudson. *The Ascent of Denali (Mount McKinley)*. New York, 1914.

Thorington, J. Monroe. "Frederick Albert Cook," in "American Alpine Club Annals." *American Alpine Journal*, vol. 6 (1946).

Washburn, Bradford. "Doctor Cook and Mount McKinley," with assistance from Adams and Ann Carter, *American Alpine Journal*, vol. 11, no. 1 (1958).

———. "Special Report to the American Alpine Club with regard to the claim that Dr. Frederick A. Cook and Edward Barrille made the first ascent of Mount McKinley in September 1906," unpublished typescript in American Alpine Club library, New York (January 1958).

7

DID PEARY REACH
THE NORTH POLE?

In 1908 the most coveted prizes in terrestrial exploration were the Poles. Antarctica had seen the dramatic rivalry of Scott and Shackleton and was to witness three years later Amundsen's clockwork success and the desperate retreat and deaths of Scott's polar party, an ordeal that still forms a canonic lesson in heroism and self-sacrifice for British schoolboys. There had been schemes for sailing to the North Pole as early as the Renaissance, but it was only after 1870 that explorers pursued the quest in earnest.

Seduced by the *a priori* idea of an "open polar sea," the first adventurers tried to push to the Pole by steamship from Spitsbergen, Greenland, and Siberia. They met, of course, unrelenting and apparently permanent ice. The 1890s gave birth to two extraordinarily innovative attempts to reach the Pole. Between 1879 and 1881 the ill-fated De Long expedition's ship *Jeannette* had drifted, frozen inextricably in the ice, from near the Bering Strait to the New Siberian Islands. The crew abandoned her and reached the delta of the Lena River, but most of them died of starvation.

Three years later relics from the *Jeanette* were discovered on the southwest coast of Greenland. Thus was the existence of the remarkable drift of the polar ice pack discovered. A plucky Norwegian named Fridtjof Nansen decided to use this discovery to "hitchhike" toward the Pole. He had his ship, the *Fram*, designed specially to resist the ice by means of a hull shape that would cause it to be squeezed up on top of the floes rather than crushed between them. In 1893 he traversed the Northeast Passage to the New Siberian Islands, headed north, and deliberately let the *Fram* get frozen in. For a year and a half the ship drifted slowly northwest with the pack. When it began to trend southward again, Nansen and one companion set off on skis, with twenty-eight dogs, three sledges, and two kayaks for crossing open leads. They had no hope of rejoining the *Fram*, but planned to reach the Pole and make their way back to civilization unaided.

This brilliant and nervy scheme was defeated by the unexpected southerly drift of the ice the two men were walking on. They were, in effect, traveling in the wrong direction on a treadmill. They did reach 86°13′6″ N, the closest to the Pole any human beings had ever been. Their eventful return journey included a successful wintering over on Franz Josef Land, where one day in 1896 they were accidentally found by an English expedition, whose ship took the two explorers home. The *Fram*, under the able captainship of Otto Sverdrup, escaped the ice in the same spring and steamed home under its own power. Not a single life had been lost.

The next year a Swede named Salomon Andrée set in motion an equally bold scheme—to balloon to the North Pole. From Spitsbergen, with two companions, on July 11, 1897, Andrée lifted off in the *Eagle*. His plan was to fly all the way across the Arctic Ocean to Alaska. A single homing pigeon launched from the balloon was captured on a Norwegian sealer. The three aviators disappeared.

Thirty-three years later, purely by chance, a scientific expedition came upon the trio's last camp on White Island. They found the remains of two of the men, the grave of the third, and numerous pieces of gear, notebooks, and diaries, all so well preserved that it was possible to reconstruct the fate of the *Eagle* in considerable detail. Film in the cameras had been kept so well by the cold that it was successfully developed after a third of a century!

The *Eagle* had lasted only three days in the air. What had caused it to come down was no miscalculation on Andrée's part, but the accumulation of ice on the top surface of the balloon. The three men had inadvertently discovered that future bane of fixed-wing planes, icing. Undaunted, the trio had set out southward over the ice and had reached White Island. Their diaries indicated that they were surviving well, with no shortage of game—but the entries stopped abruptly twelve days after the arrival on the island. Even today the cause of the three men's deaths remains a mystery. A leading theory hypothesizes that they were poisoned by an overdose of vitamin D from eating polar bear liver.

It was becoming evident that the key to reaching the North Pole would have to involve dogsledging. The single man most responsible for adapting sledging to the polar effort, as well as the one who seemed most obsessed by that goal, was Robert E. Peary, who devoted twenty-four years of his life to reaching the northernmost point on earth.

In 1885, when he was twenty-nine, having been absorbed for years in the writings of Arctic explorers, Peary wrote himself a memorandum calling for "an entire change in the expeditionary organization of Arctic research parties." The next year he made his first trip to Greenland. Six subsequent expeditions between 1891 and 1906 took Peary north, as he probed the topography for the best route to the Pole and perfected his sledging technique. On the last expedition he reached 87°6' to establish a new farthest north. By 1908 Peary was confident that he knew how to attain the Pole. His logistical attack depended on the coordination of several details, each of which gave him the maximum advantages: the establishment of a winter base at Cape Sheridan, on the north coast of Ellesmere Island, close to the northernmost land in the Western hemisphere; the use of Eskimo dogs and Eskimo drivers; and a pyramidal support system by which early parties would carry supplies successively farther north and retreat from predetermined latitudes, leaving the supplies to boost the final party safely to the Pole and back. It was analogous to the kind of pyramidal logistic effort that Scott was to utilize in reaching the South Pole, as well as that employed forty years later when the British at last climbed Everest.

The years of perfecting a system had taken their toll on Peary, however. He had lost all but two of his toes to frostbite in 1899, the amputations being performed in the field. By 1908 he was fifty-two years old, not nearly as strong as he had been when he first went to Greenland. The years of obsessive preoccupation had turned him, by some accounts, into a fanatically driven man who all too easily antagonized the very men on whose cooperation his success depended.

Peary's early years had given little evidence of the far-flung ambitions that flowered in his maturity; but there were hints. It is an eerie coincidence that, like his future polar adversary, Frederick Cook, Peary lost his father to pneumonia when very young (Peary at two, Cook at five); and like Cook, Peary suffered from a lisp which he struggled in adulthood to banish. As a child "Bertie," as his mother called him, got into frequent fights with other boys who called him a sissy. Besides the lisp, he was to suffer all his life from the sense that he was a "poor relation," inferior by breeding to the socially graceful whose acceptance he longed for. Compensation for what he perceived as innate faults may have been the seminal cause for his driving ambition.

But Bertie's biggest problem was his mother. After his father's death she never considered remarriage, but turned her smothering attention to her only child. She brought the young lad up in some ways as if he were a girl, and seems to have projected her own hypochondriacal character onto her son. Relocating in her native Maine, she at first sent Peary away to a series of boarding schools, but was dissatisfied with each and pulled him out. When Robert went to high school in Portland, his mother lived with him in a two-story house in town. When the boy went off to Bowdoin, she insisted on moving to Brunswick—"I am going to college," she announced to dismayed relatives. Throughout his years at Bowdoin, Robert lived with his mother. Upon graduation, the pair moved to Fryeburg, where Robert hoped in vain for a modest career as a civil engineer. Only at the age of twenty-three, with a job in Washington, did he escape his mother's household.

Throughout Peary's adolescence he was tortured by her ailments and illnesses, which conjured up the intolerable prospect of losing her. John Edward Weems quotes a diary entry from the sixteen-year-old Peary.

> About nine o'clock as mother got up to go to bed she suddenly became very weak and cold on her left side so she could not walk. It scared me very much, but she laid on my bed and I chafed her hands and feet till she recovered and I then got the pistol in case of emergency.

The temptation to psychoanalyze Peary is hard to resist. Certainly the Oedipal confusion that he experienced must have been massive. According to a family tradition obviously innocent of its Freudian reverberations, Peary's most vivid memory from his first two years was of watching railroad trains disappear into a tunnel and being terrified they would not reemerge. For the student of his exploration, however, it suffices to wonder how Bertie ever did escape becoming a lifelong mama's boy, how he dared to leave home and get married, let alone run off to the Arctic year after year. In a direct sense his expeditions can be seen as a dogged and continuous effort to sever his mother's apron strings.

At Bowdoin, Peary was, understandably, a loner. He became a good athlete, although he preferred individual to team sports, and an assiduous solitary walker. An influential professor bent his interests toward civil engineering. But when he set up to do business in Fryeburg he had to resort to taxidermy to eke out a living. It was in the local post office that he noticed one day in 1878 a poster advertising drafting work with the Coast and Geodetic Survey in Washington.

Peary's biographer Weems does not record his mother's reaction to the desertion at twenty-three—only that, once ensconced in his job, he often brought her to the capital to visit. Peary's love of nature produced in the deskbound civil servant an increasing wanderlust. His first chance to gratify it came at the age of twenty-four, when the Survey proposed an expedition to study the proposed canal in Central America. He wrote his mother, asking permission. For two weeks she failed to write, and then when she did, she ignored his question. He pressed her again, and at last the answer came: no. Dutifully the son obeyed his mother's wishes, immersing himself instead in reveries about Cortez and Balboa.

In 1881 he changed jobs, gaining a civil engineering post in the Navy. By managing to get himself "ordered" to participate in a Nicaraguan canal survey three years later, Peary finally, at age twenty-eight, still against his mother's wishes, got to go on an expedition. The Nicaraguan venture was followed in 1886 by a private jaunt to Greenland. For years Peary had been reading Arctic literature, and now, with the headstrong conviction that European explorers had not developed the proper system for travel in the north, he stormed off on the first of his six Arctic adventures. His mother stoutly opposed this trip too, but, curiously, lent him five hundred dollars for it.

At a dancing place in Washington, Peary in 1882 had met the charming and energetic Josephine Diebitsch, the daughter of a Smithsonian scholar. They courted for years, then married in 1888. On their honeymoon in a hotel in Seabright, New Jersey, they were accompanied by Peary's mother. Josephine joined him on two of his major expeditions, and when she gave birth to a daughter in Greenland in 1893, Peary proudly claimed that never in history had a white child been born in so northerly a latitude. The "Snow Baby," as she was nicknamed by the Eskimos, became part of the Peary legend.

All this time, in her self-pitying, guilt-laying letters, Peary's mother continued to oppose her wayward son's Arctic follies, even as he continued to seek her approval. An example, quoted by Weems:

> From my childhood, I was not strong, less so since your birth. In my weakness and loneliness I have tried hard and earnestly to do what I thought was best for you. . . . Now I cannot have your unhappiness laid at my door. Leave me entirely out of the question and do what you think will give you sunshine and happiness. The sudden though not unexpected announcement of your intentions wrung from me a cry of pain—It shall not happen again. All the clothes that you brought home I have put in as

good order as my strength and ability would admit. You have only to say what else I can do to assist your preparations. If I have caused you the loss of a night's sleep you will forgive

Mother.

This meddlesome woman enlisted Peary's wife and child as fellow sufferers, writing him in the midst of one expedition: "I can imagine how much you suffered before you decided to stay another year in that dreary place. I would have borne it for you if I could. I have a mental photograph of you as you turned your face northward away from Jo and baby." Even on her deathbed she managed to transmit her messages of guilt, conveying to the explorer through his cousin that his mother had lost the will to live because he was in the Arctic. Peary's diary entries after her death reveal the extraordinary depth of his grief.

Peary was, it seems, devoted to Josephine. But his loyalty did not keep him from taking a fourteen-year-old Eskimo named Allakasing-wah as a mistress, by whom he had at least one child. Greenland gossip suggests that "Ally" was not Peary's only dalliance. With the naïveté of the obsessive character he was becoming, he decorated one of his books with nude photos of Ally, aimed not at prurient minds but "to show physique and muscular development." In 1900, arriving unexpectedly by boat in northern Greenland to support her husband, Josephine ran into Ally, who ingenuously bragged of her relationship with the great explorer. Jo was deeply shocked, and contemplated a year's separation, but in the long run rallied to her husband's defense. "Life is slipping away so fast"—she wrote him shortly after learning about his affair—"pretty soon all will be over."

Over the years Peary's singleminded passion to get to the Pole, far from waning, continued to intensify. His drive can be deduced from the fact that within a month of suffering the amputation of his toes, he was out sledging again, although forced to ride at first or to walk with crutches.

From one expedition to the next Peary modified and perfected his system. One estimate suggests that in his lifetime the man sledged a total of thirteen thousand miles. But the Pole continued to elude him, as what he regarded as bad luck intervened again and again to frustrate his well-laid plans.

As skillful an explorer as he had become, Peary's strongest suit was his knack for drumming up institutional support. The frequent extended leaves from the Navy might have made a joke of his professional career, but by building up a network of influential backers he had made an alternative Arctic career for himself far beyond the dreams of the once-unemployed civil engineer.

By 1908, besides the strong support of the American Geographical Society, the American Museum of Natural History, and the National Geographic Society, Peary could rely on the "Peary Arctic Club" to provide a financial base, generate publicity, and lend an air of graybeard expertise to his upcoming eighth expedition. His well-chosen team included men who would become familiar names in Arctic exploration: George Borup and Donald MacMillan, for both of whom this was the first expedition; Matthew Henson; and Captain Bob Bartlett.

By this point in his life, Peary had begun to think of the region between northern Greenland and Ellesmere Island as his real estate. The route to the Pole was "his" route; even the inhabitants were "his" Eskimos. It was with considerable vexation, then, that in the middle of his preparations in 1907 he heard that Frederick Cook, who had been Peary's surgeon on the 1891–92 expedition, was planning an Arctic trip of his own. The vexation increased when Peary's party arrived at Etah, Greenland, to learn that Cook had been there and had left with two Eskimos on a sledging voyage, reportedly to try to reach the Pole. But no one in Peary's party was worried that Cook had a chance of succeeding: it was demonstrably impossible to travel such distances so light. Peary's wrath had much to do with the fear that Cook might have employed some of "his" native dogs, but was perhaps really grounded in the irrational proprietary obsession he now felt for the Smith Sound route to the Pole.

Peary was fairly confident that his eighth expedition was going to succeed. But he also knew that it was destined to be his last try: age, weariness, and the condition of his feet, which continued to be achingly sensitive to the cold, dictated as much.

The key man in his party was the Newfoundlander Bartlett, a brilliant and good-natured sledger who had proved his stuff on the 1905–6 expedition. Peary's plan put each of his principals in charge of a team of men and dogs with prearranged turnaround duties in support of his own polar party. Bartlett was to leave land first and break trail all the way to the last retreating point. There seems, however, to have been some confusion as to whether Bartlett would go on to the Pole himself.

Almost as important was Henson, Peary's oldest accomplice, a former manservant whom Peary had met in Washington and invited to Nicaragua. Henson, as that ultimate rarity, a Negro in the Arctic, has since been championed as a forgotten hero of exploration. It is interesting to look at Peary's view of the man, because he was to become the only non-Eskimo chosen to accompany the leader to the Pole itself. In *The North Pole*, a book which, curiously, Peary had ghostwritten for him, but which consistently reflects his views, he indicated about Henson: "While faithful to me, and when *with me* more effective in covering distance with a sledge than any others, he had not, as a racial inheritance, the daring and initiative of Bartlett, or . . . MacMillan, or Borup."

Because of their "racial inheritance of ice technic," the Eskimos were regarded by Peary as more necessary in his final dash than any white men—but only in a subservient role. "Of course they could not lead, but they could follow and drive dogs better than any white man." What Peary never acknowledges is that his mind may have been influenced from the start by the knowledge that neither the Eskimos nor Henson knew how to take observations of latitude and longitude. And Bob Bartlett did.

On July 6, 1908, the *Roosevelt* steamed down the East River out of New York, shortly after the President himself had come on board and eagerly approved all the paraphernalia. The ship made an uneventful trip up through Smith Sound and delivered the men at Cape Sheridan on Ellesmere Island, where they spent the winter. The following spring, on February 28, Bartlett led the first party north across the ice from Cape Columbia, the island's northernmost point of land. Other contingents, with varying orders—some were to take out loads, drop them, and return for more supplies—set off within hours or days. In all, the expedition comprised 24 men, 19 sledges, and 133 dogs.

On March 14 the first return party turned around at about 84°30′ N. MacMillan retreated the next day from a little farther north. The progress of most of the parties was smooth enough, but there were damnable open leads before which the men had to pause until enough "young ice" formed to support the sledges. The worst lead delayed Peary and Bartlett for more than a week, to the commander's infinite agitation. Borup returned on March 30, to be followed by Ross Marvin, a Cornell professor who was to die under mysterious circumstances on the way back. Before he headed for land on March 26, Marvin took a latitude observation and got 86°38′ N.

Now only Bartlett's and Peary's parties were still pushing north. The effort was beginning to show. Daily marches averaged between 10 and 17 miles, but some days saw dishearteningly meager progress. On April 1 Bartlett took an observation of 87°46′49″ N—a new farthest north, only 133 miles from the Pole. But the day before he had been told by his leader that he would have to return.

Bartlett's autobiography records a sanguine and magnanimous acceptance of the decision—while indicating that it came completely

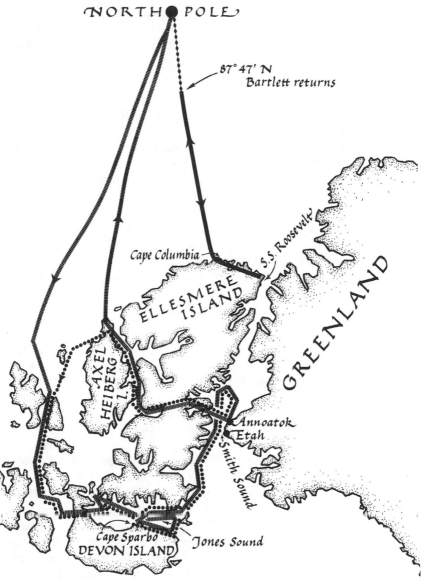

NORTH●POLE

87° 47' N
Bartlett returns

Cape Columbia

S.S. Roosevelt

ELLESMERE
ISLAND

GREENLAND

AXEL
HEIBERG
I.

Annoatok
Etah

Smith Sound

Cape Sparbo
DEVON ISLAND   Jones Sound

➤ Robert Peary's verified sledging route toward the North Pole in 1909.

•••••• Peary's unverified—and probably spurious—completion of the polar journey.

➤ The route by which Frederick Cook claimed he reached the Pole before Peary, in 1908.

•••••• Cook's probable route during the year he was absent from civilization.

out of the blue. "Don't forget that Henson was a better dog driver than I. So I think Peary's reasoning was sound; and I have never held it against him." But a 1909 interview in the *New York Herald,* when Bartlett was fresh from the Arctic, reveals him "arguing, begging, almost quarrelling" with Peary to be allowed to go on.

> It was a bitter disappointment. I got up early the next morning while the rest were asleep and started north alone. I don't know, perhaps I cried a little. I guess perhaps I was just a little crazy then. I thought that perhaps I could walk on the rest of the way alone. It seemed so near. . . .
> I felt so strong I went along for five miles or so, and then I came to my senses and knew I must go back.
> They were up at camp and getting ready to start. Never mind whether there were any words or not. . . . [Peary] said I must go; so I had to do it. But my mind had been set on it for so long I had rather die than give it up then. When I started on the back trail I couldn't believe it was really true at first, and I kind of went on in a daze.

"Peary's reasoning" has ever since puzzled students of the polar controversy. In *The North Pole* he suggests that besides the factor of Henson's superior sledging when with his commander, Peary was influenced by the reflection that "had I taken another member of the expedition also, he would have been a passenger, necessitating the carrying of extra rations and other impediments. It would have amounted to an additional load on the sledges, while the taking of Henson was in the interest of economy of weight." This is murky thinking at best. Furthermore, Peary never indicates why the order to return came as such a shock to Bartlett. On other expeditions— notably Scott's to the South Pole and the British on Everest in 1953— the leader deferred deciding who would make up the "summit" party until the last moment, basing the decision on the relative performances of the men up to that point. But the men themselves understood and accepted this procedure. And if performance was the criterion for Peary, no one deserved to go to the Pole more than Bartlett.

The progress of the expedition, then, to 87°46′ N we have on the concurring testimony of Peary and Bartlett. There are some critics who feel that even Bartlett's last observation cannot be automatically swallowed. But the essential mystery of Peary's accomplishment in 1909 begins with Bartlett's turning south on April 1. The leader's last words to his departing lieutenant were, according to Bartlett, "Goodbye, Captain. . . . If we get there it will be the South Pole next and you as leader."

Bartlett had a close call on the way back when he fell through young ice and nearly drowned: his Eskimos saved him and restored him to health. On April 18 he reached Cape Columbia once again, and six days later was back aboard the *Roosevelt*. On his return he learned of the death of Marvin, apparently by drowning. (Years later Knud Rasmussen was to win from the Eskimos involved a confession that one of them had shot Marvin in a quarrel. Though it has no direct bearing on the polar controversy, Marvin's murder may reflect the intense psychological pressure all the returning parties felt.)

Peary himself, with Henson and the four Eskimos with whom he had continued north, regained the *Roosevelt* on April 26, only two days behind Bartlett. The latter recorded the reunion thus:

> I ran out on the ice to meet him. He looked haggard but not weak. IIe grasped my outstretched hand while I exclaimed: "*I congratulate you, sir, on the discovery of the Pole!*" "How did you guess it?" he asked, laughing at my excitement.

Peary's story of his triumph, as later told in *The North Pole*, was a straightforward one, on the surface. The day after Bartlett departed, April 2, the polar party headed north. At once they made better distances than they had been able to cover at any time so far. Peary wanted to guess thirty miles for the first day's sledging, but contented himself with a conservative twenty-five. He was able to keep up that average for the next four days as well, despite numerous small leads and pressure ridges.

> Many laymen have wondered why we were able to travel faster after the sending back of each of the supporting parties, especially the last one. To any man experienced in the handling of troops this will need no explanation. The larger the party and the greater the number of sledges, the greater is the chance of breakages or delay for one reason or another. A large party cannot be forced as rapidly as a small party.

On April 6 Peary took a latitude reading of 89°57'. He was virtually on top of the Pole. To make sure, he set up camp, then made a short march until a second reading showed that he had passed beyond the Pole. He returned and set out on a zigzagging series of short marches to make sure he had got within a small margin of error of the Pole, and took thirteen separate sun altitudes over the thirty hours he lingered there. He wrote in his diary: "The Pole at last. The prize of three centuries. My dream and goal for twenty years. Mine at last! I cannot bring myself to realize it. It seems all so simple and commonplace."

Ceremonies at the Pole included the planting of five flags, one of which Josephine had given him fifteen years before and which he had carried wrapped around his body on every Arctic trip since. Another was the colors of Delta Kappa Epsilon, Peary's Bowdoin fraternity. Henson was ordered to lead "three rousing cheers," and the Eskimos "were childishly delighted with our success." Peary deposited records in a glass bottle commemorating "the last of the great adventure stories—a story the world had been waiting to hear for nearly four hundred years."

At 4:00 P.M. on April 7 they headed south. A little more than forty-eight hours later they were back at the 87°47' camp, from which Bartlett had retreated. Peary had ordered double marches for fear of the coming spring tides, and all the way back to land the party covered, on the average, what had been five outward marches in three homeward ones. On April 23 they reached Cape Columbia; three days later they were on board the *Roosevelt*.

When the ice permitted they began their nautical voyage homeward. On August 8, Peary learned from natives that Cook had returned the previous spring with his two Eskimos, no sledges, and no dogs. Later, at the Greenland settlement of Etah, the party discovered that Cook was claiming he had reached the North Pole. In a fury Peary ordered his assistants to question the two Eskimos who had accompanied Cook. In Borup's recorded interview the Eskimos testified that Cook had never gone out of sight of land. Instead of heading toward the Pole, the trio had circled along the north shore of Ellesmere Island, rounded Axel Heiberg Island and headed south, cut north of Devon Island, wintered at Cape Sparbo, and returned via the southeastern shores of Ellesmere Island and Smith Sound to Annoatok, a little north of Etah. If so, it was an extraordinary journey in its own right—but nothing remotely connected with an attempt on the Pole.

Peary reached Indian Harbor in Labrador on September 6, 1909, and immediately wired the news of his success to the States. To his deep chagrin, Cook had scooped him by five days, announcing the attainment of the Pole from Lerwick in the Shetland Islands, where he had stopped en route to Copenhagen.

Thus began the great polar controversy. In its first stages Cook won all honors. He was given a tumultuous welcome in Copenhagen. Peary seemed to damage his case by viciously attacking Cook's claim, while Cook magnanimously offered Peary congratulations for also reaching the Pole. As mentioned in the previous chapter, an early

The only known portrait of Sebastian Cabot. (*New York Public Library*)

James Bruce at the age of thirty-two. From a painting by Pompeo Batoni in the Scottish National Portrait Gallery. *(New York Public Library)*

Mount McKinley from the southeast. Frederick Cook's "Fake Peak" is indicated by the arrow. The Ruth Glacier, by which Cook claimed to have reached McKinley's inner defenses, is the major glacier ascending from the lower left corner to the center of the picture. (*Boston Museum of Science photo by Bradford Washburn*)

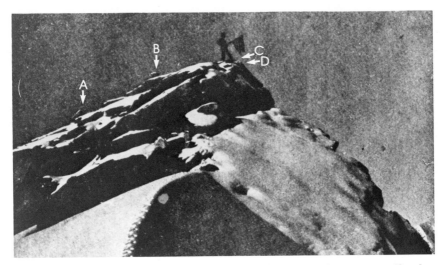

Frederick Cook's infamous Mount McKinley "summit photo," actually shot on top of an insignificant lump of rock and snow some twenty miles southeast of McKinley and 15,000 feet lower. Cook's sole companion, Montana horse-packer Edward Barrill, held the American flag in the posed photo, but later swore an affidavit to the effect that he and Cook had got nowhere near the summit of McKinley.

In 1957 H. Adams Carter led an expedition that duplicated the scene in Cook's summit photo, proving it had been shot on the insignificant "Fake Peak." Although snow cover had changed drastically over the years, by erecting and climbing an aluminum pole Carter was able to get within a few feet of where Cook had stood in 1906 to shoot Barrill. Features labeled A, B, C and D are unmistakably identical in both photos. *(Photo by H. Adams Carter)*

Dr. Frederick Cook in 1907, just before he disappeared into the Arctic, from which he would emerge to claim he had beaten Robert E. Peary to the North Pole. The year before this photo was taken, Cook had faked the first ascent of Mt. McKinley, but he had not yet been publicly discredited. *(Harvard University Library)*

One of the fuzzy snapshots Robert Peary took to document his alleged arrival at the North Pole. *(New York Public Library)*

Robert Peary's Eskimo mistress Allakasingwah, who was fourteen when she began her affair with the explorer. She later bore him at least one child. Peary ingenuously sprinkled the pages of *Northward over the Great Ice* with nude photos of Ally and other Eskimos, passing most of them off as ethnographic studies. *(New York Public Library)*

Robert E. Peary after his seventh Arctic expedition (1905-06), the strain of his life's quest evident in his face. By the time he set off on his last attempt at the North Pole in 1908, he was 52 years old and had lost all but two of his toes to frostbite. *(Harvard University Library)*

Never one to shun the limelight, Richard E. Byrd poses in full regalia for a publicity photo for Paramount Pictures' "With Byrd at the South Pole." It was his faked flight over the North Pole in 1926 that had first won Byrd his fame. *(Paramount Pictures)*

Facing page: Cerro Torre, in Patagonia—"the hardest mountain in the world." The route by which Cesare Maestri claimed he and Toni Egger climbed the mountain in 1959 is the right profile, ascending from the gun-sight notch Maestri called the "Col of Conquest." The facing ridge of the mountain is the route of Maestri's 1970 attempt, on which he used a gas-oline-powered bolt gun. *(Olaf Soot)*

Cesare Maestri, photographed during the *Mountain* interview. (Ken Wilson)

Donald Crowhurst in the months before his attempt to win the *Times* of London solo around-the-world sailing race. (*Peter Dunne, The Sunday Times*)

One of the last photos of Donald Crowhurst aboard the *Teignmouth Electron* (shot by Crowhurst with a timing device). *(BBC Copyright)*

poll of readers conducted by a Pittsburgh newspaper produced 73,238 supporters of Cook, only 2,814 supporters of Peary.

Cook's case began to crumble only when he was asked to produce the records of his observations. He delayed, maintaining that his instruments were still in Greenland. When he finally offered Copenhagen authorities only typewritten transcriptions of alleged field notebooks, the examiners rejected his claim. But Peary, too, was refusing to produce records, on the ostensible grounds that he was afraid Cook might steal his observations.

The exceptionally bitter and prolonged battle between partisans of Cook and Peary is too complex and, frankly, too tedious to summarize comprehensively here. Suffice it to say, in dealing with Cook's ultimately preposterous claim, that, despite modern "true believers," there is not even a shadow of a chance that he reached the Pole. The case against his claim rests on the probability that he did not know how to navigate out of sight of land; on the Eskimo testimony recorded by Borup; on the vagueness of Cook's own account; on the demonstrated hoax on Mount McKinley two years before; and on the logistical impossibility of reaching the Pole over four hundred miles of difficult ice, barren of game, without any help from supporting parties.

In the subsequent furor, as Cook began to be discredited, Peary was aided by a subconscious superstition on the part of the public; in such a dispute, it seemed to feel, one man had to be the charlatan, the other the honest man. If that assumption didn't hold, it was easier for most observers to entertain the possibility that both Cook and Peary had reached the Pole than to contemplate the idea that both had pretended to.

Eventually Peary submitted his records to a "subcommittee on research" appointed by the National Geographic Society. This three-man group made a rather casual investigation and certified Peary's achievement. The result was perhaps not unexpected, in view of the fact that the society was one of Peary's chief sponsors, and each of the three men was a personal friend of the explorer. Peary also hired two men from the Coast and Geodetic Survey to go over his data. They concluded that the commander had "probably passed within one and six-tenths geographic miles of the North Pole."

Encouraged by these pats on the back, in 1911 Peary supporters (and, *sub rosa*, Peary himself) lobbied to get through the House of Representatives a bill that would officially credit him with the Pole and retire him from the Navy as a rear admiral. The Senate had passed just such a bill already. But a small group of House members balked at rubber-stamping the achievement, and started asking some very close questions. Two in particular, Congressman R. B. Macon of Arkansas and Ernest Roberts of Massachusetts, displayed a rare geographical acumen, and more than once had Peary squirming before their questions. When the vote came, however, the bill passed 154 to 34. Peary was made rear admiral and given a pension of $6,500 annually for life.

He retired with Josephine and his two children to Eagle Island, Maine, where he spent the last nine years of his life in relative tranquillity. He dabbled during these years as a government adviser and champion of aviation. In 1917 he was stricken with pernicious anemia, the malady that took his life three years later. He died relatively secure in the knowledge that posterity had awarded him the palm; and in fact nearly all Americans who give the question a second thought today assume that Peary was the first to reach the North Pole.

It was not only the partisans of Cook, plugging away indefatigably for decades in their effort to restore their fallen hero, who were left uneasy by seeing Peary's claim cast in bronze. More than one explorer harbored private doubts about that final dash to the Pole; and a succession of students of the Arctic kept the controvery alive in print.

A Congressman from North Dakota, Henry Helgeson, who was originally dragged into a grass-roots pro-Cook movement, turned his scrutiny in 1916 to the loopholes in Peary's testimony. He found that five short years after the previous House investigation, he could hardly find a copy of its transcript. As he began poking into other spurious Peary discoveries, like the chimerical "Crocker Land" discovered on the 1905–6 expedition, he became convinced that Peary's 1909 claim was a fraud. He made himself a student of the journey, entering pages of informed analysis of the Peary record in the *Congressional Record*, and on August 2 introduced a bill to repeal the 1911 act that had given Peary his laurels and his pension. By now Helgeson was disenchanted with Cook, too, and dissociated himself from the forces trying to resuscitate the doctor's blasted fortunes.

Peary wrote out a court-martial threat against Helgeson, but was saved by an act of fate. The Representative died suddenly on April 10, 1917, and the budding Congressional interest in reopening hearings died with him.

Over the years some of the top Arctic explorers, like Roald Amundsen and Adolphus Greely, publicly expressed their disbelief in Peary's claim. Their demurrals were met with howls of indignation from the National Geographic Society and its brethren, for whom

Peary had begun to seem a patriotic monument. Leaving aside the confusion and vagueness about just what kind of observations Peary had taken to ascertain where he was, students of the question were most skeptical about the astounding sledging distances Peary claimed to cover once he had parted from Bartlett.

In 1929 a Britisher, J. Gordon Hayes, published what was to that date the best analysis of Peary's distances. From Cape Columbia outward to 87°47′, Bartlett's turnaround point, Peary averaged only 9.3 miles per day. His six best consecutive days yielded an average of 15.3. Suddenly, once there were no witnesses who could make observations, Peary made five days in a row to the Pole at an average, by his own reckoning, of 26 miles per day.

Were this true, it would have been remarkable enough. But the most astounding feat of all was Peary's alleged return from the Pole to 87°47′ N—133 miles at the very minimum—in 2¼ days. *The North Pole* disguises these unbelievable marches by making no mention of distances covered, but only of forced "double marches" on very little sleep. Yet the distances can be deduced easily from the text. Hayes's step-by-step analysis reveals that, according to his own text, Peary traveled 429 miles to, around, and back from the Pole between April 2 and April 9, with "a few hours" of sleep mentioned only six times. In other words, according to Peary, six already deeply fatigued men, going on virtually no sleep, are supposed to have averaged more than 53 miles per day of difficult sledging.

In 1906 Peary had claimed the world's record for speed over the ice pack, around 30 miles per day. It hardly seems credible that, had he three years later consistently doubled and at times tripled that record, he would fail to mention it even in passing. As Hayes wrote, "Is not this a peculiar, not to say a suspicious, circumstance? Everyone knows that to hide his light under a bushel was not one of Peary's failings."

An average of 50 miles per day, Hayes goes on to point out, "is comparable only to the world's walking record, made in a few ounces of clothing." Certainly no one since has been able to approach Peary's apparent sledging times: one of the greatest Arctic explorers, Knud Rasmussen, averaged 36.6 miles per day in Greenland in 1912, which may be the legitimate all-time record. And the interior of Greenland is smooth icecap, unlike the polar pack with its constant pressure ridges and open leads.

If the impossible distances were not proof enough that Peary failed to reach the Pole, Hayes amassed a bookful of self-contradictions, navigational errors, and exaggerations that further discredited the claim. Hayes was confident that posterity would soon correct the record: "It is most improbable that Arctic history will be falsified." None of Peary's defenders ever began to answer the objections of Hayes and a half-dozen other critics. Yet such is the obstinacy of "heroism," or perhaps the power of institutions like geographical societies to sway public opinion, that as the decades passed the polar controversy receded like a bad memory, leaving a paradoxical confirmation of Peary's outlandish "dash" to the Pole.

Bob Bartlett seemed to have no trouble swallowing Peary's distances. In his autobiography this uncomplicated and honest man dismissed the controversy as so much sour grapes:

> There was no point falsifying his position even if he had been that sort of man. It was an easy jaunt to the Pole from where I left him, and conditions were improving right along. Anyway, the Eskimos never keep a secret. And they knew well in which direction he was going.

In the 1960s John Edward Weems was given access to Peary's personal papers in order to write a "definitive" biography. Weems took everything in The North Pole at face value, summarized the controversy as if it were merely a nasty conspiracy of pro-Cook forces, avoided the stickier questions (like the sledging distances) entirely, and dismissed scoffers with the kind of indignation one might expect from, say, close relatives of Robert Peary. Weems's popular book did much to teach a new generation of readers that Peary had undoubtedly reached the Pole.

In 1973 Dennis Rawlins published a book that must be regarded as the definitive analysis of the Peary controversy. His conclusion is unequivocal. Peary may have gotten within 100 miles of the Pole, but he could not possibly have reached it. Besides reviving the qualms of Hayes and others about sledging times and sharpening the unanswered questions from the Congressional cross-examination, Rawlins, who was trained as an astronomer, made a devastating attack on Peary's "observations." The crux of this fairly technical matter is as follows. In the far North, observations of latitude are fairly simple to make: they require only a record of the sun's altitude at local noon time. Even if one does not know what time noon is, a series of altitudes through the day will yield a highest one, which determines one's latitude. Because this observation is easy to make in the field, it is also quite easy to fake.

Where Peary's observations are most suspect is in the matter of direction-finding. All the explorers who have ever sledged across the Arctic ice pack have had a great deal of trouble keeping a straight line. There are, of course, no fixed landmarks to take position by; the pack itself is constantly drifting; and the numerous detours forced by pressure ridges and leads defeat dead reckoning as a directional resource. In essence, a traveler in the Arctic is lost without regularly noting not only latitude and compass bearing but also what is called transverse position, or deviation from the beeline between land and Pole. Yet Peary nowhere mentions the latter. Going by compass and dead reckoning alone, he claims to have struck a beeline from Cape Columbia to the Pole and back with an error of less than 0.6°. This "most superhuman aiming achievement in the entire history of Polar exploration," to quote Rawlins, would be the equivalent of "expect-[ing] a rocket aimed from Cape Kennedy to hit the moon without any in-flight guidance system."

Some critics have entertained the possibility that Peary was the unwitting dupe of his own observational errors, that he genuinely believed he had reached the Pole even though he had not. Rawlins rejects this speculation on a number of grounds. For one thing, Peary's earlier writings make it clear that he knew full well the failings of dead reckoning. He understood the need for observations of transverse position, but those were virtually impossible to fake. Sending back Bartlett, moreover, looks like the premeditated act of a man who knows that even his observations of latitude will not stand up to the checking of a single competent ally.

Peary's defenders have long maintained his innocence on the grounds of character as well as "fact." A man, they claim, who had never lied to anyone would not be the sort to pull off such a colossal hoax at the age of fifty-three. But as Rawlins, Hayes, and even Representative Helgeson made clear, Peary's whole record as an explorer was checkered with spurious discoveries, exaggerations, and boasts. If we add to that unreliability the personality of a fanatically determined man who had devoted twenty-three years of his life to a goal that now seemed to be slipping away from him for good, we can perhaps understand why he decided to fake the last hundred miles or so to the Pole. His greatest virtue as an explorer was his obsessive will. As Hayes admiringly recalls, "He could stand any amount of physical pain, and stumped about for weeks, after losing nearly all of his toes, with eight open wounds on his feet!" But the "*daimon*" that "drove him mercilessly" northward on eight succes-sive expeditions must in the end have driven him into the refuge of a hoax.

An interesting question remains: was Matthew Henson privy to the fraud? Rawlins thinks not. Like the Eskimos, Henson had no independent way of knowing whether he was at the North Pole or not. He never directly confirmed the astounding sledging distances claimed by Peary; in fact his own account tends to emphasize that the final marches were only slightly more successful than those just before Bartlett turned back. Henson wrote an article for the *Boston-American* which Rawlins rediscovered after fifty years of neglect. It casts a fascinating light on Peary's behavior during the crucial days of April 6 and 7. According to Henson, as soon as Peary had made his observations from the last camp on April 6 (which he was to claim was situated only six miles from the Pole), he and two of the Eskimos "witnessed the disappointment" of their leader. "His face was long and serious." At first Peary would not speak to Henson.

> "Well, Mr. Peary," I spoke up, cheerfully enough, "We are now at the Pole, are we not?"
> "I do not suppose that we can swear that we are exactly at the Pole," was his evasive answer.

Peary then spent some time deep in thought—while, we may imagine, he faced the fact that he would never reach the Pole, and pondered exactly what he would have to do to convince the world—and Matthew Henson—that he had done just that. Abruptly he confessed his surprise at being at 89°57′, "having fooled himself in the matter of distance." Henson took off his glove to shake his leader's hand in congratulation.

> But a gust of wind blew something into his eye, or else the burning pain caused by his prolonged look at the reflection of the limb of the sun forced him to turn aside; and with both hands covering his eyes, he gave us orders not to let him sleep for more than four hours.

And from that moment on Peary treated his assistant in a strange fashion:

> From the time we knew we were at the Pole Commander Peary scarcely spoke to me. . . . It nearly broke my heart on the return journey from the Pole that he would arise in the morning and slip away on the homeward trail without rapping on the ice for me, as was his established custom. . . . On board the ship he addressed me a very few times. When he left the ship [for good] he did not speak.

BIBLIOGRAPHY

Bartlett, Captain Robert A. *The Log of Bob Bartlett*. New York, 1928.
Hayes, J. Gordon. *The Conquest of the North Pole*. New York, 1934.
———. *Robert Edwin Peary*. London, 1929.

Peary, Robert E. [ghostwritten by A. E. Thomas]. *The North Pole.* New York, 1910.

Rawlins, Dennis. *Peary at the North Pole: Fact or Fiction?* Washington, 1973.

Weems, John Edward. *Peary: The Explorer and the Man.* Boston, 1967.

Wright, Theon. *The Big Nail: The Story of the Cook-Peary Feud.* New York, 1970.

8

ADMIRAL BYRD AND THE
NATIONAL GEOGRAPHIC
SOCIETY

If Peary did not reach the North Pole, then who was the first to do so? For almost two decades after 1909, Arctic exploration confined itself to other goals, doubtless in large part because public opinion held that Peary had vanquished the elements and arrived at 90° N. When interest in the Pole was revived, it was as the object of a new medium of travel: by airships.

The pioneer of this new thrust of discovery was the man who, it can be convincingly argued, was the greatest polar explorer in history: Roald Amundsen. By 1925, at the age of fifty-two, the Norwegian had behind him, among other adventures, the discovery of the South Pole in 1911 and the first continuous traverse of the Northwest Passage in 1903–6. With the American Lincoln Ellsworth and four crew members he organized the flight of a pair of clumsy Dornier-Wal amphibious planes to Spitsbergen—no mean feat in itself. From there the plan was to fly in one jump the 670 miles north to the Pole and back to land. When they were only 156 miles short of the Pole, one of the engines on Amundsen's plane quit and he had to land in an open-water channel. Ellsworth landed beside him.

The doughty aviators managed to drag Amundsen's craft up onto an ice floe before the lead froze up and imprisoned her. Ellsworth's plane had been damaged so seriously on takeoff that the men gave up on her and put all their efforts into rebuilding Amundsen's. For twenty-four days they worked on the engine, cut a path to move the plane to a larger floe, and built a runway. Finally all six men climbed into the single Dornier-Wal and apprehensively revved up for the takeoff. After lumbering along for fifteen hundred feet, the craft wobbled into the air. Later that day it brought the men safely back to Spitsbergen with half an hour of fuel to spare.

The flight had demonstrated what the experts suspected from theory: the distance from land to the Pole and back was at or beyond the maximum range for the kinds of airplanes in which a polar flight was likely to be made—unless a plane could refuel. But without any known land in a circumference of four hundred miles from the Pole, this was not a serious possibility.

Undaunted, Amundsen and Ellsworth returned in 1926 with another kind of aircraft: a dirigible piloted by the Italian Umberto Nobile. With a much heavier carrying capacity and the ability to drift before favorable winds with the engines off, the *Norge* (as it was renamed) seemed to combine the best qualities of an airplane and a balloon. Just as Salomon Andrée had planned to do, Amundsen expected to drift across the North Pole all the way to Alaska. Nobile came along as a paid professional, accepting a fee of ten thousand dollars to pilot the ship.

The party was ensconced in Kings Bay, Spitsbergen, on April 29, 1926, when to their surprise a steamship came into view. On board were fifty members of an American expedition headed by Richard E. Byrd, and a Dutch tri-motor Fokker named the *Josephine Ford*, after Edsel Ford's daughter. Byrd too was planning to fly to the North Pole.

At the age of thirty-eight, Commander Byrd had been officially retired from the Navy for ten years because of a bad leg. He had learned to fly in Florida, where he picked up a young mechanic named Floyd Bennett to serve as his official pilot. Bennett was a superb airman, but having attained the rank of only chief machinist's mate, he stood in perpetual awe of Annapolis graduates like Byrd. A deference arising from that awe may have helped Byrd perpetuate the fanciful version of the story of the polar flight he was about to attempt.

The year before, Byrd had been to Greenland under Donald MacMillan, a veteran of Peary's 1909 expedition. The National Geographic Society had sponsored MacMillan in an ambitious scheme to explore Ellesmere Island by air; but difficulties had hindered the effort. This year Byrd again had the backing of the NGS, as well as the financial support of such men as John D. Rockefeller, J. Vincent Astor, and Edsel Ford. That Byrd was the brother of Harry Byrd, later senator from Virginia, had done him no harm in cultivating such connections.

It now seemed that a race to the Pole was in the offing. But Amundsen magnanimously played down any hint of rivalry, vowed that the two efforts were both in the name of exploration, and even offered the services of pilot Bernt Balchen to help Byrd out in any way he could.

If Amundsen seemed unconcerned with the "race," Byrd was

chafing at the bit. He made a test flight on May 3, before the *Norge* had arrived by ship. Balchen offered advice having to do with wax on the plane's ski landing gear. A second test flight cracked a ski. Balchen suggested reinforcing the ski with an oar from the lifeboats aboard Byrd's ship. The third test ended up flipping the plane onto its side, fortunately leaving it undamaged. Byrd undertook a wholesale effort to lighten the plane, dumping three hundred gallons of gas, among other cargo. Balchen suggested taking off at midnight, when the snow would be frozen hard.

On May 9, 1926, at 12:37 A.M., with Byrd as navigator and Bennett as pilot, the *Josephine Ford* took off at last on its all-out effort to fly to the Pole and back. Shortly before leaving, Byrd had told a Norwegian journalist that he expected the round-trip flight to take about twenty hours. He had fuel, he figured, for from twenty to twenty-four hours in his tanks.

At 4:07 P.M. the plane touched down again at Kings Bay. When the two men emerged, they were surrounded by a wildly cheering crew from the expedition ship, Amundsen embraced Byrd and congratulated him, and Ellsworth seconded the gesture. A *New York Times* reporter radioed the news back to the United States, and within hours Richard E. Byrd was an international hero.

There were those present at the scene who wondered from the moment of Byrd's arrival how the flight could have been accomplished in only fifteen hours and thirty minutes. But no one was about to accuse the handsome, well-connected explorer of falsifying his data. There was another evident fact to give the skeptical observer pause: when it landed, the *Josephine Ford* was leaking oil from the right engine.

Two days later the *Norge* cast off from its moorings carrying sixteen men and a dog. Good weather held, and the ship drifted at a steady fifty miles per hour north. At 1:25 A.M. on May 12 the *Norge* passed directly over the North Pole. The men stood with "uncovered heads" and dropped ceremonial flags from the dirigible onto the ice pack. After a brief circle of the area, the crew set the ship on a course for Point Barrow, Alaska. In another day the ship came in sight of the Alaskan coast, but a sudden onset of heavy fog and icing supplied a dramatic conclusion to the voyage. Finally on May 14 the dirigible landed at Teller, Alaska, north of Nome.

The international acclaim due Amundsen and Ellsworth was relatively slow in coming. Byrd had indeed "scooped" the competition. On May 27 his ship arrived in London, where the aviator was lionized by press and public. Here however, the first skeptics surfaced: Scandinavian and Italian journalists who, championing their own heroes aboard the *Norge*, denied that a fifteen-and-a-half-hour trip in a three-engine Fokker could have gotten the *Josephine Ford* to the Pole and back. Byrd held a press conference and announced that he was planning to submit his proofs to the National Geographic Society as soon as he got back to the United States.

As Byrd's official biographer puts it, "the carping of foreigners made no difference to Americans." Proof or no proof, the moment Byrd steamed into New York Harbor he was mobbed by a virtually hysterical public. Mayor Jimmy Walker declared the day of arrival a city holiday; at noon Byrd was presented the keys of the city; there were speeches and a ticker-tape parade up Broadway; and by late that evening Byrd was in Washington.

The society had appointed a committee, just as it had seventeen years earlier in the case of Peary, to examine Byrd's reports. The committee was headed by President Gilbert Grosvenor himself. They had received the records, they averred, well before Byrd's arrival, and now, with exquisite timing, they certified that five days' nonstop scrutiny had verified Byrd's claims in every particular. In the late evening of the same day that Byrd had arrived in New York, President Coolidge presented the explorer and his pilot Floyd Bennett with the National Geographic Society's Hubbard Gold Medal, an honor previously reserved for explorers of the caliber of Amundsen, Shackleton, and Stefansson.

Even Byrd was surprised by the intensity of the reaction. In the next few months his wife and mother joined him in the entourage of honors; he spoke at town halls and universities; and eventually he took the Fokker on a tour of the nation. In the initial reception in New York, Bennett had been subdued, while Byrd accepted the adulation of the crowds as naturally as a politician. Now, although Bennett had actually flown the plane, the hero worship focused not on him but on Commander Byrd. Along with the honors which he mutely accepted, Bennett was promoted from machinist's mate to machinist.

The wild enthusiasm of the public swept away the grumblings of the doubters: Byrd was established for life as an American hero. But especially in Europe, skeptics clung to their reservations. The crux of the case against Byrd was a simple matter of flying time and the plane's top speed. Bennett himself in 1927 calculated the Fokker's top speed during the cross-country tour. He could never exceed an average of seventy-five miles per hour, and he was flying without the ski landing gear which, tests showed, slowed the plane by another five miles per hour. The distance from Kings Bay to the Pole and back was at least 1,330 miles. Thus the *Josephine Ford* had to average eighty-seven miles per hour to perform the round trip in fifteen and a half hours. The times of takeoff and landing were not in dispute, since there had been so many witnesses.

Byrd accounted for the unprecedented speeds as the result of a helpful tailwind all the way north which, once they reached the Pole, "began to freshen and change direction"—by 180°, in fact, so that all the way home it was boosting the plane to a speed of over a hundred miles per hour. The oil leak, Byrd maintained, had been noticed just before reaching the Pole. (Had it occurred earlier, any sane pilot would immediately have headed for safety.) At the Pole no flags were dropped, despite a thirteen-minute circling maneuver. One other important event occurred: just after turning back, Byrd's only sextant fell accidentally and was broken.

Byrd, of course, went on to fly across the Atlantic, to establish Little America in Antarctica, and to fly over or near the South Pole. Floyd Bennett caught influenza on a flying effort in Labrador in 1928, and before an emergency shipment of serum could arrive, he was dead. Bernt Balchen was one of the last to see him alive. As Balchen was departing for a flight north, the bedridden Bennett said weakly, "Have a good trip."

> "I'll see you when I get back, Floyd." There is a trace of a wry grin at the corners of his mouth. "That depends how the sock blows." His eyelids lift a little. "One thing I want you to promise me, Bernt. No matter what happens, you fly to the South Pole with Byrd."

Throughout his lifetime, Byrd floated, like his rival Charles Lindbergh, on the apparently inexhaustible fame the single flight had first brought him. But within the close-knit polar exploring community, a much-tarnished image of the gallant airman and explorer developed. A gentleman's code kept the gossip from reaching the ears of the public. But when Bernt Balchen came to write his memoirs in the mid-1950s, he decided at last to tell what he knew. Byrd was still alive, in his late sixties, a kind of national monument.

In the midst of writing the book, Balchen learned that Byrd had died. The news made him all the more determined to set the record straight. In a hotel in Chicago in 1927, Balchen revealed, after he had repeatedly queried his good friend Floyd Bennett about the apparently impossible times logged by the Fokker, Bennett at last admitted that he and Byrd had gotten nowhere near the North Pole. Balchen went on to claim that on the trans-Atlantic and South Pole flights he had piloted for Byrd, the navigator had not taken a single sextant reading. Because of this, even the South Pole flight could not be verified. What was more, Balchen reported, while flying in Antarctica

Byrd drank cognac steadily from a secret stash he had brought on board. After one flight he was so drunk that he had to be carried from the plane.

E. P. Dutton & Co. had printed four thousand copies of *Come North with Me* when Byrd supporters got wind of the book's revelations. Though Byrd was dead, lawyers representing him threatened Balchen with libel, slander, and defamation of character suits, and talked of arranging to have him deported back to Sweden, even though he had become an American citizen. Dutton buckled under the pressure by hastily running off a bowdlerized second edition. Balchen was forced to pay for the rewriting and other expenses. He acquiesced because he thought it was the only way to keep his book from going under.

In 1971, after Balchen's death, Richard Montague and Random House courageously laid bare the censorship of the airman's autobiography. In his delightful *Oceans, Poles and Airmen*, Montague published excerpts from *Come North with Me* as Balchen had originally written them side by side with Dutton's final version. The unexpurgated passages reveal a Commander Byrd far removed from the National Geographic boys' hero of Little America. Among the revelations was a strong streak of "cold detachment" and aloof isolation in the leader. In Little America, "We have been living together half a year now, and still I do not know Commander Byrd any better." What was more, Balchen indicated, Byrd had a habit of taking his men out one by one for walks and telling each that he should watch the others carefully and report any disloyal behavior. As a result the morale had plunged to a very low ebb. Byrd apparently played each of his pilots off against the other, hinting to each on the short walks that he would be chosen to be at the helm for the South Pole flight.

Considerable insight into the possible fakery Byrd engaged in is offered by another passage which did not appear in the second edition. Right before the South Pole flight, Balchen, trying to be helpful, rubbed Byrd the wrong way.

> "I'll go over the whole engine installation thoroughly," I promise him, "to make sure my figures are right." I take out of my pocket my little slide rule, the same one I used in crossing the Atlantic. "I've been keeping very careful figures on mileage and fuel consumption, just as I did on the *Josephine Ford* and the *America*—"
>
> He interrupts, his eyes full of cold fire. "Forget about that slide rule. From now on, you stick to flying, I'll do the figuring."

Balchen's own calculation was that, on the North Pole flight with

Bennett, the closest Byrd could have got to the Pole was 88° 15′ 30″ N. But the scrutiny of his former commander in *Come North with Me* is no mere hatchet job. Balchen concludes by arguing that it doesn't really matter whether the *Josephine Ford* actually reached the Pole and that Byrd was a great man who "dreamed a big dream," albeit a difficult and inscrutable man as well.

In 1960 a Swedish professor of meteorology, G. H. Liljequist, made the definitive analysis of the plane's flying times. In an article in *Interavia*, Liljequist deduced from the weather maps for May 9, 1926, that the flight must have taken place in an essentially "no-wind atmosphere." Byrd's helpful tailwinds, then, were spurious. Liljequist also made a thorough study of the Fokker's performance capabilities, and concluded that the plane's absolute top speed with ski gear would have been seventy-five knots, so that in fifteen and a half hours the closest Byrd could have come to the Pole was 88° 36′ N. With gentlemanly restraint, the Swedish scholar refrained from hammering home the allegation of a fraud, and closed his article with a polite appeal "that a committee of aeronautical and meteorological experts be given access to the flight log and all available data to study the question whether in actual fact he did reach the Pole."

What exactly were Byrd's data? Trying to answer that question led Dennis Rawlins, who had convincingly debunked Robert Peary's "discovery" of the North Pole, back to the National Geographic Society. The official NGS report on its certification of Byrd's records, published in the September 1926 issue of the society's magazine, had been, Rawlins found, deliberately doctored by Gilbert Grosvenor in some crucial ways. The five-day study of the records, Rawlins discovered, was originally reported as taking place between June 23 and June 28. But Byrd had been awarded the Hubbard Medal on June 23—just as the inquiry was beginning! For the magazine Grosvenor adjusted the dates so that the apparent conclusion of the study was June 23. Obviously, then, the certification was an after-the-fact effort if it took place at all; and the NGS was not about to embarrass itself by withdrawing credit from the man whom it had just given its highest award.

Rawlins tried to locate the "original report," but found that it had disappeared from Navy files. The NGS said it had misplaced its carbon of the report. Rawlins finally found a copy of a "navigation report" which Byrd had typed on a train in November 1926. The "observations" in this report are of the kind that could easily be calculated afterward, and the rest of the "proof" is a disjointed and impressionistic prose narrative.

After the publication of Rawlins's book, the columnist Jack Anderson challenged the National Geographic Society to meet Rawlins for a decision on Robert Peary's claim before an expert panel appointed by a top navigational institution of the NGS's choosing. The society backed off from the confrontation.

In 1977 another student of Byrd's flight in the *Josephine Ford*, William Fantini, tried to penetrate the murky cloisters of the controversy. The National Geographic Society wrote him, too, that their archives did not contain any of the 1926 records. Instead they offered, at eight dollars apiece, a raft of reprints of *National Geographic* articles by and about Byrd. Fantini was able to find some of Byrd's correspondence in the library of the more cooperative American Geographical Society. In his letters to Isaiah Bowman, then the society's president, Fantini found three peculiarities. Byrd asked Bowman for a copy of Fridtjof Nansen's *Farthest North* when he was preparing to write (actually to have ghostwritten) his own *Skyward*. Might he, Fantini wondered, have wanted Nansen's descriptions of the Arctic ice to supplement his own?

Byrd apologized to Bowman for the delay in supplying the society with his navigational records because, he said, he had not yet "mathematically worked [them] out." What did this mean? Why were they not worked out at the very time of the flight? Finally, Byrd insisted to Bowman that the data be kept strictly confidential. To Fantini this suggested fear of exposure.

Indeed, Byrd's whole life was conducted in a shroud of secrecy. Twenty-three years after his death most of his papers remain locked up by relatives in the family house in Boston. Even the loyal biographer Edwin P. Hoyt was denied access to the private papers, and so was forced to acknowledge that his lengthy opus was not in fact a definitive biography.

Fantini's inquiries brought a candid shot from Dean C. Smith, one of Byrd's Antarctic pilots whom he had played off in 1929 against Balchen and others. Smith wrote Fantini in 1978:

Byrd is considered by many to be a great aviator, navigator, explorer, Virginia officer and gentleman. He did not fly, he was flown, he did no navigating at all on any of my flights with him, nor, according to Balchen, did he do any on his transatlantic flight. He did very little exploring in the Antarctic, he had been preceded to the Pole by Amundsen and Scott. Once the Polar flight was made, he curtailed further flying into the unknown territory to the east, only making one modest flight with Alton Parker, on which he got so drunk he had to be carried out of the plane and dumped into his bunk. As for the gentleman bit, he once gave me his word of honor that he knew nothing about the whereabouts of my diary. Actually, he ordered [fellow pilot] Harold June to confiscate it. . . . June told me this after he returned from the second expedition, disillusioned. Corroborating this, Charles V. Bob, angered at Byrd, told a friend of mine that he, Bob, had seen a copy of my diary at Byrd's home.

In 1979 Captain Finn Ronne, who had been a colleague of Byrd's at Little America and who had traveled to Antarctica for nine separate expeditions, cast another vote against Byrd's North Pole flight. Ronne's informant, he revealed in his autobiographical *Antarctica, My Destiny*, was none other than Isaiah Bowman. At Bowman's summer home in New Hampshire one day in 1949, the former president of the American Geographical Society unburdened himself of a secret, on the condition that Ronne keep it to himself as long as Bowman lived.

"Upon Byrd's return from the Arctic in 1926, I had doubt that he ever flew over the North Pole. I asked to see his compilations and what navigational aids were used to prove that he had reached 90 degrees north. Byrd always gave evasive answers and said no one should question his integrity. But he had no proof of having passed the northernmost point of Ellsworth and Amundsen the year before. I got my answer to my suspicion when Byrd returned from the Antarctic in 1930. Byrd visited the AGS and after lunch we went for a walk. . . . It was raining that afternoon and with raincoats on we kept walking and talking for almost two hours around the blocks of Broadway and 156th Street. By that time I managed to break down Dicky-Byrd, and the time it took to do so was worth it. Byrd confessed . . . that he had not reached the North Pole, but had missed it by about 150 miles."

Bowman kept quiet, he told Ronne, because he sensed that Byrd was such a national hero no one would believe a detractor.

It was the 1926 flight that made Richard E. Byrd world-famous. But fame had been his goal ever since childhood, and the privilege and status of growing up in what was perhaps Virginia's leading family only goaded "Dicky" to a more intense determination to succeed. The competition of his two able brothers seems to have spurred him as well. As a child he had been, according to Hoyt, "small, almost girlish in stature and muscle structure." He compensated by an intense application to sports and the boyhood resolve to be the first man to reach the North Pole.

At Annapolis, however, he was academically undistinguished. His career was nearly ended in 1911 when he shattered his right foot trying a gymnastic stunt. A year later he slipped aboard ship and broke the foot again. In surgery his weakened bone was fastened with a metal pin, which he kept, along with a telltale limp, for the rest of his life. It was this injury that seemed to forestall his Navy career and that caused his official retirement at the unusual age of twenty-eight.

He turned to flying, and became a minor politico and lobbyist in Washington, constantly at odds with that other champion of aviation Billy Mitchell. On Capitol Hill he seems to have learned the ins and outs of "leadership," which in his maturity was to mean, as much as anything, the skillful manipulation of underlings and the promotion of his own designs. He made many enemies; and it may have been during these years that his penchant for secrecy, his almost paranoid fear of disloyalty, developed. By the age of thirty-eight he had fallen far short of the high goals he had set himself as a child. His best remaining hope was his earliest one—to reach the North Pole. Though Peary, he thought, had beaten him there, he could still be the first man to fly to the Pole—unless an Italian dirigible got there first.

Amundsen, Ellsworth, Nobile, and their crew, then, it must be concluded, were the first to reach the North Pole. The first men actually to stand there were four members of the crew of a ski-equipped American C-47, who landed at the Pole on an old thick ice floe on May 3, 1953. The men spent a little over three hours at the spot, taking measurements of the depth of the ocean and the pull of gravity. The first party to travel by surface to the Pole was Ralph Plaisted's in 1968, who, having arrived by snowmobile, boarded an airplane that met them there and flew home to hold a press conference.

BIBLIOGRAPHY

Balchen, Bernt. *Come North with Me.* New York, 1958.

Byrd, Richard Evelyn [ghostwritten by Fitzhugh Green]. *Skyward.* New York, 1928.

Crary, Mildred Rodgers. Personal communication. July 19, 1973.

Fantini, William. Unpublished ms. Amherst, Mass., 1978.

Hoyt, Edwin P. *The Last Explorer.* New York, 1968.

Liljequist, G. H. "Did the 'Josephine Ford' Reach the North Pole?" *Interavia,* no. 5 (May 1960).

Montague, Richard. *Oceans, Poles and Airmen.* New York, 1971.

Rawlins, Dennis. "Paper Flight." Unpublished ms., n.d.

————. *Peary at the North Pole: Fact or Fiction?* Washington, 1973.

Ronne, Captain Finn. *Antarctica, My Destiny.* New York, 1979.

9

THE HARDEST MOUNTAIN
IN THE WORLD

The ten years from 1950 to 1960 are known as the Golden Age of Himalayan mountaineering. Beginning with the legendary French ascent of Annapurna in 1950, the decade saw nearly all of the highest dozen mountains in the world, including Everest, climbed for the first time. With perhaps one exception—the four-man Austrian ascent of Hidden Peak, led by Hermann Buhl—those ascents were triumphs of massive expeditionary build-up. As many as twenty climbers, scores of Sherpas, hundreds of porters, and hundreds of thousands of dollars worth of supplies were combined in methodical sieges on the high places of the earth. Success depended less on the technical abilities of the lead climbers than on smooth logistics and dogged load-carrying.

During the same decade, in a range halfway around the world from the Himalayas, a quite different mountaineering era was unfolding. At the southern tip of the Andes, in Chilean Patagonia, in a small massif named after Robert Fitzroy (Darwin's commander on the *Beagle*), some of the best climbers in the world put their skills to work on the striking spears of granite and ice that rise dramatically between the pampas on the east and the icecap on the west. These jagged peaks are distinguished not by height (the highest, Fitzroy, is only 11,073 feet above sea level), but by sheer steepness and difficulty exacerbated by some of worst weather on earth. The Patagonian winds, unrelenting gales that fray nerves and ropes and that cause baroque mushrooms of ice to accumulate on the mountains' upper ridges, are a constant threat even during the rare spells of clear weather.

The first milestone of the 1950s in Patagonia was the plucky ascent of Fitzroy by a French team in 1952. The summit pair of

Lionel Terray and Guido Magnone were reduced to their last piton before making the summit. Terray, the greatest expeditionary mountaineer of his generation and a veteran of Annapurna two years earlier, gazed from Fitzroy at an even more fearsome pinnacle nearby, called Cerro Torre, and later expressed the opinion that it might never be climbed.

Throughout the 1950s newspapers heralded the ascents of Everest, K2, Kangchenjunga, and Nanga Parbat; Edmund Hillary was knighted and Maurice Herzog (leader of the Annapurna expedition) became a Minister of Sport. But in the pubs and huts where the best alpinists gathered the chat took on a special electricity when Patagonia came up. In particular Cerro Torre—a mountain that had never even been attempted—came to loom as an ultimate test. More than one expert suggested that the 9908-foot pinnacle might be the hardest mountain in the world.

It was the Italians who finally rose to the challenge. In early 1958, at the peak of the South American summer, two of the world's most accomplished mountaineers made a serious attack on Cerro Torre from the west—the iciest of its faces, lashed by the heavy wet winds that sweep across the icecap, but even so the side that seemed to offer the best climbing possibilities. Walter Bonatti had been a prime mover in the raising of standards on the most dangerous faces in the Alps, and had been the strongest member of the successful Italian K2 expedition four years before. Carlo Mauri had a record almost as distinguished. In 1958 the pair were at the peak of their form. The following August they would make the first ascent of Gasherbrum IV in Pakistan, technically the most difficult Himalayan climb done up to that date.

But they failed on Cerro Torre. A sustained effort got them to a high pass on the southwest flank of the mountain. They named the pass the "Col of Hope" and climbed a few hundred feet higher, but were still several thousand feet below the summit. Realizing they had underestimated the mountain, they retreated and climbed some much easier summits in the range.

Bonatti and Mauri were in competition with a team led by a fellow countryman named Cesare Maestri that was simultaneously attacking the mountain from the opposite, or eastern, side. There was no love lost between the two parties, who perceived their rivalry as an out-and-out race. Maestri was Bonatti's equal in many technical respects and his superior in the extremely dangerous art of climbing solo, in which sphere his only rival in Europe was the great Hermann Buhl. But Cerro Torre was too much for Maestri, too. The year 1958 closed with the mountain still unclimbed. However, Maestri, unlike Bonatti, decided to return.

While it is more accepted today, solo climbing was practiced by very few alpinists in the 1950s. How-to manuals routinely equated it with suicidal impulses. In the United States, with rare exceptions, it simply "wasn't done." In Europe it was the mark of the loner. And both Buhl and Maestri seem to have been spiritual loners throughout their lives—despite eventually marrying, despite inspiring the deep loyalty of climbing comrades.

Cesare Maestri's early development as a climber and as a person, as revealed in a 1972 interview in the British magazine *Mountain*, offers some interesting clues to the controversy that was to surround him and Cerro Torre. He was born in Trento in 1929, the son of a man who ran a traveling theater. His father had opposed the Austrians in World War I, and when the Nazis took over Trento in World War II they condemned him to death, but were unable to catch him. Cesare, as a youth, fought against the Nazis. He was later to claim, perhaps in jest, that his first climb was a secret raid on a German barracks to steal food.

Like so many other men who were later accused of exploration frauds, Maestri lost a parent when young: his mother died in 1936, when Cesare was seven. He seems not to have reflected in public upon the impact of the loss. When father and son moved during the war to the Bologna area, where Cesare's mother had come from, he quickly embraced the Communist movement that flourished in the area. Later he would describe himself not as a communist, but as an anarchist. The designation has import for his views of climbing.

After the war Maestri dabbled with theater and art, and began climbing in earnest. He would later brag that after following a leader on his first six routes, he would never again—except for one climb—submit to being second on the rope. If a partner chose to climb with Maestri, he must understand that Maestri would lead. The headstrong will to excel combined with his insistence on leading brought him by a natural progression to soloing. Influenced by a dictum of the alpinist Paul Preuss, Maestri began soloing not only up his routes, but back down them—a much more difficult business. In the 1950s he acquired the *nom de guerre* "spider of the Dolomites," in reference to the steep limestone crags in northern Italy where he made his most daring climbs.

The 1958 attempt on Cerro Torre was Maestri's first major effort abroad. On that attempt only one companion, the Argentine Cesarino Fava, was in anything close to Maestri's league. When he decided to go back in 1959, Maestri invited a friend who he thought would be as likely as any climber in Europe to better the odds of success: the brilliant Austrian Toni Egger.

Maestri had met Egger in a hut in the Dolomites but had never climbed with him. What influenced him most, he later acknowledged, was the need for a partner with more experience on ice than Maestri himself had. Egger was renowned for his fast, daring ice routes and particularly for his masterly climb of the most difficult mountain yet ascended in the Peruvian Andes, Jirishhanca, in 1957. The most extraordinary aspect of that climb was that it was accomplished in what climbers call "alpine style." On most hard mountains in remote ranges at that time, and indeed for fifteen years thereafter, the method of attack was to move upward in small daily increments from well-stocked camps, "fixing" the pitches gained by leaving ropes strung over them to facilitate each day's return to the previous high point. This "expeditionary style" tended to be slow, cumbersome, and tedious, but relatively safe from the threat of sudden storms. To climb Jirishhanca alpine style, Egger and his partner had eschewed fixed ropes, camped in bivouacs rather than in tents, and gone very fast up to the summit and back. Climbing alpine style on a major Peruvian peak was decades ahead of its time; few mountaineers in 1957 were willing to make themselves as vulnerable to objective dangers as Egger had done.

Even though it meant being the sole Austrian on an Italian expedition, and even though he and Maestri had been on opposing sides in the war, Egger asked if he could join the second Cerro Torre expedition. Maestri later recalled the warm phrases of Egger's letter: "Dear Cesare, I offer you all my help and hope that I may be able to join you. It's time the Torre was climbed."

In the initial stages of the 1959 expedition, however, things looked bad for Egger. He developed an infection in his foot that rendered him useless on the mountain. Climbing with Fava, Maestri pushed the route up to the base of the gigantic eastern precipice of Cerro Torre proper. They needed to establish three camps just to get to that point. In early January Fava and Maestri climbed 450 feet of the wall and fixed ropes. Egger gamely joined Maestri to push the route along a 1200-foot groove that diagonaled up and to the right—the key to the lower half of the face.

Two weeks of snow and wind drove the men down to their lowest camp and eventually out to the nearest human settlement, where they waited for better weather and for Egger's foot to heal. The whole party knew that Maestri and Egger ought to be the lead pair. Among the others only Fava was a top climber, yet he was not close to Maestri in ability; moreover, he had seriously frostbitten his feet the previous year rescuing some climbers on Aconcagua.

On January 26 the trio regained the foot of the face. They had cached a hundred pitons there, but now the precious hardware was buried under new snow. They dug a trench forty-five feet long but never found the pitons.

Maestri had approached the expedition with an uncharacteristic fatalism. In 1972 he recalled, "I left for Cerro Torre in 1959 convinced that I was going to be killed." Face to face with the intimidating mountain, stunned by the loss of the pitons, his mood continued to darken. "I felt in me all the weight of our enterprise," he wrote after the expedition:

> . . . above us, white and tragic, the Cerro Torre. Even my equipment, my sleeping bag, seemed mysteriously to sense my loss of heart on the night before we set out. This was the psychological turning point. I thought about what I had to lose, my friends, the young girls with whom I had walked in summer, my family, the woods in autumn, the glittering stars in winter.

On January 28 Fava, Egger, and Maestri pushed up the diagonal groove toward a gunsight notch, the north col of the mountain, "which we had already christened 'the Col of Conquest'—because in the mountains 'hope' is a vain word, only the will to succeed counts. Hope is the weapon of weaklings." The obvious snub to Bonatti would reverberate throughout the climbing world.

The account from here on of the trio's movements is Maestri's. That afternoon, he asserted, the three men reached the col. From this eyrie the upper wall of the mountain rose 2500 feet at a dizzying angle, much of the rock coated with ice, for the north ridge was the dividing line between the icecap weather to the west and the sheltered rain-shadow of the east face. Fava wished the two men luck and began to descend alone. "His look pleaded with us to 'come back,' and even before the tears could come to our eyes he had disappeared down the abseil [rappel]." Egger and Maestri dug a snow hole, settled in to bivouac, and brewed up some tea. Fava regained the ice cave at Camp 3 and waited, alone.

He waited, in fact, for six days. Egger and Maestri, he knew, were planning to go alpine style for the top. They did not have enough food for a long stay on the mountain. The weather held for the first three days, then it began to blow, an unusual warm wind that melted the ice on the peak and sent it crashing down in huge avalanches. Unable to see Egger and Maestri, completely in the dark about their progress, undoubtedly oppressed by his solitary vigil in the dank cave, Fava's worry mounted daily. On the sixth day he decided to set out for the lower camps to get help, convinced that his friends were in trouble.

Just as he was leaving the cave, he saw a dark object in the snow at the edge of a large crevasse nearby. He went over to look at it. It was Maestri, half buried in snow, almost delirious. He had slipped on the snow cone below the rock face; only the crevasse had stopped him from sliding farther. Fava got him back to the ice cave, revived him, and listened to the exhausted man's story.

Maestri and Egger had reached the summit three days before. The descent had taken its toll on them, as they constantly battled the wind and the deteriorating ice, but finally they had reached the comparative calm of the east face. They were almost down to the highest fixed rope when disaster struck. Egger was sixty feet below Maestri, in the middle of a rappel. Suddenly, out of the mists enshrouding the upper reaches of the mountain, they heard the unmistakable roar of an avalanche. Maestri shrank into the wall, gripped the ropes of his anchor, and yelled, "Toni—look out!" Egger tried desperately to climb back up to his partner, but the avalanche engulfed him. When the air had cleared of the fine powdered ice an avalanche leaves in its wake, Maestri saw that his partner had simply vanished, together with both rucksacks.

Maestri crawled into the snow and managed to get through a grim, sleepless night; then,

> at dawn I got up like a condemned man, who, indifferent and worn out, goes forth to the execution chamber. I used the bits of rope which remained to descend towards the fixed ropes. I safely reach[ed] the top of the groove. I was in a trance. The noise of the avalanches seemed distant and did not worry me any more. I continued to descend over the sections which Toni and I had climbed several times, when we were preparing the groove, but now I was alone. Never did these words seem sadder and more meaningful. Me, the famous solo climber, and now I am really alone.

With Fava's help, Maestri regained base camp. As soon as the party emerged from the Fitzroy massif, word of the ascent spread through the climbing circles of Europe and North America. Terray, who had thought Cerro Torre impossible, summed up the opinion of many when he declared Maestri's and Egger's achievement "the greatest climbing feat of all time."

An unliterary sort, Maestri published only a short account of his monumental climb in several mountain journals. The details of the actual climbing, however dramatic, were presented in vague, general terms, and tended to be subsumed by reflective and polemical passages. On January 29, the day after Fava's retreat, wrote Maestri, he and Egger climbed in clear weather out of the Col of Conquest.

For the only time in his maturity Maestri let someone else lead—because, he said, Egger was lighter than he, and the ice crust was very thin, requiring the most delicate of movements. On a loosely affixed sheet of ice varying between ten inches and three feet thick Egger progressed with only the crampons on his feet, his ice axe, and an occasional ice piton. At the top of each pitch Egger dug through the ice to reach the rock beneath, into which, because there were no piton cracks, he laboriously hand-drove a drill hole for an expansion bolt to serve as an anchor. Each bolt, Maestri said, took five hundred hammer blows to drive.

Ice of this character, at the dizzying angle of the upper 2500 feet of Cerro Torre, had perhaps never before been climbed: it was simply beyond the technique of alpinists in 1959. Maestri gave Egger due credit for the feat: "It seemed unreal to be by the side of such an extraordinary climber, one capable of climbing on ice with as much assurance as going up his stairs at home."

The pair slept the first night on a tiny ledge, anchored by expansion bolts and ice pitons. The second day the going was more consistently icy, and the weather held. Maestri tunneled through an ice overhang that could not be otherwise turned. That night they dug a hole and bivouacked only 450 feet below the summit.

The morning of the third day Maestri's barometer indicated "storm." Again Egger led all day, and a little before 4:00 P.M. they reached the summit. They were immediately blasted with a violent gust of warm wind, a harbinger of the deteriorating weather. "We had a quick look round at the view, then embraced each other, hiding from the other our faces filled with the prospect of death. . . ." Egger took a few photos, the two men ate the last of their sweets, and they left a slip of paper with their names on it in the tin.

The winds were so high that the ropes were blown out horizontally from the rock. In order to descend, the first one down had to be lowered "like a sack of potatoes"; then he would hold the bottom ends of the ropes so the second could rappel normally. They regained their previous night's bivouac hole. ". . . [I]t seemed as if we were in the trenches during the war. The noise of the wind prevented us from sleeping, its howling frightened us, the stuffiness almost suffocated us. Toni kept repeating, 'Let's hope we don't die a white death.'"

The next day the avalanches began falling on every side. Sometimes Maestri and Egger rappelled off bollards—uncertain knobs of ice carved with the axe. On other rappels the first man down had to hang from the end of his rope and drill a bolt to anchor the succeeding rappel. The men were out of food and approaching exhaustion. It was too windy to light their stove. They spent a sleepless night, "staring into the darkness. Each time we tried to speak, we fell silent after only a few words."

By the next afternoon—the fifth since parting from Fava—the pair regained the Col of Conquest and started down the diagonal groove on the east face. Just as they were beginning to believe they were safe, only 300 feet above the fixed ropes, the avalanche struck from above, taking Toni Egger with it. And with Egger—so Maestri averred—the camera recording their climb.

Maestri desperately continued down alone, reached the snow cone below the wall, slipped on a patch of ice, and hurtled down the snow. The crevasse near Camp 3 caught him up, and by the luckiest of chances Fava, setting out for help, saw him lying helpless and half-comatose in the snow.

It was several years before doubts about Maestri's integrity surfaced. The journals that published his article presented it without a breath of suspicion. The climb quickly became legend. Terray, who was later to doubt the authenticity of climbs that were thoroughly legitimate, uncritically hailed Maestri and Egger as heroes.

The first public note of skepticism was sounded by Carlo Mauri. To an Italian climbing magazine he contributed an article about Cerro Torre which, instead of directly contradicting Maestri's claim, simply implied that the mountain had never been climbed. Mauri, of course, had a strong vested interest as Maestri's chief rival (along with Bonatti) in 1958.

The character of Maestri's own climbing in the years following Cerro Torre undoubtedly hurt his credibility. The man whose reputation had been built on an extreme purism of style—soloing up and down difficult routes in the Dolomites—came to be scorned for "over-bolting," when he took an inordinately long time and relied on what others thought excessive use of artificial aids on a number of Italian routes.

Adding to the skepticism among climbers was the incredible steepness of the upper 2500 feet of the mountain, as revealed in photographs. The best ice climbers in the world had only to look at a photograph of that plastered, near-vertical nightmare to doubt seriously whether they could have climbed even a few pitches of it. Toni Egger was one of the very greatest, they agreed; but could even Egger have pulled that off? Finally, Maestri's account was so damnably vague about details, and the loss of the camera with Egger so damnably convenient.

For all these reasons, the climbing grapevine began to buzz with suspicions about the Cerro Torre ascent. In the 1960s no topic provoked more heated debate in the bars and campgrounds where climbers congregated. The controversy called up all kinds of emotional issues: whether climbers ought to be taken on their word; whether other "established" ascents ought to be similarly scrutinized; whether the whole thing mattered.

The controversy intensified in 1968 when four of the finest climbers in Britain decided to try for a "second" ascent of Cerro Torre. They were joined by an Argentine who had made the second ascent of Fitzroy by a bold new route in a very fast time. These five were arguably as strong a team as it was possible to put together anywhere in the world. And between 1959 and 1968 improvements in gear and technique had revolutionized mountaineering. Routes in the Alps that had been desperate ten years before had become almost routine. The clincher was that the British expedition would try a route apparently easier than that supposedly climbed by Egger and Maestri.

Despite a dogged effort over several months, the British failed on Cerro Torre's southeast ridge, well below the summit. They found the climbing fiendishly difficult, far more intricate and demanding than they had expected. And the toll exacted by the high winds and insidious wetness on both morale and gear seemed to these veterans of the worst storms in the Alps quite overwhelming. In the wake of their defeat, the claims of Cesare Maestri began to ring all the more hollow.

Suddenly everyone wanted to climb Cerro Torre. During the next two years Japanese and Argentine expeditions failed on the southeast ridge, well below the British high point. In 1970 Carlo Mauri returned to the west face, the route he had tried twelve years earlier with Bonatti. His very strong team managed to surmount an amazing tower of ice and rock that stands like a shoulder on the main peak; on its summit, called the "Helmet," they pitched an advance camp. But even from this solid outpost they were unable to reach the summit. Gruesome "cauliflowers" of ice blocked their progress 600 feet below the top. A dejected Mauri declared that he would never return to the mountain, scornfully implying that he was surer than ever that no human being had yet stood on Cerro Torre's summit.

The most bizarre chapter in the mountain's history was about to be written. To silence his detractors, Maestri decided to go back and climb Cerro Torre *again*. Disguising his expedition at first as an assault on the unclimbed satellite of Cerro Torre, called Torre Egger after his dead comrade, Maestri boldly set out for Patagonia in the middle of the South American winter.

Whereas his 1959 ascent, if genuine, represented a triumph of fast, light climbing, the 1970 expedition outdid many logistically top-heavy Himalayan assaults in its cumbersome overkill. Despite the short approach march, Maestri had the party's gear helicoptered to base camp. There, incredibly enough, the members built a wooden hut out of imported materials. Obviously Maestri was determined to stay until the mountain was climbed. And his chief weapon against the peak was a device the likes of which no mountain range on earth had ever seen: a gasoline-powered compressed-air drill for placing bolts.

With Maestri, now forty-one, relentless in the lead, the team stormed Cerro Torre's southeast ridge—the route first attempted by top British climbers in 1968. For fifty-four consecutive days they worked on the route, but the bitter winter conditions made progress tediously slow. Contributing to the snail's pace was the awkward effort of winching as much as three hundred pounds of gear—compressor, drills, oil, gas, and ropes—up each pitch so that the infernal machine could be directed at the next one.

From a point only a little above the Britishers' highest, Maestri retreated because of weather. But he was not ready to give in. His party loitered for five months in Argentina, then returned during the Patagonian summer. With a new motor for his compressor Maestri went back to work. Ten days got him to the winter high point, from which he bolted on. After drilling holes in a total of 1200 feet of virgin rock Maestri reached a ledge only 150 feet below the summit. The last remaining obstacle was a horrendous mushroom of ice—a feature the bolt-gun was powerless to attack. Instead of trying to climb it, Maestri dismissed it as irrelevant and claimed the ascent. Later he would sneer in print, "It's just a lump of ice, not really part of the mountain—it'll blow away one of these days."

Maestri returned to a hero's welcome, and eventually produced a popular book about his "triumph." But most of the climbing world was appalled. The British journal *Mountain* headlined its account, "Cerro Torre: A Mountain Desecrated." As he might well have foreseen, Maestri's "comeback" backfired: it convinced climbers the world over that the 1959 ascent had been a hoax. As *Mountain* editorialized, "How . . . could Maestri, a man who claimed to have ascended one of the world's hardest mountains in perhaps the boldest and finest climb of all time, think of returning to make a second ascent by means of such despicable tactics, thus befouling and polluting the whole aura surrounding this romantic peak?"

Soon thereafter *Mountain* editor Ken Wilson and Cerro Torre veteran Leo Dickinson, with two others, visited Maestri in his home in the Dolomites to interview him for the magazine. The resulting exchange quickly became the hottest journalistic item in the climbing world. Although Maestri received his guests cordially and was open and candid about his past, as the debate waxed more and more acrimonious the interview began to resemble a prize fight. Wilson, in particular, perhaps motivated by the British tradition of austere denial of mechanical climbing aids, pushed the attack on Maestri. He challenged the Italian to mark his 1959 route in detail on a photograph; Maestri declined. Wilson eventually published a route diagram based on "information . . . gleaned from our recent interview" and pointed out the discrepancies with a route diagram published a decade earlier in the French journal *La Montagne*.

At one point, when Wilson denigrated the style in which Maestri had completed a recent climb in the Dolomites, Maestri baited him by threatening to take him out on the peak. Wilson backed off, insisting he was "here merely as a journalist." Instead of rationalizing his use of the bolt-gun, Maestri brazenly flaunted his background as an anarchist, insisting that as he did not care what style other people climbed in, it was none of their business how he chose to go about his own climbs. "I can't understand why it concerns you," he told Wilson. "I haven't come and put expansion bolts in the wall of your house, have I?" The interview broke off abruptly after Maestri made a derisive jab at the 1969 attempt by his long-time antagonist Carlo Mauri: "He was getting a bit past it then. He had a good team, but he himself. . . What is impossible for Mauri may not be impossible for others."

Far from dwindling, interest in Cerro Torre burgeoned in the next years, largely because most climbers were now convinced that the mountain still awaited its first ascent. In 1974 a strong Italian team from Lecco under the leadership of Casimiro Ferrari approached the west face, the ice-covered route first attempted by Mauri and Bonatti. After a long battle three climbers stood beneath the summit mushroom that Maestri had dismissed as "not really part of the mountain." It turned out to demand some of the fiercest climbing on the whole route. At last Cerro Torre had received an undisputed ascent. On the summit the trio left a memento of their own. They did not find—and did not expect to find, given the seasonal variations due to ice and wind—the tin can in which Maestri and Egger supposedly had left a slip of paper with their names in 1959.

In January 1979 two Americans, Jim Bridwell and Steven Brewer, made a brilliant ascent of the southeast ridge in only two days. Near the very top of the rock wall they found Maestri's compressor—as he had boasted successors would—and marveled over the sheer will power required to lug so heavy and clumsy a piece of gear so far up a sheer precipice.

The most provocative discoveries bearing on the Cerro Torre controversy, however, had occurred several years earlier. An Anglo-American group had come to Patagonia in late 1974 to climb a peak near Cerro Torre called Cerro Stanhardt. After a retreat in December, the American Jim Donini was crossing the glacier with the Englishman Mick Coffey. Coffey noticed some odd debris scattered on the ice. To their wonderment, as they identified a pair of worn boots, a piece of rope, and assorted hardware, the two men realized they were looking at the remains of Toni Egger. One of the boots had the bones of a leg and foot in it. Having vanished under the snows almost sixteen years earlier, Egger's body had traveled, like any object suspended in a glacier, a full mile and a half within the ice, only to emerge in the summer thaw of late 1974. In Donini's laconic words, "We felt it was a good resting place for a climber so we left his body there." An extensive search failed to discover the camera that might have cleared up the whole mystery about Maestri's claim.

The following summer Donini was back with John Bragg and Jay Wilson to attempt the still unclimbed Torre Egger. The first half of their route would duplicate Maestri and Egger's progress up the lower part of Cerro Torre's east face to the Col of Conquest. They would be the first climbers ever to retrace the first half of the controversial 1959 attempt. Donini carried with him a single carabiner he had picked up from Egger's remains; he hoped to leave it on the summit of the mountain named after the valiant Austrian.

Donini had cut his teeth climbing in Yosemite, where, he later recounted, he first heard the rumors about Cerro Torre. "I was one of those who believed in Maestri. I took him at his word." Now, in the summer of 1975-76, "A lot of the appeal of climbing Torre Egger by way of the Col of Conquest was the fact that we would be repeating three thousand feet of climbing that was done in 1959 by Toni Egger and Cesare Maestri." The three Americans soon found that climbing much more difficult than they had expected. And they found signs from 1959 everywhere.

I remember in the first seven or eight hundred feet finding all sorts of remains of their route, little shards of rope hanging from wafer pitons and wooden wedges—I hadn't seen wooden wedges before . . . We were following history as we climbed the first thousand feet, also it helped us find the correct way. They had done the route finding for us essentially.

The Americans reached a point just below the prominent triangular ice field on the east face. A few rope-lengths took them to "a one hundred foot aid pitch bristling with gear left behind by Maestri and Egger." There Donini found a sight so puzzling it haunts him years later. For a hundred feet, he found a piton nailed into the aid crack every three or four feet. A single rope ran through the succession of carabiners clipped in to the pitons. The rope was tied in a knot called a clove hitch to approximately every other carabiner. At the top of the pitch, the trio found a pack with pitons, wooden wedges, and three or four ropes—an obvious equipment dump.

And from that point on the Americans found not a single sign of human passage. They climbed two thousand feet farther—up the diagonal groove Maestri had indicated—to the Col of Conquest. They felt that their very difficult route was the only likely line. And after having found traces of Maestri and Egger everywhere in the first thousand feet, they found not a single carabiner, not a piton, nothing at the Col of Conquest. "If you found a piton," Donini says, "you would know that, okay, they got to this point without a shadow of doubt." But there was nothing, except that puzzling series of clove hitches—unlike any arrangement a climber might leave for any imaginable purpose—a scant fifty feet below the triangular snowfield.

Donini, Bragg, and Wilson went on to forge the very difficult ascent of Torre Egger. On top Donini left Egger's carabiner as a tribute to the man who had first climbed Jirishhanca in an equally bold alpine style. Even now Donini is unwilling to call Cesare Maestri a fraud. He acknowledges only "grave reservations."

But the evidence—or rather the lack of it—is hard to ignore. It seems virtually impossible that if Maestri and Egger had reached the summit, the American trio would have found not a single rappel anchor, not a trace of the purported bivouac at the Col of Conquest—especially after coming across so much debris from the 1959 ascent in the first thousand feet. The implication is glaring: Maestri and Egger did not even reach the Col of Conquest, much less climb Cerro Torre. Probably they climbed only a little less than 1000 of the full 6000 feet of the route.

A host of mysteries remains. What do those alternating clove hitches on the highest rope signify? At what point did Toni Egger die, and how? What happened during the six days after Fava's retreat? If Maestri lied at the moment Fava found him half buried in the crevasse, was it out of delirium or shock? Did he then feel compelled to stick to his perhaps impulsive claim? Or did Maestri perhaps delude himself, under the strain of his ordeal, into a genuine belief that he had reached the summit?

The vast majority of the climbing world today is convinced that Maestri's 1959 climb of Cerro Torre is a hoax. A few climbers—some of them top-notch—stubbornly persist in crediting the ascent, on the grounds that a climber's word must be taken on faith, and that Maestri in 1959 was as fine a climber as Europe had to offer, as was Toni Egger. Maestri is still alive; but it is unlikely that anything he has to say in his remaining years will clarify the murky circumstances surrounding what Lionel Terray earnestly called the greatest climbing feat of all time.

Cesare Maestri himself remains an enigma. The core of his being, perhaps, is the paradox of the brilliant loner who nevertheless wins the adulation of followers. A man who would never let anyone else—except Toni Egger—lead him on the rope, a man whose reputation was forged in a series of daring solo climbs in the 1950s, Maestri may well have found his whole life dominated by the compulsive challenges of the need to excel, even to annihilate, competitors. Supremacy, one suspects, was everything for him, so that he had to sneer at the greatest Italian climber of his generation for naming a resting place on Cerro Torre the "Col of Hope"—even if Maestri himself never reached his own "Col of Conquest."

In such a man, even intimacy is subordinate to achievement. Maestri bragged to Ken Wilson that in the 1950s, when he was in his best shape, "Even when I made love to a girl I did it in a press-up position to strengthen my arms!" A final footnote might call attention to the simple matter of names. Imagine the shadow destiny seems to cast on a boy who, his mother dead at seven, his father hunted by Nazis, bears the name Cesare Maestri—in English, roughly, "King Master."

BIBLIOGRAPHY

Bridwell, James D. "Cerro Torre—Alpine Style," *The American Alpine Journal*. New York, 1980, vol. XXII, no. 2.

Campbell-Kelly, Ben. "Cerro Stanhardt Attempt" [note], *The American Alpine Journal*. New York, 1976, vol. XX, no. 2.

"Cerro Torre: A Mountain Desecrated," *Mountain*. London, September 1972, no. 23.

"Cerro Torre, Patagonia" [note], The *American Alpine Journal*. New York, 1959, vol. XI, no. 2.

"Climbing in Patagonia," *Mountain Craft*. London, Autumn 1968, no. 81.

Heppenstall, Alan. "Cerro Torre" [note], *Mountain*. London, May 1971, no. 15.

Maestri, Cesare. "The Conquest of Cerro Torre," *Mountain Craft*. London, Autumn 1968, no. 81.

_____. [Interview conducted by Ken Wilson, Leo Dickinson, Peter Gillman, and Alan Heppenstall], *Mountain*. London, September 1972, no. 23.

Mauri, Carlo. "Cerro Torre: The West Face," *Mountain*. London, September 1970, no. 11.

McNaught-Davis, Iam [narrator]. *The Cerro Torre Enigma* [film script]. [London, n.d.]

Tomkins, Douglas. "Second Thoughts on Cerro Torre," *Ascent*. Oakland, California, July 1971, vol. 1, no. 5.

"Torre Egger/Cerro Torre" [note], *Mountain*. London, September 1970, no. 11.

10

ALONE IN THE ATLANTIC

The men who perform exploration hoaxes almost never confess. Theirs is a solitary conspiracy against the world. And when the world conspires against them, daring to doubt the claims by which they climbed to fame, they react with bitter and pedantically consistent indignation, clinging doggedly to "the true story" in the face of any number of discrepancies and improbabilities.

Explorer-frauds lie to their own diaries—so sure is their conviction that to confide is to invite betrayal. And yet there seems to be, in the common pattern of their crimes, nothing like the careful premeditation of a good bank robbery. For the most part these men seem to have wanted some goal so badly, and to have pursued it so relentlessly by fair means long before fictional ones occurred to them, that their patched-together frauds bear the unmistakable stamp of improvisation.

In all the annals of exploring shams there is no story quite like that of Donald Crowhurst. Nor is there a hoax better documented, at least in its perpetrator's own hand, however cryptic the mode was in which he set it down. Thanks to the superbly balanced and diligent work of two journalist-biographers, Nicholas Tomalin and Ron Hall, posterity may gain access to the subconcious workings of a mind struggling with the Hamlet-like dilemma—to fake or not to fake—in greater depth than it is likely to come across anywhere else.

The story of Crowhurst's attempt to steal instant fame, unlike any other saga of a hoax, depends hardly at all on conjectured reconstructions of what "must" have happened. Nor does the case against Crowhurst depend at all critically on the argument from probability.

In an oblique way, we know exactly what he tried to fake; and thanks to Tomalin and Hall's excellent book, *The Strange Last Voyage of Donald Crowhurst*, we can know in surprisingly intimate detail just what the man went through trying to pull the thing off.

Born in 1932 in British India, Donald Crowhurst grew up as a mama's boy. His largely absent father was a drunk who died when Donald was sixteen, occasioning in his son the deep adult regret that he had never really gotten to know his sire. Until the age of eight Donald was dressed as a girl, and his hair was allowed to grow long, because his mother had hoped for a daughter. Crowhurst's relationship with his mother seems to have been every bit as close as Robert Peary's.

Throughout his childhood, adolescence, and early adulthood, Crowhurst seems to have had a penchant for self-destruction. He was famed among his classmates for being absolutely fearless, for climbing water towers and dancing blithely along the vertiginous catwalks that circled their summits. Once he learned to drive, he was involved in several potentially serious auto accidents. He was also an intensely self-critical child, given to fits of philosophical rumination of the most ingenuous and at the same time the most gloomy kind. In a school exercise, for instance, he posed the dilemma, "The two questions that vex mankind more than any others are perhaps 'Why do I live, and what am I when I live no more?'"

By the time he was twenty-six Crowhurst had flunked out of three careers. As a young officer in the Royal Air Force he had shown more verve for wild partying than he had for military discipline, and had been asked, for reasons mysterious to this day, to leave the service. Apparently unfazed, he joined the army, but after he was arrested for suspicion of auto theft (the deed may well have been only a drunken prank), he was once again asked to resign. He met his future wife, Clare, at a party in 1957, courted her in an outrageously cocky style, and talked her into marriage within the year. That year he also took up sailing.

As he had in his two short-lived military careers, Crowhurst botched up his first job as a married man, working for an electronics firm called Mullards. A car crash in a company vehicle led to an official reprimand; Crowhurst responded candidly, and was fired.

He managed to wangle a series of unimportant jobs with electronics firms, but gradually turned inward and became a kind of crank inventor. During these years Donald and Clare became the parents of four children. Living in a small village in England's Quantock Hills near Bridgewater, they became a fixture of the community. Donald started a firm of his own called Electron

Utilisation, acted in local theatricals—and got more and more interested in sailing.

Despite—or because of—his numerous personal failures, Crowhurst began to develop a sense that he was invincible. A close friend from these years, interviewed by Tomalin and Hall, reflected, "The thing about Donald is that he thought himself God. Everything in his life revolved around his belief in himself." He ran for a minor local public office and won. But after yet another car crash in his new Jaguar, Crowhurst became, according to his wife, more moody and violent than she had ever seen him.

In May 1967, when the man was thirty-five, the event that would shape the rest of his life occurred. Francis Chichester sailed into Plymouth after his one-stop, solo circumnavigation of the globe and became, much to his surprise, a national hero. Donald Crowhurst was one of Chichester's most loyal fans, having read all his books and followed his career closely. Yet on the day of Chichester's tumultuous welcome, Crowhurst and a friend went sailing in Bristol Channel. Listening to the radio coverage of the event, Crowhurst pranced around the deck, parodied the announcers, and complained that the fuss was wildly exaggerated: the only remarkable thing about Chichester's feat, he sneered, was that the man was in his sixties when he performed it.

For the first time Crowhurst revealed to his friend that for four years he had cherished a plan to make the first *nonstop* solo circumnavigation. He was not the only man to nurture such ambitions: by 1967 there were at least four other sailors seriously engaged in planning such a feat. It was, indeed, the logical next step in sailing circumnavigation, just as Chichester's extraordinary speed in his *Gypsy Moth* had represented the ultimate up to 1967. Thanks to the spillover of publicity that Chichester had generated, several of these men managed to get backing from newspapers and publishers by early 1968.

Donald Crowhurst followed all these doings avidly and enviously. When a newspaper clipping informed him that Chichester's *Gypsy Moth* was going to be embalmed in concrete in Greenwich as a memorial to the deed it had performed, Crowhurst wrote a letter to the Greenwich Town Clerk suggesting instead that he be allowed to sail the *Gypsy Moth* on the first nonstop circumnavigation. If the authorities would lend him the boat for a year, Crowhurst grandly promised, he would hand over all the profits that would undoubtedly ensue. The letter was never answered.

On March 17, 1968, the London *Sunday Times* announced that it was "sponsoring" an around-the-world race. Since it was clear that some of the competitors already had their own sponsors and would decide their own starting dates, the Sunday Times announced two separate prizes: a "Golden Globe" trophy for the first boat home, and an award of five thousand pounds for the fastest circumnavigation.

Four days later Donald Crowhurst announced himself an entrant. The press, whose interest in the story daily increased, began to refer to Crowhurst as the "mystery yachtsman." Unlike such other competitors as the already legendary French sailor Bernard Moitessier or the well-advertised Robin Knox-Johnston, Crowhurst was a complete unknown in sailing circles. And what the press did not know those close to Donald Crowhurst knew all too well; they were beginning to worry about their friend's mental stability. At the time of announcing his candidacy, Crowhurst did not own a boat, nor did he have enough money to buy one.

The Sunday Times had set the dates June 1 to October 31, 1968, as the outer parameters for starting the race. Crowhurst thus had six months to find himself a boat and learn enough about sailing—he was still not much more than a Sunday yachtsman—to attempt a solo circumnavigation. In late May he got his break in an astonishing fashion. A man named Stanley Best, who had invested in Crowhurst's shaky firm, Electron Utilisation, decided after looking at the books that he wanted to pull out. In an exchange of letters Crowhurst managed to persuade the normally skeptical Best that building a trimaran in which Crowhurst would win the race would be the soundest investment Best could make. "My wife tells me I must have been mad," Best said later. "I, who have always invested in a certainty or a rigorously calculated risk, suddenly jumped into this mammoth undertaking, which I didn't really comprehend, with only the shadowiest prospect of a proper reward."

All through the hectic summer the building took place in an Essex shipyard. Crowhurst supervised every detail, and kept up his spirits by making charts of his competitors' likely speeds and departure dates which demonstrated that even with a four-month-late start he would overtake and beat all the others. He gave the brilliant Moitessier, for instance, a likely elapsed time of 234 days; himself, 130. Given that the builders were in effect designing the trimaran as they were constructing it, and trying to incorporate in it some of Crowhurst's quirky intuitive notions, it is no wonder that major snags soon hindered progress. As late as mid-September Crowhurst was commuting daily to Bristol to take an intensive course in radio-telegraphy. He managed to attract a press agent named Rodney Hallworth, whose gift for hyperbole would later stand Crowhurst in good stead. All through the feverish planning, Crowhurst's spirits, on the surface, were maniacally high. But by late September the strain was getting to him. The earliest of his competitors had sailed on June 1, and it was beginning to look as if all eight of them would beat Crowhurst's launching date. On September 21, in the midst of a design dispute over the telephone, Crowhurst's patience snapped, and his anger exploded. That night his wife, Clare, tried to talk him out of the race. In his angry, pessimistic mood he considered her arguments seriously. According to Tomalin and Hall, he said to Clare that evening, "I suppose you're right, but the whole thing has become too important to me. I've got to go through with it, even if I have to build the boat myself on the way round."

On September 23 a trial voyage of the *Teignmouth Electron* was launched. It was a disaster. Crowhurst expected the short journey from Brundall to Teignmouth to take three days; in fact it took two weeks. Crowhurst had two friends aboard with him, and it was a good thing he did, because he was violently seasick much of the time he was aboard. At first Crowhurst had miserable success simply figuring out how to sail the unusually shaped trimaran. His anger and impatience disconcerted the two friends who were aboard. He managed to burn his hand badly on the generator exhaust pipe, but concealed the injury. The maiden voyage made clear a host of design problems in the trimaran which, for a single man out at sea, could well spell disaster.

Crowhurst reached Teignmouth again with only sixteen days left before the race deadline of October 31. The last of his competitors had set sail a full month before, though another late entrant had leaped into the fray. In the midst of frantic last-minute work on the boat, Crowhurst gave a BBC interview, in which he managed to appear the soul of romantic self-confidence. The real state of his mind may have been reflected in the anonymous reminiscence of one of the boatyard workers whom Tomalin and Hall later interviewed:

> You couldn't tell what was going on inside of him. He just wasn't integrated with us, if you know what that means. He was in a daze. We'd have admired him much more if he'd simply said "I've lost me nerve. Let's drop the whole business." Obviously he was in a blind panic and didn't have the guts to call it off.

Preparations got so chaotic as the deadline loomed near that the head of the BBC crew filming Crowhurst's efforts finally told his men to put down their cameras and help with the work. The last trials revealed that the boat still had serious basic sailing faults. On the day before Crowhurst would have to launch or miss the deadline, a close friend recalled,

"Round about teatime we dragged him off to a local tea shop with Clare to have a snack of some sort. He was in a terrible state, quivering from lack of sleep and food. There was no doubt he clearly didn't want to go. He kept murmuring 'It's no good. It's no good.' He knew it could kill him, but he could never quite bring himself to say so."

In bed with Clare on the last night on shore, according to Tomalin and Hall, Donald

said in a very quiet voice: "Darling, I'm very disappointed in the boat. She's not right. I'm not prepared. If I leave with things in this hopeless state will you go out of your mind with worry?" Clare, in her turn, could only reply with another question. "If you give up now," she said, "will you be unhappy for the rest of your life?"

Donald did not answer, but started to cry. He wept until morning. During that last night he had less than five minutes' sleep. "I was such a fool!" says Clare Crowhurst now. "Such a stupid fool! With all the evidence in front of me, I still didn't realise Don was telling me he'd failed, and wanted me to stop him."

Four months after Crowhurst set sail in the *Teignmouth Electron*, Clare came across the draft of a letter to be given to her in the event of Donald's death. Clare gave Tomalin and Hall permission to publish it. It is a heart-rending document, thanking Clare as it does for making "my whole existence a great and powerful rapture for 12 years," bespeaking a deep capacity for intimacy which the secretive Crowhurst of the last summer must have rarely exposed to anyone— not even his wife. But the eeriest thing about it is its tone: the letter reads as if from the grave, as if Crowhurst were already convinced of the inevitability of his death at sea.

Nothing is certain—least of all life, from day to day, minute to minute, or even second to second. This *was* the manner of my death. What does that matter? A car crash, a falling slate, thrombosis . . . ten thousand alternatives lie ready waiting to sever the tenuous links of circumstance that keep us alive.

Just before 5:00 P.M. on October 31—only seven hours before the deadline—the *Teignmouth Electron* was towed over the harbor bar in a cold drizzle, and Donald Crowhurst began his solitary ordeal. Even the last few hours were inauspicious, as an attempted start at 3:00 P.M. had to be aborted because two sails had been attached to the wrong stays.

For the first two weeks the *Teignmouth Electron* made abysmal progress. All kinds of minor mechanical problems beset her, as well as several major ones, including the failure of Crowhurst's radio equipment to work, snafus with the ship's self-steering gear, a leaking float, and a breakdown of his electricity generator.

From October 31 on, the record of what happened to Crowhurst depends almost entirely on the logs he kept aboard ship. The analysis upon them performed by Tomalin, Hall, and experts whom they consulted is what allows us to follow with reasonable certainty not only the erratic progress of the forty-one-foot trimaran, but the eccentric course of its pilot's mental journey. Through November 15, 1968, the logs give no reason to believe that Crowhurst intended to falsify anything. The jottings therein—both navigational and impressionistic—bespeak a dismal series of setbacks, but they seem lucid and honest. Besides the mechanical problems with the boat, Crowhurst suffered from adverse winds blowing out of the southwest. When he slept one night for seven hours, the winds carried him north; it required four hours to get back to where he had started from—a "total waste of 11 hours," as he recorded in self-castigation, just before the stern words in capitals, "I MUST NOT ALLOW MYSELF TO BE LAZY."

By November 15 he was still only off the coast of Portugal, at a point it had taken Chichester only six days to reach. His progress thus far was slower than that of any of his competitors in the yacht race. Besides the poor sailing, he had suffered physically, cutting a finger badly and giving up trying to lance a boil, relying instead on penicillin to clear it up.

Though his navigational record seems precise and ingenuous so far, there was already emerging, as Tomalin and Hall see it, a kind of double personality in Donald Crowhurst. By prior agreement, the sailor had arranged to tape-record himself at various intervals for the BBC. Around November 15 he made a long tape, which played down any fears he might have had at that point and played up the jaunty, swashbuckling image he had culled from the dozens of sailing memoirs he had read. "Of course single-handing has its compensations," his voice coyly bragged. "No matter how schizophrenic you are, it's difficult to fall out with the crew, they're excellent people from the captain to the cabin boy."

On or about the same day Crowhurst's log records a close analytical account of everything that was going wrong. The tone was antipodes apart from that of the BBC tape. Nine pages full of carefully itemized mechanical and navigational impossibilities led him for the first time to face squarely the question of whether he ought to quit the race.

The anguish in those pages is unmistakably deep and genuine. To be weighed in the subjective scales were his promises to Clare, his boasts to his backer Stanley Best, his potential financial ruin if he gave up, and his own precarious self-esteem. He recorded bluntly that his only chance now of winning the race was if everybody else dropped out; even so, he thought his chances of survival only fifty-fifty. The man, it is clear, was on the verge of heading, defeated, for the nearest port. Almost having decided to do so, he rationalized giving up by attributing the failure to an unwillingness to worry Clare beyond reasonable lengths.

Yet, on the verge of throwing in the sponge, Crowhurst decided that some sort of spectacular stunt was necessary to save face. He wrote down alternatives—whether to try to push on to Australia at least, or go as far as Capetown—farther than one of his adversaries, who, Crowhurst knew from incoming radio reports, had given up the race short of that mark. He pondered landing in America and trying to sell his boat. "Money," he lamented. "This area is the most worrying."

The long, agonizing self-examination of November 15, penned into his log by precious flashlight, served only to leave Crowhurst with a determination to muddle on for a few more days while he tried to fix his generator so that he could contact Stanley Best and discuss the situation.

As Tomalin and Hall convincingly demonstrate, this early point in the voyage was the crucial psychological turning point. After November 15 Crowhurst's log ceases to be reliable. Thus the saga "becomes a detective story, and all his records become evidence (some of it accurate, some not) from which to deduce what really happened." What Crowhurst apparently decided to do, as a grand gesture in the face of failure, was to claim not victory in the round-the-world race, but "only" the record single-handed sailing distance for one day.

On November 16 he got his generator working and sent off a message to his agent, Rodney Hallworth, explaining his radio silence and claiming vaguely "GOING ON TOWARDS MADEIRA." The day after this he wrote in his log a despairing list of alternatives open to him— none of them involving continuing the race, but one foreshadowing his first fraud: "4) Return to UK for record-breaking attempt." Yet on November 18 he made two radio telephone calls, one to Clare and one to Best, indicating in neither that anything was amiss.

Incoming radio broadcasts may have fueled a remote hope in Crowhurst that there was still a chance of staying in the race. The news was that there were only three other contestants still trying to win. Robin Knox-Johnston was off New Zealand; his boat was in very

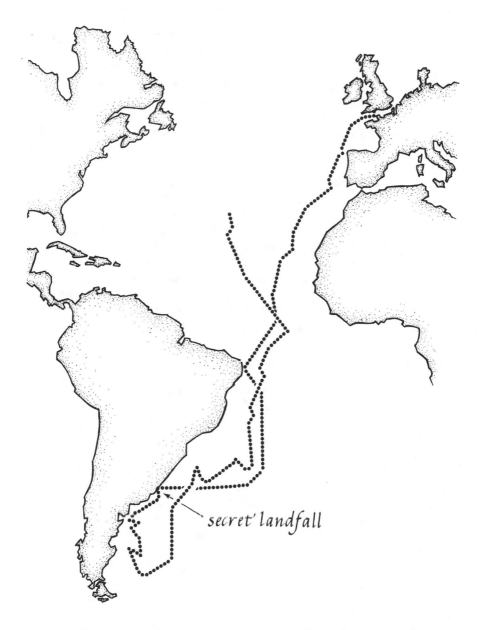

As reconstructed from his log, the actual route Donald Crowhurst sailed in the Teignmouth Electron from October 31, 1968, to July 1, 1969, while he pretended to sail around the world in the race sponsored by the Times of London.

bad shape, but he intended to continue. Bernard Moitessier, who had refused to take along a radio on the grounds that it was a distraction from serious sailing, was catching up to Knox-Johnston despite having embarked more than two months later. Nigel Tetley, who had left England on September 16, was approaching the Cape of Good Hope. All the others had retired from the race, some barely clinging to their lives.

On December 10 a radiotelegram from Crowhurst reached Hallworth. Exuberantly it claimed a week of over-100-mile days in the trade winds, capped by a "SUNDAY 243 NEW RECORD." If Crowhurst had sailed 243 miles in a single twenty-four-hour period, he had indeed eclipsed the record of 220 set six months earlier by Geoffrey Williams. Hallworth made the most of the news, and despite skepticism from Chichester and others, the newspapers uncritically headlined the feat, spurred perhaps in part by a lack of previous information about the laggard fourth-runner in the race.

The certainty that Crowhurst's "record" was a hoax is provided by two intensely worked-over sheets of calculations that later came into Tomalin and Hall's hands. In parallel columns these list Crowhurst's actual distances—as high as 177 miles in one day—and his claimed distances, peaking in the record 243. The calculations work out with elaborate care the navigational observations that Crowhurst would have had to have made to sail the record distances. Meanwhile the narrative log, no longer truthful, records joyful sentiments like "If this wind holds I will do it!" So skillful was Crowhurst's fakery that an expert asked later to read only the log found nothing seriously to discredit either the navigational data or the narrative. Had the hoax proceeded no further than this, there is a strong likelihood Crowhurst would have pulled it off.

The first indication that Crowhurst intended a larger hoax—namely, to fake the entire around-the-world journey—appears on December 12. It was, to the casual observer, a subtle clue: Crowhurst stopped writing in his official log and began a new one in a blue exercise book. The implication is unmistakable: the first log was being set aside for later doctoring with appropriate data and comments. Meanwhile in the new log an apparently honest account of the actual progress of the trimaran was put down. This log obviously was never meant to see the public eye. But Tomalin and Hall believe that Crowhurst, during these several days, was still uncertain about the larger hoax. His telegram messages grew curt, ambiguous, and vague. The new log is spare, all data. Perhaps the man was trying to weigh all the possible fates by which his grand scheme could be exposed: an untimely sighting by another ship, the wrong weather recorded at a given place, the barrage of questioning upon his return. On an Admiralty chart he started to sketch out a plan of false positions. Then on December 17 he sent his first blatantly untruthful radiotelegram to Hallworth: "THROUGH DOLDRUMS OVER EQUATOR SAILING FAST AGAIN." Five days later he cabled his position as "OFF BRAZIL," and claimed he was again averaging 170 miles a day. By Christmas Crowhurst was reporting his position a full 550 miles ahead of where he was actually sailing, which was near the northeast coast of Brazil, trying to avoid the shipping lanes where he might be seen and located by passing commercial vessels. He made a hearty and nostalgic BBC tape on Christmas Eve, playing "God Rest Ye Merry, Gentlemen" on his mouth organ. For the first time his recently shelved original log became the receptacle for original poetry. Christmas seems to have affected him deeply and unhappily, but he was determined to keep up the facade of the dashing sailor.

On Christmas Eve he radiotelephoned Clare. When she at once demanded his position (which Hallworth had been clamoring for), he refused to give her one, claiming he hadn't had time to take sun sights. (She thought his voice strangely clipped.) At this point the first messages in Crowhurst's hand indicative of severe emotional distress and perhaps imbalance appear. His first poem was doggerel, a sea chanty of recognizable derivation. Soon after, perhaps in the grips of Einstein's *Relativity, the Special and General Theory*, which he had aboard, the verses begin to include lines like

> *My footstool's a 10 lb case of rice*
> *To the North-east 2.5 x 10³ miles,*
> *250 x 10³ babies will slowly die, too weak to fuss.*

On Christmas Day Crowhurst's actual position was within twenty miles of the Brazilian coast. Perhaps the loneliness of the holiday and the emotional strain of talking to his wife had made him steer suddenly toward land.

By the New Year Crowhurst had evidently entered uncompromisingly into the labyrinth of his hoax. His movements during January 1969 are an aimless series of zigzags off the coast of Brazil, where he was in effect hiding from the commercial traffic. But during that time he was assiduously copying every message he could receive on his set into a radio log. The reason is clear: he knew that he would have to fake a knowledge of the weather and sailing conditions at every stage of his pretended voyage.

His own broadcasts had continued to be vague about his position. Finally on January 19, responding to Hallworth's entreaties, he sent out a telegram giving a precise location—way down in the windy latitudes called the Roaring Forties, weeks ahead of his actual position. Hallworth converted the message into a press release, and the *Sunday Times* told its readers that Crowhurst was probably already in the Indian Ocean by the time they opened their papers. This leap of faith put the *Teignmouth Electron* a full four thousand miles ahead of where it actually lay.

Then, after broadcasting on January 19, Crowhurst lapsed into a radio silence that was to last for months. The entries in his logs give clues as to what was going on inside the man's head. He wrote a kind of prose vignette, entitled "The Misfit," about a stray owl that had landed on his dinghy. The plight of the bird, "bedraggled, shivering, eyes closing with heavy fatigue, head withdrawn," is unmistakably self-referential. On February 2, worried about a damaged starboard float, he decided to make a secret landing on the coast of Argentina.

On March 6, after much deliberating, Crowhurst chose the estuary of the Rio Salado for his illicit landing spot. It was a clever choice: though within a hundred miles of Buenos Aires, the remote coast-guard outpost at the river's mouth had no telephone or railway connecting it to civilization, and only three men on duty. What Crowhurst's feelings must have been as he stepped on dry land for the first time in more than four months we can only imagine. This episode in his desperate saga is known not from his log, but from the assiduous researches of Tomalin and Hall, who traced down the witnesses to Crowhurst's two-day visit to the outpost, gathered their recollections, and copied the entries in their official logs.

After miming unsuccessfully to indicate to the Argentinians what materials he needed to repair the float, Crowhurst was driven to the rancho of a French-speaking ex-sergeant. There the sailor informed his audience that he had left England four months before as part of a "regatta," had rounded Cape Horn, and would win the race home if they could supply him with plywood, screws, nails, and timber. The sergeant's wife remembered, "He laughed a lot, as though he were making fun of us. We thought that something was wrong, that he might be a smuggler."

Finally Crowhurst was given the materials he requested. With them he patched his boat, drank a glass of wine, told jokes in mime, and set sail again on March 8. For all the curiosity he had aroused, no word of his visit got back to England.

For the next month, still in radio silence, Crowhurst sailed in a wandering loop off the coast of Argentina, drifting as far south as the Falkland Islands before wandering back almost as far north as where he had made his secret landing. His thinking, logistically speaking, is fairly clear: he needed to kill time until a plausible interval had passed before he could resume radio contact from the Atlantic. To make a phantom voyage from a point northwest of Cape Horn in the South Atlantic all the way through the Indian Ocean and the Pacific and around Cape Horn, even if he traveled at the very wildest speeds, three months were marginally brief. He set himself April 15 as the date for claiming to have rounded the Horn.

Meanwhile Crowhurst was keeping track of the positions of his three remaining competitors. Moitessier, clearly the class of the lot, had in fact already passed the Horn and was in position to head home the winner. But this lyrical vagabond had so fallen in love with the Roaring Forties that he decided to sail on in the southern latitudes and circle the world once again! He wrote a long letter explaining his decision which he intended to catapult to some passing ship. Moitessier eventually went halfway, stopping in Tahiti for several months before he returned to France. Knox-Johnston, though himself out of radio contact for months and feared dead, had coaxed his ship around the Horn and into the Atlantic. On April 6 he was spotted by a tanker; the press began to hail him as the winner of the Golden Globe trophy for first home, but at an average of less than a hundred miles per day he was widely regarded as likely to lose out to both Tetley and Crowhurst for the monetary prize—if they finished. And Tetley had rounded the Horn on March 20 and was trailing Knox-Johnston home.

For a long while during his time-killing loop Crowhurst evidently pondered a fake telegram to Australia or New Zealand. The scrap of paper on which he drafted and redrafted the possible message was found later. The gist of the unsent telgram was an effort to find out whether he had been spotted during his long silence—a possibility that must have weighed on his spirits hourly. But apparently he could not think of a way of asking this without also volunteering his position.

Finally, on April 9 he made radio contact with a station in Buenos Aires. His deliberately cryptic indication of position was summed up in three lines: "HEADING DIGGER RAMREZ." It may be that the Buenos Aires station raised Crowhurst when they heard him trying to reach Wellington, New Zealand. In any case, the sailor consistently evaded the query "QTH?" ("What is your latitude and longitude?").

Rodney Hallworth, overjoyed to receive his first message in eleven weeks, deciphered it as indicating that Crowhurst was near the tiny island southwest of Cape Horn called Diego Ramirez. The surprisingly uncritical newspapers swallowed it whole. Only Sir Francis Chichester himself was skeptical enough to approach the race officials with his suspicions.

The aimless meandering seems to have plunged Crowhurst into a more digressive, whimsical, and even childish mood than he had previously indulged in. He wrote a succession of bawdy limericks, and got drunk one night and taped a BBC broadcast. The rambling monologue, though on the surface full of the boisterous cheer of an old "tar," had a despairing undertone to it: "Actually matey, I tell you this matey, I've got a hell of a lot of tape to record on. I don't have the faintest notion matey how I'm going to fill it, but if I keeps this up much longer somebody's gonna shoot me."

In an altogether different mood he began to record metaphysical thoughts like his "Cosmic Integral":

$$_{-\infty}^{+\infty} \int \text{Man} = [0] - [0].$$

A rough prose translation is, the total extent of mankind from minus infinity to plus infinity is zero.

Other ramblings were preoccupied with God and a sense of sin. In an oblique parable Crowhurst seems to have decided that lying to others was justifiable if it gave them pleasure. At this point—if there ever is such a point in the progress of mental deterioration—the man may have passed the illusive boundary between sanity and madness. While waxing far more verbose than he had in the gloomy weeks previous, Crowhurst now was not entirely in control. Yet he kept any direct acknowledgment of the hoax he was perpetrating out of the zany entries in his logs, even when drunk.

At this point in the race Knox-Johnston was the imminent winner of the Golden Globe. Only Tetley and Crowhurst were left to challenge him for the other prize, for fastest circumnavigation: if either finished, he would surely better Knox-Johnston's elapsed time. The resurfacing of Crowhurst panicked Tetley's supporters, who never suspected a hoax. Hallworth, rejuvenated by the "DIGGER RAMREZ" telegram, wired back to tell Crowhurst that he was only two weeks behind Tetley. The effect of the telegram must have been to confirm Crowhurst in the knowledge that he had indeed fooled everybody. And now the awesome reality that he was committed for good to the hoax must have come home. On May 4 Crowhurst stopped killing time and began to sail for England in earnest. He made steady progress throughout the month up the coast of South America. And he finally sent off a pair of jaunty telegrams confirming his reentry into the race.

Hallworth sent back cables urging his champion not only to beat Tetley's elapsed time, but actually to close the gap and pass him in a neck-and-neck race. One of his telegrams ingenuously gushed: "TEIGNMOUTH AGOG AT YOUR WONDERS   WHOLE TOWN PLANNING

HUGE WELCOME—RODNEY." Strangely enough, Crowhurst's response was to reassert that he thought he had no chance of overtaking Tetley. Yet at second glance, as Tomalin and Hall point out, losing to Tetley was a logical way of handling the pressure Crowhurst had put himself under. If he won, all his records would be subject to the closest scrutiny. If he made a gallant try and lost, then he would be soon forgotten.

Tetley solved the dilemma for him. Less than 1,200 miles from home, near the Azores, desperately pushing ahead of his phantom pursuer, he got caught in a violent storm. On May 21 the *Victress's* port float bow broke loose and smashed into the center hull of the trimaran. Helpless, Tetley abandoned his ship in a rubber life raft and watched the *Victress* sink. Knox-Johnston had reached England weeks before. This left Crowhurst the only contender still in the race—and the certain winner of the five-thousand-pound prize if he could only sail up the Atlantic and make it home.

Meanwhile the man had been suffering some very real nautical problems. Virtually all his food supplies were either growing short or spoiling; there were numerous mechanical problems with the boat; and most important, he developed genuine broadcasting problems that culminated in the complete breakdown of his radio. He could still receive messages, but for several weeks in late May and early June he was unable to send them out. His logs reveal that he was at this point desperately eager—and completely unable—to have a long radiotelephone conversation with Clare.

While his ship sailed desultorily northwest across the Equator, Crowhurst occupied himself with trying to fix his radio and with talking for hours into his tape recorder. An incoming BBC cable reconfirmed the tumultuous welcome that was awaiting him. He was now given to lounging nude all day in the tropical heat, and his penchant for self-documentation went so far as to persuade him to shoot some film of himself.

Finally on June 22 Crowhurst got his radio working. He sent off messages to the BBC, to Hallworth, and to Clare, then relapsed (as his tapes record) into a euphoric mood of self-congratulation. The tone was that of his early boasting, with no trace of the delusional "revelation" that was about to take over his mind.

On June 23 he made his last tape, and recorded in his log his last navigational observation. His last spoken words recorded by the machine were: ". . . the poisons in your body, you must get rid of them. I don't know what they are, but they've got to go. The sea's the way to get rid of them I'm sure. I feel in tremendous shape. I've never felt so . . ."

The rest of the record of what happened to Donald Crowhurst

depends on the words he wrote in his logs. The final break from sanity seems to have been sudden, no matter how persistently it had been foreshadowed. The last week of Donald Crowhurst's life can be known only by the fascinating pencil record he scratched into the pages of his "diary." The entries are analyzed by Tomalin and Hall as skillfully as the most probing witness could ask for; yet there remains an essential mystery about those last days that will never be dispelled.

Crowhurst had a revelation. It had to do with Einstein. Under a new heading, "PHILOSOPHY," he tried to summarize it for the world. For the most part it reads as the raving of the sort of "philosopher" one avoids on the streets of big cities, on the soap boxes of Hyde Park. "No real classification possible until advance stage reached," Crowhurst confidently wrote, and "I introduce this $\sqrt{-1}$ because [it] leads directly to the dark tunnel of the space-time continuum," and "'Love thy neighbor's ideas as thine own' will lead us through the tunnel." Passages are underlined, or emphasized with as many as eighteen successive exclamation marks. When the entries verge on coherence, they seem to bespeak a wish on Crowhurst's part either to leave his body or to become God. Yet the delusional system on which the "truths" are based escapes even Tomalin and Hall's sympathetic analysis. We finally have no real idea what Crowhurst thought was happening to him.

Meanwhile Hallworth was preparing his hero's welcome. He cabled his friend, promising a crowd of 100,000 to greet his arrival at Teignmouth. The threat of others may have driven the solitary sailor deeper into his theorizing. He poured out in his logbooks thousands of words of revelation. More and more the biblical themes of justice, godhead, and retribution merged with the Einsteinian pseudo-science. "This is probably true, *alas I shall not see my dead father again unless* for I see no way in which the system benefits by the retention of a computer incapable of action within the system . . ."— such a fragment gives a taste of the bizarrely fluctuating tone of these desperate last ruminations. "I knew everything from Julius Caesar to Mao Tse Tung. I had a complete set of answers to the most difficult problems now facing mankind."

One of the last entries comes as close as any to confession.

> Nature does not allow
> God to Sin any Sins
> Except One—
>
> That is the Sin of Concealment

Near the end Crowhurst adopted a chess metaphor. "During his lifetime," he wrote relatively lucidly, "each man plays cosmic chess against the Devil." The sense of having sinned against his father—put in a third-person parable—also recurs. And so does the messianic voice proclaiming answers to all mankind's problems.

On or about June 30, having let his chronometer run down, Crowhurst came to his partial senses long enough to make an effort, patchily recorded, to reorient himself in space and time. His terse log entries record: "Clock started approx. 5.10. Just before moon went down," and "June 30. 5.10. MAX POSS ERROR." But instead of regaining control of himself and his boat, he seems to have used the occasion to pen what must be one of the most bizarre suicide notes ever retrieved.

It begins with the heading "EXACT POS July 1 10 03." Then with eerie pedantry, a series of time observations in the left margin, specified to the second, mark off the telegraphically clipped last words Crowhurst set down opposite them. It was the *reductio ad absurdum*, in a sense, of the self-documentation the man had engaged in for the past eight months.

> 10 14 30 My folly gone "forward" in imagination
> Wrong decision not perfect   Time
> no longer computed   Had disorganises Clocks

The minutes ticked away.

> 10 15 40 Clocks   Think no need worry
> about time ± but only elapsed time
> ±   May be meaningless?   Important
> reason for work is (lost)   understand

> 10 17 20 right Sorry waste of time

The momentary allusions to his real-life situation, as in the above "but only elapsed time ±" blur into the overall madness.

> 20 22   Understand two "reasons" for task of
> conflict. Rule of game unsure. If
> 10 23 30 game to put everything back? Where is back?

Crowhurst's "resignation," tied up in a way no one will ever fathom with the father who had died when he was sixteen, figured in the quasi-confessional entry that announced:

> I will only resign this game
> if you will agree that   on
> the next occasion that this
> game is played it will be played

> according to the
> rules that are devised by
> my great god who has
> revealed at last to his son
> not only the exact nature
> of the reason for games but
> has also revealed the truth of
> the way of ending of the
> next game that
>
> > It is finished—
>
> > It is finished
>
> IT IS THE MERCY

The last entry in the log apparently records to the very second Crowhurst's suicide, which must, Tomalin and Hall conclude, have taken the simple form of jumping overboard.

> 11 15 00 It is the end of my
> my game the truth
> has been revealed and it will
> be done as my family require me
> to do it
>
> 11 17 00 It is time for your move to
> begin
>
> I have not need to prolong
> the game
>
> It has been a good game that
> must be ended at the
> I will play this game when
> I choose I will resign the
> game 11 20 40   There is
> no reason for harmful

"Harmful" was the last word Donald Crowhurst wrote.

England was waiting to welcome home the winner of the prize for the fastest solo circumnavigation. Donald Crowhurst was about to be acclaimed as a hero. But for more than two weeks only silence greeted the news-hungry public. There was no transmission from the *Teignmouth Electron*, but that was not so alarming, given that Crowhurst's last broadcasts had complained about radio problems.

On July 10 a Royal Mail vessel heading from London to the Caribbean came in sight of a trimaran floating in an unusual spot in the mid-Atlantic, some eighteen hundred miles from England.

Captain Richard Box hailed the ship with his foghorn, but roused not a single crew member. A chief officer boarded the ship, searched its quarters, and found nobody there. There were two days' dirty dishes in the sink, radio parts strewn everywhere, an old sleeping bag on a bunk. Slowly it dawned on the crew, some of whom had followed the round-the-world race in the *Sunday Times*, that they had discovered the *Teignmouth Electron*. And there was no sign of Donald Crowhurst. The mail boat searched for a day, joined by a U.S. Air Force plane. They found nothing on the smooth surface of the sunlit sea.

Captain Box cabled England about his discovery, affirming that the whole business was a complete mystery to him. Then, as the vessel headed on to Santo Domingo, he began to read the voluminous logbooks he had retrieved from the trimaran. Only in the last pages did he begin to glimpse the fact that something terrible had happened to Donald Crowhurst.

When two Bridgewater policemen informed Clare Crowhurst about the discovery, she was at first not greatly alarmed. She guessed that Donald had simply rowed off on a side trip in his dinghy. It took several days for the shock of the true facts to dawn upon her. Meanwhile Donald Crowhurst's name attained the celebrity he had always dreamed of, as papers blazoned the romantic story of his tragic failure all across England and even the world. But there was still no suspicion that he had attempted a hoax. Rumors of his survival sprang up from the Azores to France.

It was only a week later, when Rodney Hallworth led a small party by airplane to the island of Santo Domingo to greet the mail vessel, that Crowhurst's hoax reached the public eye. Captain Box had been so disturbed by the discovery of the confessional last pages that he urged Hallworth to tear them out of the log so that Crowhurst's family would never learn the truth. Hallworth did so. But it soon became apparent that the log itself testified to the hoax. Hallworth admitted the truth to the papers, and Nicholas Tomalin, who had accompanied him to Santo Domingo, got the journalistic scoop of his life.

Despite the sensation, Crowhurst's memory was honored. The Golden Globe celebration dinner for Knox-Johnston was called off, and its winner magnanimously urged that the five-thousand-pound prize for elapsed time be donated to a Crowhurst Appeal Fund set up for the family. Tomalin managed to gain the cooperation of virtually everyone involved, from Clare Crowhurst to Sir Francis Chichester, and within the year had collaborated with Ron Hall to publish one of the best nonfiction adventure books of our generation. In the pages of *The Strange Last Voyage of Donald Crowhurst* the reader has the opportunity to gain access to a unique internal drama—as well as the best-documented exploring hoax of all time.

Tomalin and Hall's conviction is that Crowhurst set out from Teignmouth to win the race fair and square. Only the combination of multiple setbacks, the enormous publicity surrounding his effort, and the prospects of financial ruin and personal humiliation drove him to attempt a hoax which, had he completed the run to England, he might actually have pulled off. If he premeditated the fraud, he never breathed a word of it to his wife.

Only one hint of forethought looms in the meticulous record compiled by Tomalin and Hall. On board the *Teignmouth Electron* during its disheartening maiden voyage, Donald Crowhurst sat one night drinking coffee with his old friend Peter Beard, while his other companion slept belowdecks. Beard was raising potential obstacles; Crowhurst confidently dismissed them. But suppose the prevailing winds weren't favorable, Beard asked.

"Well, one could always shuttle around in the South Atlantic for a few months," said Crowhurst. "There are places out of the shipping lanes where no one would ever spot a boat like this." Then he took Beard's logbook to show how it could be done. He drew Africa, and South America. He placed two small triangles between them to represent the Falkland Islands and Tristan de Cunha. With his pencil he lightly traced a lozenge-shaped course, round and round, between the two. It would be simple, he said, no one would ever find out. Crowhurst laughed: it was obviously a joke. The diagram is still in Peter Beard's logbook.

BIBLIOGRAPHY

Tomalin, Nicholas, and Ron Hall. *The Strange Last Voyage of Donald Crowhurst*. New York, 1970.

EPILOGUE

Cesare Maestri's mother died when he was seven. Pneumonia took Robert Peary's father when the future explorer was two, as it did Frederick Cook's sire when the boy was five. Donald Crowhurst lost his absent alcoholic father at sixteen. The only thing we know about Sebastian Cabot's youth is that his father, whose whole career Sebastian was to appropriate as his own, was lost at sea when the boy was in his teens. The facts about the parents of Father Hennepin and Captain Samuel Adams have eluded history. Robert Drury's mother died of grief while he was stuck on Madagascar—if he existed. But Drury's hoax—if it was a hoax—was perpetrated by someone other than Drury. Only Richard E. Byrd, among the men surveyed in this book, is known to have seen both his parents live until he reached adulthood.

Cook and Peary, those archrivals in the polar controversy, both suffered all their lives from humiliating lisps. Peary's suffocating mother called him "Bertie" all his life, tried to keep him from going to the Arctic, and managed to live in the same house with her only son until well into his adulthood. Crowhurst's mother, who wanted a daughter, dressed him in girl's clothes until he was eight. Byrd, according to his biographer, was "small, almost girlish in stature" as a youth; he also suffered from adverse comparison with his successful brothers.

The striking recurrence of a missing parent and a childhood "defect" or "fault" tempts one into facile psychologizing. The explorer, perhaps, embarked on a lifelong quest whose real, underlying object was to find the lost parent, to repair the fault, to determine what his own identity was. Failure was intolerable—a confirmation

171

of all one's deepest fears about the self—and so the hoax was born.

But such an explanation remains procrustean. Abyssinian Bruce, who faked nothing, lost his mother at two, had a sickly childhood, and was feared to be consumptive. It may be that explorers in general fit the "profile" of missing parent and childhood defect; among them, perhaps, a peculiar subset ends up perpetrating hoaxes. Our sample of nine—seven, really, since we know almost nothing about the early years of Hennepin and Adams—is too small to draw reliable conclusions from.

All the same, there are similarities among our exploration hoaxers that cry out for attention. The essential question is the simplest: why? What drove these men, some of them highly esteemed explorers on the merits of their real deeds, to try to hoodwink the world? Without being able to penetrate to the heart of that question, since history is only rarely capable of revealing private motivation, we can speculate, on the grounds of common patterns.

The men who perpetrated exploring hoaxes all wanted the genuine achievement very badly. The classic case is Peary, with seven Arctic expeditions behind him, his toes lost to frostbite, realizing at the age of fifty-two that the goal of a lifetime was oh-so-slightly out of his grasp. Many explorers have suffered that frustration with grace and honesty: Eric Shipton on Mount Everest, Ernest Shackleton near the South Pole, Belmore Browne on Mount McKinley. But when the North Pole and victory in the solo circumnavigation race and the ascent of Cerro Torre began to loom as impossible, Robert Peary and Donald Crowhurst and Cesare Maestri grasped at what must have seemed to them the only remaining straw: the pretense of having made the actual achievement.

Thus exploring hoaxes tend to be poorly planned. They are last-ditch improvisations in the face of failure. There is not a single case among our nine—unless it be Sebastian Cabot's—of a clearly pre-meditated, cynically choreographed hoax. Sam Adams really tried to descend the Colorado; Father Hennepin probably wanted to explore all of the Mississippi; Richard Byrd would have been glad to fly over the North Pole; Donald Crowhurst tried desperately to win the race. Only when the goal was recognized to be unattainable did these men scrounge about and patch together the illusory data to support their hoaxes.

Another feature common to exploring frauds is the identification of an enemy—usually one's chief rival. Cook and Peary, despite having been teammates on an earlier expedition, became the bitterest of antagonists when the Pole was at stake. Earlier Cook had turned his fellow mountaineers Belmore Browne and Herschel Parker into his chief detractors, when he claimed to have stolen Mount McKinley from them. Maestri sneered at his rivals Walter Bonatti and Carlo Mauri, and it may have been Mauri who drove him to his ill-conceived return to Cerro Torre. Hennepin could not bear the fame of his former commander La Salle, and so tried to steal his cardinal accomplishment after the greater man had died—as did Cabot with his own father. Byrd was driven to hoax by the impending success of Nobile, Amundsen, and Ellsworth. Crowhurst worshiped Sir Francis Chichester, but could only make fun of his grandest feat; later he found insupportable the thought of losing out to rivals like Bernard Moitessier and Robin Knox-Johnston. Sam Adams, having failed to join John Wesley Powell, felt the burning need to supersede him. In each case, it seems apparent, the potential success of the rival had much to do with motivating the fraud.

Exploring hoaxes have no element of the playful. The kind of *jeu d'esprit* embodied in the Piltdown Man is altogether absent in the machinations of Hennepin or Peary. There is no hint of a lark, a joke on the world. The solitary conspiracy is a grimly serious effort to fool the whole world. There is nothing even in the vein of the misanthropically satirical, as one finds, for instance, in the "hoax" of Swift's Isaac Bickerstaff's almanac.

And solitary the effort inevitably turns out to be. Out of necessity Cook tried to conscript Edward Barrill in his bogus Mount McKinley climb, as Byrd did his pilot Floyd Bennett, and Peary did Matthew Henson and his Eskimos. In each case the principal banked on the inferior social status of his unwilling or unknowing accomplices. The world's spotlight was aimed only at the man who craved notoriety; his competent companions nervously dodged attention. Crowhurst and Maestri simplified things by being the sole witnesses to the feats they claimed to have accomplished. It is interesting, if perhaps logical, that an exploring fraud seems never to have resulted from the careful collaboration of conspirators, but rather was always the product of a single iron will.

Nor did any of the men ever confess, even to their wives—unless Finn Ronne's recollection of Isaiah Bowman's memory of Richard Byrd's collapse on a walk one day in New York City represents the sole exception to the rule. Crowhurst chose suicide over exposure. Cook lived out his pitiful later years patiently explaining how he had been misunderstood. The question raised by Stegner about Adams's last years could be applied to all our men: did the years of living with their lies spawn the delusion that they had actually accomplished the feat the world had mocked them for faking?

Psychology, after all, may help to elucidate. In David Shapiro's

Neurotic Styles (New York, 1965) we may find a description that fits remarkably well the men whose company this book has kept. Shapiro is discussing what he calls "paranoid style."

> There are, descriptively and quite roughly speaking, two sorts of people who fall within the category of this style: furtive, constricted, apprehensively suspicious individuals and rigidly arrogant, more aggressively suspicious, megalomanic ones.

Exploring hoaxers, of course, fit the latter category.

According to Shapiro, "suspicious cognition" has some quite distinct formal qualities. It is characterized by a "rigid directedness" of attention. Suspicious people

> are, in actual fact, extremely keen and often penetrating observers. They not only imagine, they search. And they not only search, but also search with an intensity of attention and an acuteness that may easily surpass the capacity of normal attention.

Crowhurst and Peary come most vividly to mind; but the quality seems characteristic of others among our hoaxers as well.

The paranoid person, Shapiro continues, imposes his anticipations on the facts he encounters, even when mutually contradictory. "He is bound to 'find' what he is looking for. . . . This keenness enables suspicious people to make, as they often do, brilliantly perceptive mistakes." If Shapiro's condition applies to men like Cook, Adams, and Maestri, it lends support to the possibility that delusion took charge, that they ended up believing they had actually accomplished what they claimed.

Indeed, Shapiro describes the "paranoid loss of reality" as a process in which the most obvious truths—such as not having reached the North Pole—are dismissed as not really true, as superficial and hence misleading. "A subjective world comes into being that is a peculiar blend of the autistic and the factual." Crowhurst again comes to mind—and perhaps even Cabot and Hennepin. One of the most surprising characteristics of this state of mind is, according to Shapiro, that it can involve quite severe distortion of reality without the impairment of logical processes.

If the "paranoid megalomanic" style describes our hoaxers' dealings with the world, that diagnosis raises not only the possibility that they believed in their claims, but the deeper question of its personal genesis. Here Shapiro's work is most suggestive, in the end most tantalizing. So many traits that he describes fit our heroes: they are threatened above all by the unexpected; their psychological condition can be described as "hyperintentionality," or an extreme purposiveness directed at a single goal; they feel the need to thwart tender or sentimental feelings; they tend to have an abiding interest in things mechanical; they despise weakness in others; and "Playfulness disappears, and playful interests are usually absent."

Shapiro is much more cautious in suggesting the etiology of paranoid style than he is in describing it. He does link it to "exceedingly frail autonomy." Paranoid people, he says, are likely to grow up with a strong sense of personal shame, often centered around a perceived physical defect. Shame for them tends to replace any sense of guilt. They are exceedingly aware of rank and power (Hennepin, Cook, Byrd, Adams, to name a few). The key to the dynamic of paranoid style is revealed in this remark:

> It is a special fact of the psychology of a person of rigid, unstable autonomy that he must always defend that autonomy on two fronts at the same time. He must defend it against internal and external threat. The battle on the one front results in rigidity; that on the other front in defensiveness.

The paranoid person's weapon in this struggle is what psychologists call projection. Whatever is intolerable in the self is projected onto another person, perceived as an enemy; in fact, Shapiro says, it is essential for such a person "to construct an image of the enemy" out of one's defensive biases. The threat that sets this whole train of perceptions in motion is the sense of unstable autonomy, perceived by its bearer as "the threat of 'giving in' to external domination and the threat of 'giving in' to internal pressure."

The syndrome seems to fit too well to be coincidental. It explains the need each of the men we have surveyed had to construct an enemy out of his rival. And it explains why hoaxes are not premeditated, like bank robberies: it is the intolerable internal threat of failure in an exploratory effort that triggers the need to lie, to escape the external threat of a rival who might get there first and thereby conquer.

Shapiro's analysis is fascinating—but one must step back and allow for skepticism. He himself is reluctant to assign reasons why one person develops a paranoid style, another, say, an obsessive-compulsive or hysterical style. An unstable autonomy could arise from hundreds of causes, among which might be the loss of a parent when young—especially if it occasioned, as in Peary's case, the smothering possessiveness of the remaining parent. It could also result from a boy's growing up dressed as a girl, like Crowhurst. But it may also be determined by pure biology. Far more women than men,

Shapiro observes, develop a hysterical style; far more men than women an obsessive-compulsive style. The question of what causes a future explorer to adopt a paranoid style—even if we accept the characterization as fitting the men in this book—remains a murky one. Finally, it is worth bearing in mind that even at their most severe stages, neurotic styles are, according to Shapiro, strategies of coping with the world—not "sicknesses." And except for Donald Crowhurst, our heroes—whatever the strain or tragic consequences—coped with the world and lived to a reasonable age.

The question of sexual preponderance among neurotic styles raises an interesting issue. Women do not seem to be very good at hoaxes. Of course the history of exploration is so dominated by men it is not surprising that we find no examples of women hoaxers—there are few enough examples of women explorers. But it is hard to think of examples of women attempting hoaxes in any field. Shapiro's analysis may gain pertinency here, simply because very few women tend to be paranoid megalomanic types. Rosie Ruiz, the runner who tried to fake victory in the 1980 Boston Marathon, made a very bad show of it compared to men like Peary. Cross-examined on television, challenged to run other courses, she took refuge in tears and a short memory. Within weeks her claims were demolished, and she raised scarcely a whimper. In the blare of publicity around her deception, the Boston Globe revived the story of an English Channel swimming hoax from the 1920s. Like Ruiz, the woman who had ridden in a boat most of the way and then claimed a record wilted under examination; unlike Ruiz, she confessed within the week. What both women lacked was that dogged, secretive fanaticism that allowed Frederick Cook to insist up to his dying days that he had been wronged, that he could still demonstrate his triumph, that future ages would vindicate him.

The case of Rosie Ruiz raises another point. In the future it will be much, much harder for explorers to get away with their frauds. Her "victory" collapsed under the scrutiny of the electronic media, when videotapes and films failed to show her passing checkpoints, when similar footage from the New York Marathon showed the same thing, when coordinated eyewitness reports established a pattern of deceit. Donald Crowhurst's problem was not the simple one of staying out of view of other ships. It was how to fake telegrams, weather reports, photographs—documentary evidence routinely required of his competitors. The effort to fake those data may well have driven him insane. Nobody in 1508 asked Sebastian Cabot for a photograph of Hudson Bay. Nobody in 1680 could check weather reports against Father Hennepin's fantasies of the Lower Mississippi. Whether exploring hoaxes completely die out as a phenomenon in succeeding ages remains to be seen.

Another thing remains, and may forever remain, to be seen. Throughout the researching and writing of this book two questions teased me constantly. The first I have acknowledged, in the chapter on Abyssinian Bruce. What if the whole world turned out to be wrong, and Frederick Cook really did, somehow or other, despite the evidence, climb Mount McKinley? But the more mischievous qualm is the mirror image of the above. Who in history—and there must have been some—got away with an exploring hoax scot-free? What hoaxes worked perfectly, fooled everybody? Suppose Lewis and Clark never did ascend the Missouri, never crossed the Rockies, never wintered on the miserable Pacific coast near the mouth of the Columbia? Suppose they simply holed up a little upstream from St. Louis, and later spun out a marvelous yarn about the West they had "discovered"? We can lay that fantasy to rest . . . but when one stops to think why one trusts so implicitly the deeds of Lewis and Clark, one begins to wonder. If not those two, then how do we know Cortez conquered Mexico? Why do we believe Hannibal crossed the Alps, or Balboa "stared at the Pacific," or Marco Polo dined with Kublai Khan?

Somewhere men lie buried who fooled every one of us, whose brilliant voyages each succeeding century commemorates, whose "records" satisfied the most critical judges. In their dusty sleep they are laughing at us all.

INDEX